Slow Road TO BROWNSVILLE

DAVID REYNOLDS

Slow

TO

Road BROWNSVILLE

A Journey Through
the Heart of the Old West

GREYSTONE BOOKS
Vancouver/Berkeley

14 15 16 17 18 5 4 3 2 1

Greystone Books Ltd.
www.greystonebooks.com

Cataloguing data available from Library and Archives Canada
ISBN 978-1-77164-049-7 (pbk.)
ISBN 978-1-77164-053-4 (epub)

Editing by Nancy Flight
Copyediting by Maureen Nicholson
Cover design by Jessica Sullivan and Nayeli Jimenez
Text design by Nayeli Jimenez
Cover photograph by shutterstock.com
Map by Eric Leinberger
Printed and bound in Canada by Friesens
Distributed in the U.S. by Publishers Group West

We gratefully acknowledge the financial support of the Canada Council for the Arts, the British Columbia Arts Council, the Province of British Columbia through the Book Publishing Tax Credit, and the Government of Canada through the Canada Book Fund for our publishing activities.

Greystone Books is committed to reducing the consumption of old-growth forests in the books it publishes. This book is one step toward that goal.

For Penny

and
for Stuart,
who showed me the road
and kept the postcard.

CONTENTS

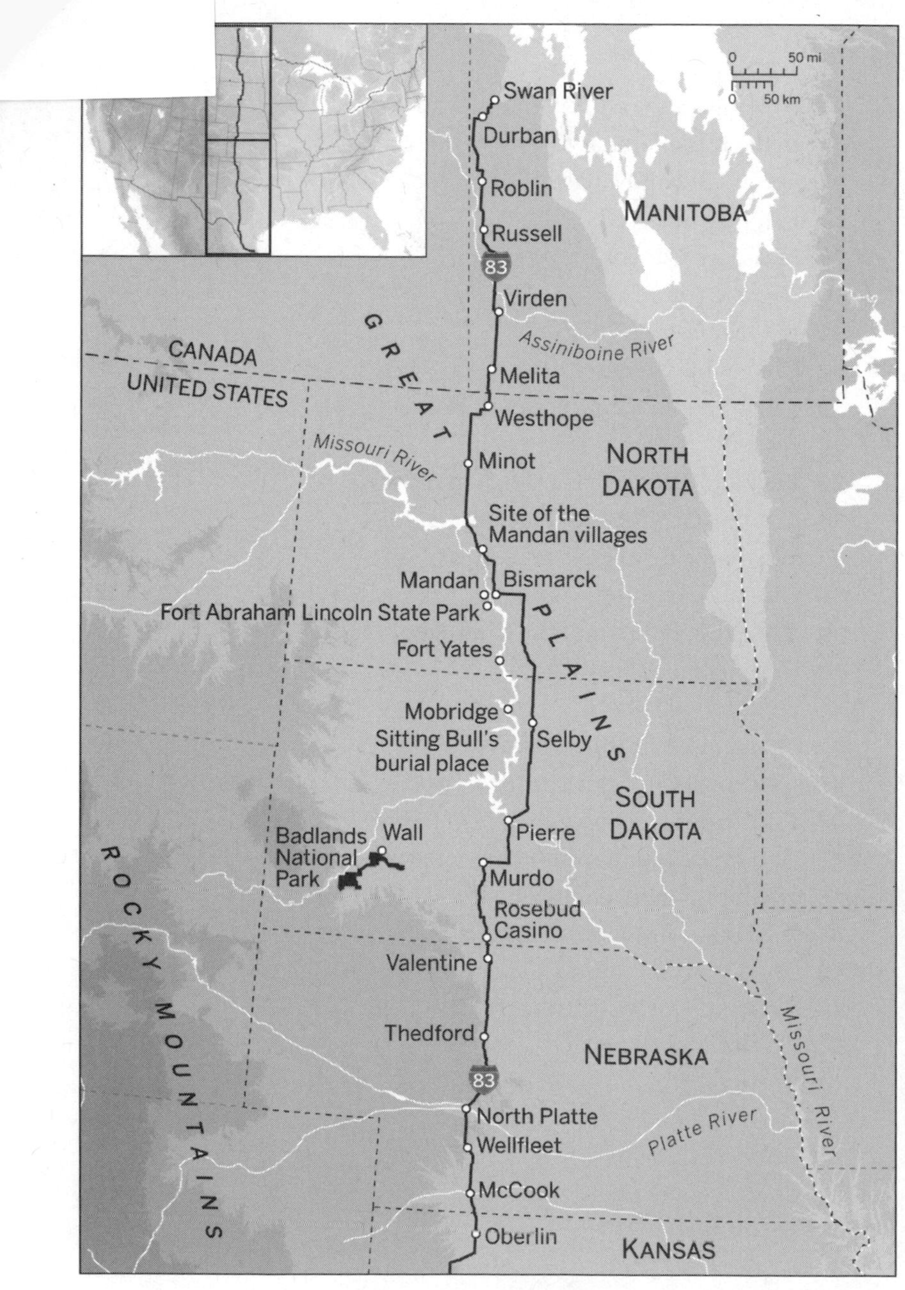

0 50 mi
0 50 km
Swan River
Durban
Roblin
MANITOBA
Russell
83
Virden
GREAT PLAINS
Assiniboine River
CANADA
UNITED STATES
Melita
Westhope
Missouri River
Minot
NORTH DAKOTA
Site of the Mandan villages
Mandan
Bismarck
Fort Abraham Lincoln State Park
Fort Yates
Mobridge
Sitting Bull's burial place
Selby
SOUTH DAKOTA
Pierre
Wall
Badlands National Park
ROCKY MOUNTAINS
Murdo
Rosebud Casino
Valentine
Thedford
NEBRASKA
Missouri River
83
North Platte
Wellfleet
Platte River
McCook
Oberlin
KANSAS

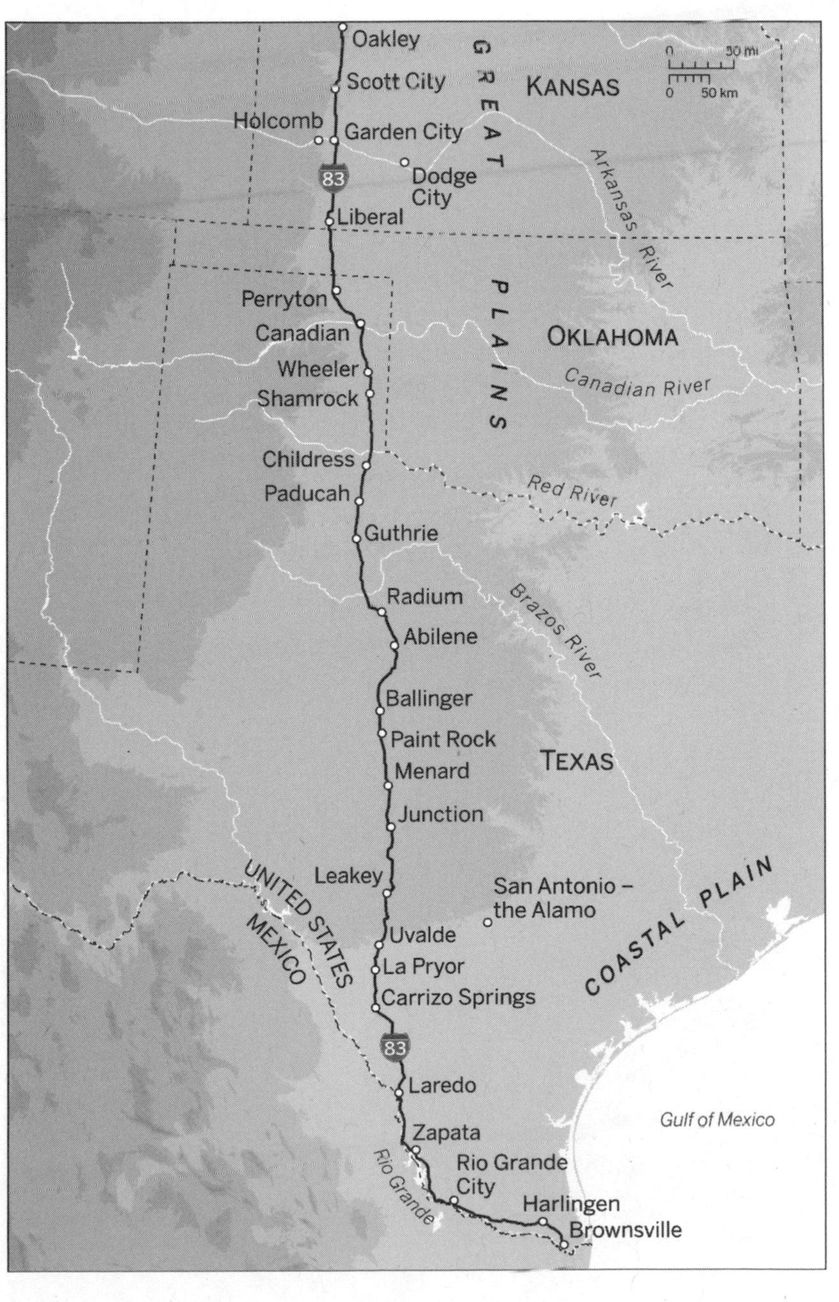
Oakley
Scott City
Holcomb
Garden City
Dodge City
Liberal
83
KANSAS
GREAT PLAINS
Arkansas River
Perryton
Canadian
Wheeler
Shamrock
OKLAHOMA
Canadian River
Childress
Paducah
Red River
Guthrie
Radium
Abilene
Brazos River
Ballinger
Paint Rock
Menard
TEXAS
Junction
Leakey
San Antonio – the Alamo
UNITED STATES
MEXICO
COASTAL PLAIN
Uvalde
La Pryor
Carrizo Springs
Laredo
Zapata
Rio Grande
Rio Grande City
Harlingen
Brownsville
Gulf of Mexico
0 50 mi
0 50 km

"Tourism has a privileged character in America; it doesn't cut you off from the country it's revealing to you; on the contrary, it's a way of entering it."

SIMONE DE BEAUVOIR, *America Day by Day*

(Translator: Carol Cosman)

"THAT ROAD GOES TO MEXICO"

I LEARNED ABOUT THE ROAD in 2002, during my second visit to Swan River. I was there in May, when the land warms up after the great freeze that lasts five months. I had driven with Stuart to the west end of Main Street. We were planning to eat at the Chinese café, but it was shut. As I turned the car round, Stuart flipped his thumb over his shoulder and said something I didn't catch—which was strange because he usually draws out his words in a soft, deep lilt which is easy on the ear and easy to understand.

It sounded as if he had said, "That road goes to Mexico."

But he couldn't have; we were thousands of miles from Mexico, in the remote north of Canada. I replayed the sound of his words in my mind. "Did you say, 'That road goes to Mexico'?"

"Sure. You bet. It does. I been down there. To Texas. And Arizona. It goes on down to the Mexican border."

"Really?" I was driving east again. We were well past the road now. I had barely noticed it: a blur of gray tarmac, wide enough for perhaps two cars.

"Yep. Highway 83. Goes from here to Brownsville, Texas, right down there in the south, as far as you can go in the USA. Drive across a bridge and you're in Mexico."

"You mean it starts *here*—Highway 83?"

"Yep."

"Why?"

"I don't know." He raised a hand. "Would've been Indian trails at first. They were everywhere—from here, north of here, right down through the prairies and into Mexico."

"Why does it start here? There's a road north from here, isn't there?" I knew there was. It went to places even farther north, places I hadn't been to, with exotic names—like Le Pas and Flin Flon.

"Yep. You just carry on past Mr. Ribs, past the Westwood Inn, and you can drive north for two hundred miles—more if you want to. But that's not Highway 83. That's Highway 10. It's different. Comes from southeast, from Brandon. Highway 83 runs due south from here, almost straight south all the way to Laredo, which is on the Rio Grande, which is the border with Mexico." He cleared his throat and tugged at the peak of his baseball cap. "Then it goes on, southeast along the Rio Grande, to Brownsville, which is near the sea, the Gulf of Mexico."

"And all that began as Indian trails?"

"Sure. Like most roads in North America—except interstates, that is."

EIGHT YEARS LATER I am back in Swan River. It's a gray day, a Sunday, and the Westwood Inn is shut. The solitary receptionist, a middle-aged woman, is polite; she gives me a key and a room number, but otherwise the place is closed—no bar, no restaurant—till tomorrow. I hesitate before phoning Stuart. It is 6 PM. Is it too late to call him? He is an old man. There is no doubt about that. He would say so himself; how could he say otherwise? He is ninety-six.

I am afraid he may not answer. Though he is in fine health as far as I know, something can happen to someone of that age—

someone of any age, come to that, but more likely of that age—at any time.

I give it a minute, then put the phone down. Two weeks ago, he answered quickly when I called to say I was coming. I stare out at the rain in the car park and at the road that leads north, and wonder what I will do if Stuart is dead.

Unwittingly, he inspired the adventure that will soon begin. So he has to be here at the beginning, to send me on my way. Would anyone have told me if he had died? Probably not. I'm not close to his sons; they wouldn't think to get in touch. They are lucky; their father has lived a long time, and he is a great man, a man's man—and, in the best way, a ladies' man.

I turn on the TV, flick through the channels, push the off button, and go back to the window. The sky has lightened a little; this far north, in June, there will still be hours of daylight.

I think about what I am doing here, why I am going to drive that long road.

Because, I tell myself, I am connected to it through my grandfather and my friends in Swan River. Because I am curious about what lies along it: the Great Plains, Middle American towns and cities, almost one thousand miles of Texas, and then the Rio Grande. Because I feel an affinity with North America derived from music, novels, films, television. Because I grew up watching Westerns and road movies, and I want to look for the realities behind the myths. Because of *Bury My Heart at Wounded Knee,* Dee Brown's account of the defeat of the Indians of the American West, a book that roused me to anger, despair, tears. It was on the plains, which these days lie on either side of Highway 83, that the Indians between 1860 and 1890 fought, raided, stood their ground, retreated, fled, hid, and often tried to make peace. And it was there that they lost thousands of lives, their way of life, their freedom, and, what the white men wanted most, their land—land on which for thousands of years they had lived until the white men came. They—the Sioux, the Cheyenne, the Comanches, the Apaches, Sitting Bull, Crazy Horse, Red Cloud, Quanah Parker, Geronimo—were on my mind when I planned this trip. I want to see the country where they lived and died, and look at how the descendants of the survivors live now.

I ring Stuart's number again, and he answers, as usual, with one word: "Harris." He has been out all day with his sons. "No. It's not too late. Let's meet today. For sure." His voice is soft and deep. With the Westwood Inn closed, he suggests we meet at Chicken Chef on Main Street in ten minutes.

As I park opposite, the familiar white car comes round the corner. I climb out and he's there, his hand raised. I run across through the rain. He looks a little older, a little more frail—but still like a man approaching eighty rather than one hundred—and he has the same bearing, the same modest authority.

The place is crowded with families and couples eating chicken dinners. We find a table and order coffee; it is all he wants.

It is awkward at first. We look at each other, smile, and mutter, and I say something about the trip I am about to make. He nods and from time to time murmurs the words he uses to show he is listening: "For sure," "Sure," "You bet." He is wearing a baseball cap, a smart, dark blue one with something that I can't see written in small white letters at the back, and I remember that I have brought him a present, a baseball cap that announces, not too garishly, that it is from London. He takes it and smiles and seems to like it. Then, only to confirm that he likes baseball caps and can't have too many of them, says that his son Garry has brought him some from Texas.

When our coffee is cool enough to drink, he takes off the cap and begins to talk. He has been thinking about the road, about the history. He has spoken to people, friends and friends of friends who have traveled it, and has tried to find people for me to talk to. He seems disappointed—too few people are around—but he will make more calls tonight. He apologizes for not emailing. He had a detached retina, and hasn't driven or used a computer for three months. But now his eye is almost better. He is driving again and will soon be emailing.

He is a little thinner than when I last saw him, three years before—and a little gaunt around the face. As always, there are subtle signs of the dandy: a patterned shirt and a black jacket. The bald, brown dome of his head, with its silky white hair falling straight at the sides, is as strong and imperious as ever, the skull of a philosopher who has lived his life outdoors.

I say that I think the book should start with him, because he told me about the road—and he has driven on it.

He grips his coffee cup with both hands, saying nothing—telling me, I think, that he has no opinion about that. But I can't be sure. I'd heard that he was pleased by his role in my earlier book—about the grandfather I never knew—that he liked the pages in which he featured, that he reread them sometimes. He had given that story an ending, had told me where my grandfather had lived, and how he had lived.

He continues to talk about the road, and I ask if he'd mind my switching on the little recorder I'd bought in London. "Sure," he says, and just carries on talking—first of all about buffalo: how they would have found their way between hills and around lakes, creating trails; how they ranged from Alaska south through the Great Plains and down into Mexico; and how the Indians, who depended on them for food, shelter, and clothing, followed them. The Indian trails became roads and eventually highways like 83.

Many people who live in this part of Manitoba, Stuart says, drive south on 83 in winter because it takes them directly from frozen Canada to sunny Texas. Perhaps as many as half a million people, nicknamed "snowbirds," drive from Canada and the northern United States to the Rio Grande Valley in the far south of Texas. There they live in trailers—many of which are towed back and forth—in hundreds of trailer parks.

One trailer park, the Pine to Palm Resort Park, was founded not far from Brownsville by people from Swan River in the 1950s. “It became popular,” Stuart says. “It still is.” And the road too became popular—so popular that a Highway 83 Association was formed with members from both ends and from places in between. “Americans and Canadians would meet, often for a week in the summer and have a picnic and a get-together—one year down there, the next year up here.”

Stuart has driven down 83 many times, stopped and lingered in many places, and turned off to drive east or west. In 1974, with his wife and another couple, he went all the way to Brownsville and on into Mexico. That evening, in Chicken Chef, he was wearing a silver ring with a red stone that he bought that time in Mexico.

83 was built in the 1920s when the roads—around a hundred of them—that were to be known as U.S. Highways, or more colloquially U.S. Routes, were planned. Most were put together by linking and improving existing country roads. Fifty or so ran north-south and fifty ran east-west, forming a grid across the United States. A few crossed the border into Canada and continued with the same numbers, because that made sense to the Canadians. This frenzy of road building provided work for the unemployed during the Great Depression while catering for a surge in the numbers of cars and trucks.

In the 1950s, the U.S. Interstates—multilane highways uninterrupted by traffic lights or conventional road junctions—began to be planned and built. But the network wasn’t completed until September 1991, when the last traffic light was removed from an interstate, I-90, in Wallace, Idaho. By then some of the U.S. Highways had gone completely and parts of many others had disappeared. Hundreds of miles of the most famous U.S. Highway, Route 66, are buried beneath five bland, efficient interstates; the rest survive as highway, but with other, newer names and numbers. Route 66 was officially "decertified" in 1985, and the remaining shields that carried the number 66 were removed from the sides of the road. (Now, however, after pressure from conservationists, signs have been put up directing tourists to Historic Route 66.)

"83 is one of the very few highways left that is complete," I say to Stuart.

"That's right," he says.

"And one of the longest as well."

"One of the longest, if not *the* longest."

"*Maybe* the longest."

"I think it's the longest north-south."

Whether 83 is the longest is contentious. One source says it is the fifth longest, but takes into account only the 1,894 miles within the United States. Only two other U.S. Highways still continue up into Canada (Highways 1 and 59). Neither reaches as far north as 83. Going south, once it leaves Manitoba and enters the United States, 83 travels through six states: North Dakota, South Dakota, Nebraska, Kansas, a narrow strip of Oklahoma known as the Panhandle, and Texas. From Swan River to Brownsville on 83 is 2,271 miles.

Stuart and I sit over our coffee and talk about Westerns and the Wild West.

Stuart's favorite cowboy actor is John Wayne.

I tell him how much *The Alamo,* with Wayne as Davy Crockett, thrilled me as a child.

"And *The Searchers, Rio Bravo*." He pauses, looking down and up again. "*True Grit*. That was a good movie."

We keep talking until almost nine o'clock. Then we part: Stuart to make phone calls on my behalf; I to get something to eat.

MR. RIBS

THE CARPET AND CURTAINS and the fabric covering the seats that form the booths in Mr. Ribs have faded to calm pastels. Otherwise the place is as it was when I first visited it eleven years before. I sit on a padded bench that I have sat on many times—sometimes alone, sometimes with others—and gaze at the road north. There is only one other person in the room: a slow, likable, apparently teenage waitress wearing a loose black polo shirt and black trousers.

She brings me a beer, Rickard's (rhymes with flickereds) Red—and I think about my grandfather. He lived here in the Swan River Valley from 1905 until he died of consumption in 1910. Stuart once told me that a man who lived here in those years was a pioneer; the first homesteaders arrived in 1898, with Stuart's father and grandfather among them.

My grandfather, Tom Reynolds, died almost forty years before I was born. When I was a child no one spoke about him and there were no photographs—which may be why I became interested in him. Later, in my teens, I discovered that he had married my grandmother in 1890 and had been an upright kind of man, an accountant, a proud husband, and the father of two children. But for some reason he had taken hold of the whiskey bottle and hadn't, couldn't, let go. This was perhaps because my grandmother had married him on the rebound from an illicit passionate relationship, and hadn't loved him, or hadn't loved him *enough*. Drunkenness lost him his job. He couldn't get another and eventually behaved so badly that he was thrown out of his home by his in-laws and lost everything. For four years, without a reference from a former employer and therefore unemployable in a time of mass unemployment, he lived as a vagrant on the streets of London. And then two kind friends paid his passage to Canada where people were needed to build a new country. It was a one-way ticket, all the way to Winnipeg, subsidized by the Canadian government. It cost four pounds.

He fetched up here, 350 miles northwest of Winnipeg, and here—I discovered with Stuart's help—he did three notable things. With three other men he spent a year, in the stifling summer and freezing winter, building fences beside the new railroad line to prevent cattle and horses straying onto the track. That railroad line led twenty miles or so from Swan River to the next stop, a pioneer boomtown called Durban. Tom settled in Durban, lived alone in a wooden cabin, and started a new life as a cobbler, making and mending the townspeople's boots and shoes. And he continued to drink, illegally, behind the town's livery stable, with a small group of friends who, Stuart told me, were known as "the bachelors."

In 1999, almost ninety years after his death, something about this grandfather—the alcoholic whom his family tried to forget, who suffered and caused suffering, not least to my father whom he deserted at the age of ten—prompted me to follow him across the world to this remote town that lies in a lush valley at the northern edge of the prairies in Manitoba.

The waitress is approaching. I am staring out at the still gray sky. I read the menu while she holds a pad and pencil with her head tilted sideways. I ignore the "combos"—"steak *and* lobster," "baby back ribs *and* a seven-ounce New York steak"—and eventually the waitress and I decide that I will have a six-ounce filet mignon that comes with salad, garlic bread, and stuffed potato. The last of these, she reminds me, is a baked potato cut in half with its insides removed, mashed with cheese, and shoved back in again, before being pushed under the grill for a few minutes.

I like this waitress; she seems to be a bit of a dreamer, to be thinking about things other than this restaurant and its menu. She brings the food and another Rickard's Red, and, as I chew a mouthful of steak and load my fork with stuffed potato, I remember what Stuart said and how the road began as Indian trails.

INDIANS—THAT WAS WHAT they were called then—played a big part in my childhood. They entered my life soon after the coronation of Queen Elizabeth II, an event I watched on a tiny television, sitting cross-legged on the floor at the home of my mother's aunt. I was four years old and spellbound—more by the sight of moving pictures inside a box than by the pretty young woman wearing a crown.

Soon after that my father brought home a television for us: him, my mother, and me. Stuck to the cabinet below the screen was a brown plastic label with the word "Murphy" embossed in gold. Murphy became my companion every evening at six thirty as I ate my dinner. My mother would place a green table mat, knife, fork, and spoon on a small table in front of my child-sized chair. I would put one of my guns beside the knife and the other beside the fork, so they were to hand when I needed to help Hopalong Cassidy or the Cisco Kid in their battles with outlaws and Indians. My guns were Colt 45s, loaded with caps. I would shoot, *bang!*, when my heroes were in danger. And let my Birds Eye Steaklets turn cold.

Soon there were more TV series, among them the *Lone Ranger*, with his sidekick, the likable and puzzling Tonto. Why was Tonto a friend of the Lone Ranger? I wondered. In the other series, the Indians were baddies.

The waitress comes, takes my plate, suggests another beer.

I drink it slowly, stare out of the window, and think again about Tonto. I know now that there were friendly Indians and hostile ones—and that the one frequently became the other, according to how they were treated by white men. And, it seems to me, that more often the former became the latter.

ANCESTRAL LAND

NEXT MORNING I SIT over coffee at the Westwood Inn with Stuart and his son Garry.

Garry is a lean, taciturn, but not unfriendly, man, who I guess is in his sixties, though it's possible that he is over seventy, considering the age and fitness of his father. He knows a lot about Highway 83, though he doesn't think he does—or maybe it's that he doesn't think there is much to know.

On every one of the last thirteen New Year's Days, Garry and his wife, Gay, have left Swan River on Highway 83 and have driven for four days to reach the Rio Grande Valley. He travels on 83 because "I live on it so there's no sense in me going over to Winnipeg to get on the freeway." But he prefers 83 to a freeway or interstate anyway. There's little traffic and few cities. "I enjoy the driving. It changes. It's ranching. It's farming. And then, when you get to Texas, you get into that hill country which is very pretty."

I ask father and son to explain the difference between farms and ranches, and am told that crops, usually cereal crops, define a farm—though a farmer may give some land over to livestock. Ranchers, on the other hand, raise cattle.

"Just cattle?" I ask.

"Cattle or horses."

At a nearby table, as if on cue, three men are discussing the wet weather and the trouble it is making for farmers.

I ask what Garry and his wife do down there in Texas.

"Oh! Well, we play golf—"

"Dance," Stuart says. "He dances."

Garry smiles. "We go dancing there."

"But you could dance here too, couldn't you?" I say.

"No, you couldn't." He laughs. "Not every night you couldn't. You can dance every night down there. Oh, there's lots to do."

I ask Garry if there is anything on the road that I should look out for. I mean towns, buildings, monuments, landscapes that I should be sure to look *at,* but, understandably, Garry takes my question another way.

"You gotta watch for pheasants."

"Pheasants!" I have a vision of Englishmen in plus fours shooting at birds.

"Oh, they're a bugger."

"On the road?"

"Yeah."

"Whereabouts?"

"North Dakota, South Dakota."

"Really! What? You drive into them?"

"Well, they're on the edge, eating stones, and they're flying up from around the ground."

"Eating stones?"

"Yep. They need small stones to help them digest."

"So people breed them for shooting?"

"No, they're wild. They're a pain in the ass. I've hit two or three of them."

I remember a scene from my childhood: my father driving into and stunning a pheasant as we drove across Salisbury

Plain. He got out of the car, picked it up, and wrung its neck. Then he had an argument with my mother because he wanted to take it home and cook it. My mother prevailed. She pointed with distaste to a swelling on the bird's side where the car had hit it—and she knew that she would have to pluck it and gut it.

"Are there still people who would be called cowboys?" I ask.

"It's a lifestyle," Garry replies immediately.

"And they're like in the Westerns, except they don't have guns I suppose." I realize straightaway that I've made a naive assumption. "Or they *do* have guns?"

My confusion makes Garry laugh.

And then I reveal yet more ignorance. "Or they don't have *pistols,* presumably?"

Garry smiles. "Well, they're not going to be armed totally, but they'll have a gun around, no doubt about that!"

"Right," I say. And straightaway, it seems a feeble response to news of guns being around.

"When you get south of Pierre, South Dakota, you'll see them."

"Right." I say it again. And then I think of something more interesting to say. "Did you employ cowboys? You used to ranch cattle?"

"No," Garry glances across at his father. "We did our own cowboying."

"So you *were* cowboys?"

"Yeah," Stuart says, as if it means little to him.

"Some days we were, yeah." Garry says. Father and son look at each other—and laugh.

Stuart says. "Lots of cowboys these days don't have any cattle. That's their lifestyle. They wear . . . "

I say, "You mean people dress up to look like cowboys?"

"It's just their standard way of life," Stuart says. "They wear the clothes."

I ask about real cowboys, who actually work with cattle. Are there any?

"Oh, for sure. They're working in those big ranches. Lots of cowboys," Stuart says.

And then we talk about Indians. I've heard that some Native Americans who live on reservations spend their time drinking; I ask if that's true.

"Well, there's that kind. There's two kinds of them," Garry says. "There's some that are all right. Lots of them are friendly."

"So they just work like anyone else? Drive trucks . . . "

Stuart answers, "Lots of them do that."

"Do you have friends here who are Native American?"

"Oh sure," Stuart speaks again. "I know lots of them. They live around here, Swan River. They don't have to live on a reservation."

"So the Indians are not a big issue nowadays—in Canada?"

"Well, they kind of are." Garry sighs. "Because there's a welfare system set up for the Native people. You can call it Indian Affairs or whatever you want to call it." He chuckles. "It's just a way of making a living off somebody else. They don't have to work, so some of them work the system." He looks down at the table. "But some of them just get sick of it. They just want to get out of there and do something else. But others are just born and raised in it and never get out of it."

There's a silence. At a distant table an elderly man is gazing at an elderly woman, with his hand resting on hers.

We walk to the hotel entrance where they climb into Garry's pickup. Stuart and I will meet later in the day. Garry waves, wishes me good luck, and drives slowly away.

I AM STILL thinking about the Indians, for whom I have great sympathy—as surely does everyone who knows their history. In the four hundred years following the arrival of Christopher

Columbus, most of them died; those who weren't slaughtered by superior firepower contracted European diseases against which they had no immunity. The survivors were driven off their land, either by force or by unscrupulous politicking, which led them to sign treaties the white men almost always broke. Many died of starvation on reservations, far from their traditional lands, where they were unable to feed themselves in the ways that had kept them healthy for generations. Red Cloud, warrior chief of the Oglala Sioux, described perhaps better than anyone what the white men did to the Indians: "They made us many promises, more than I can remember, but they kept only one; they promised to take our land, and they did."

On previous trips to Canada and the U.S., I've asked North Americans how they feel about the Indians, and there is often a sigh and a downward glance before they answer. I suspect that they feel ambivalent; that they wonder whether they have the right to complain when, so recently, their ancestors stole the Indians' lives, land, and livelihoods.

However, the love of money often outweighs considerations of conscience, and so the uprooting of indigenous people continues. If their ancestral lands happen to be where those who hold power want to build a dam, or drill for oil, or run a gas pipeline, that's often just their bad luck. The case of the Lubicon Cree of northern Alberta, whose land has been pillaged since 1970 by loggers and oil and gas companies, with the approval of the Alberta government, is just one of many.

SINCE MY FIRST visit I have returned to Swan River four times. It's a long way from London, but I go, I tell myself, in part to honor my grandfather, a man whom no one else honors and who has been dead now for a hundred years. You could call it ancestor worship. I don't worship any god. I respect nature, and I feel that history is important and therefore ancestors must be too. And I now have a sense, which has grown in me slowly, of being part of this place, here in the remote north.

Stuart and I talk about this. "You kind of feel that you belong, eh?" he says, and he seems to speak with enthusiasm, as if he is pleased at the idea.

"I do a bit," I say. I suppose I don't want to push it, to suggest too wholeheartedly that I belong in a place that belongs so unequivocally to him and to others who were born there, including, of course, the local Indians.

"You've got some roots here." He says it as if it's a fact.

I tell him what happened when I drove into Canada from the United States a few days ago: how the customs officer was puzzled by my arrival until I told him that my grandfather once lived in Swan River; how he smiled then and told me about his own grandfather who came to Canada from Ireland; and how he went on smiling as he stamped my passport and waved me through.

It isn't just a customs officer. It's Stuart and a handful of others who seem to see it as fitting, unremarkable almost, that I turn up from time to time. And I have grown a little used to the place, a little less awestruck by it, fond of it, in fact—fond of the flatness that is broken by forests and low hills, fond of the sharp light, and of the vast, dome-like sky that forms a roof over land that stretches so far in every direction that at its farthest edges the earth seems to curve down and away.

The sense of belonging makes it easier, more appropriate, to leave the place, to strike out from it in a new direction, south—to treat it as the point of departure for a new adventure.

GENIUSES OF LOCAL LANDSCAPE

SWAN RIVER IS SMALL—THE population just short of four thousand—and exists to serve the farming community that fills the valley. The town is laid out on a grid. Main Street and one cross street, Fifth Avenue, are given over to shops, banks, and a few eating places. Otherwise, apart from schools, a hospital, and a sports ground, the streets are sprinkled with trees and neat family houses. The place feels cozy: every home standing in its own grassy plot, and most of them low, single-story with a basement that provides cool in summer and warmth in winter.

I visit my friend Dale at her bookshop on Fifth Avenue. I haven't seen her for a few years. She is busy with customers and doesn't notice me at first. I drift to the back of the shop where she keeps a gallery of work by local artists, and gaze at a painting of an old wooden grain elevator standing gaunt and majestic against the sky. When I first went to Durban, the town twenty miles away where my grandfather once lived, there was a beautiful elevator like this one beside the railway track. Since then it has been torn down. The old wooden tower was no longer useful—farmers were moving their grain around in trucks. Left standing—some pencil pusher had decided—the tower would become a health hazard.

Dale's customers leave. She turns and blinks a couple of times. Side-to-side rocking bear hugs and much shouting follow. (Is it me? Or do most Canadians love to hug their friends loudly?) And then she tells me how pleased she is still to be in this small town, and how there is a freedom, of which city dwellers know nothing, that comes with living in such a place. Her shop makes little money, but she enjoys herself and meets people. "Who needs money, if you're happy?" she says.

I tell her about the trip I am about to make, and about the cowboys and Indians of my childhood. And does she think it is all right to use the word "Indians"?

"It's good with me. Some people might tell you to say First Nations, or First Nations people. But, David, in your case it doesn't matter." She lets out a yelp of a laugh and pats my arm. "You're from England, so you can say what you like."

If I want to meet First Nations people, I should visit the town's friendship center, she says. Everyone there is very friendly. She yelps again.

I WALK TOWARD the friendship center wondering what to say when I get inside. I push open a swing door, cross a polished wood floor to a reception counter, and manage to say that I am from England, have heard about their center, and wonder what happens in here. I'm speaking to two well-dressed women who don't look like Indians; one has fair skin and blond hair. They explain with smiles that this is a meeting place for First Nations people and for Métis, people of mixed blood. They are both Métis, which means, they say, still smiling, they receive no benefits. They speak readily about "aboriginal people," of how most of them live their lives like anyone else. Some, not many, live on reservations. They describe one reservation to the east of Swan River and another to the north.

A polite and smiling teenage boy speaks to me. He knows about Highway 83, that it goes right through the United States to the Mexican border; one day he wants to get a car and drive down there. A brown-eyed girl, about sixteen, is listening—and amazed. She has been to Winnipeg on Highway 10, but, to her, 83 is just a route to local lakes, farms, and small towns.

I DRIVE TO the Esso station at the east end of Main Street, fill the tank, ready for tomorrow, and pay a man with curious facial hair: a goatee beard with a soup-strainer mustache that covers his mouth. He knows where Highway 83 goes. "I saw a film," he says. "It ended with a man standing on a street in Brownsville beside an 83 shield."

"What film?" I say. "What's it called?"

"I don't know, can't remember. But you can see that shield here, three blocks west of the railroad crossing on Main Street. Turn left there on to Centennial Drive," he says. "That's 83. That's where it starts."

I'm not sure he is right, but I drive there anyway. I turn left where the man said, and there is indeed an 83 sign a little way down Centennial Drive.

It doesn't matter to me precisely where 83 begins, because it certainly begins somewhere in, or on the edge of, Swan River and ends 2,271 miles away at the Veterans International Bridge which crosses the Rio Grande, connecting the United States and Mexico. But I drive back along Main Street, past the Esso station, and over the crossroads at its eastern end, where Highway 10 brushes the edge of town and carries on north. I drive a mile out of town, make a U-turn and drive back. Some three hundred yards before the crossroads, a metal post embedded in the grass at the side of the road displays the word "JUNCTION" above an 83 shield which sits beside another shield that announces 83A.

From this junction a newish road loops left, around the town to the south, and connects to Centennial Drive. According to Wikipedia, this bypass is 83, while Main Street, which was there before my grandfather arrived in 1905, is 83A. If Wikipedia is right, then the first mile or so of this so-promising highway is a little-used ring road flanked by a few warehouses and gloomy edge-of-town fields. Sometimes, however, Wikipedia is wrong, and I would like it to be in this instance. In the coming weeks I was to discover that 83 is the main street of several towns in North America. So, in my book, *this* book, it starts at the east end of Main Street, Swan River, and continues along it, west, until it turns south on to Centennial Drive.

AGAIN STUART AND I meet in Chicken Chef and sit drinking coffee, surrounded by families eating chicken—and again, at first, we are a little formal. He has arranged for me to speak to friends of his who know 83, and he tells me about these people.

As the time for parting comes near, we seem to grow closer. We speak for the first time on this trip like old friends, which we are though we don't meet often. We talk about clothes, his adventurous taste in shirts, and where he buys them—from many places, including a branch of the American chain J.C. Penney in Minot (rhymes with why not), North Dakota, three hundred miles south of Swan River—and about mobile phones, and the way that women use phones for chatting, while we men just want to say what we have to and hang up.

Perhaps it is the knowledge that I am leaving next day and that we won't meet again during this trip that leads to this mateyness. Added to that is the hard fact—at least in my mind and, I have a suspicion, in his—that he is ninety-six, and that I won't get to Swan River again this year or perhaps next. We part in a cold wind on the pavement outside Chicken Chef with a handshake and a shoulder clap.

STUART'S FAMILY CAME to Swan Valley in covered wagons from Ontario with a team of horses, a couple of cows, and shingles and lumber for the roof of the home they would build. Many of the descendants of such homesteaders lived—and some still live—a type of life that not long ago was commonplace all over the world, but is now becoming unusual; they lived in one place all their lives and gained their livings from the land.

In an essay titled "The American Geographies," the American writer and champion of the natural world Barry Lopez laments his fellow Americans' ignorance of the geography of their own country and of the world, but takes comfort in the knowledge that there are "men and women more or less sworn to a place, who abide there, who have a feel for the soil and history, for the turn of leaves and night sounds." He calls such people "geniuses of local landscape... the antithesis of geographical ignorance." These are perfect words to describe Stuart.

I once drove with him on the dirt roads around Durban, roads—some would call them tracks—that were put in place more than a hundred years ago to divide the land into square-mile sections, which were themselves divided into quarter sections: 160 acres, the area that made up a homestead in many parts of Canada and the USA. It was late July. Fields brimming with green and gold stretched away from the roadside, often ending a half mile away at a clump or line of trees that perhaps marked a creek. Stuart knew every farmhouse, barn, field, and creek—and he knew who had lived where throughout the whole twentieth century. He showed me his own farm where one of his sons now lives and, beside it, a sturdy wooden barn that he built himself in the 1930s.

Many fields were planted with wheat, but in some a crop was growing that I didn't recognize. Stuart said it was a hybrid called canola, bred from rapeseed in the 1970s and sown on a wide scale on the Canadian prairies since the 1990s. Its name is an acronym (*Can*adian *O*il *L*ow *A*cid), and it is crushed to make oil which is consumed by humans and cattle.

In Chicken Chef, Stuart had read out the names and phone numbers of his friends for me to write down. I asked how the name "Schoenrath" is spelled. For a moment he seemed surprised. He spelled the word for me. Then he said, "There may have been German ancestors but nothing German about him." Reflecting on this, I felt parochial. In England, we cannot help speculating on the origin of a name. But to Stuart, German names, Ukrainian, Swedish, Irish, Russian, any European names, are all the same: labels, not guides to race or nationality, nor, I am sure, to class. And it isn't just Stuart; it's North Americans—most of them, anyway.

That night, again at Mr. Ribs with the waitress who dreams of elsewhere, I eat a halibut steak which is the shape of an old clinker-built rowing boat, along with salad, garlic toast, and fries. Toward the end of a marathon of munching, I order another beer. The waitress brings it, puts it on the table, gives me a long look, and says, "Where are you from? I can't help noticing your accent."

"London, England," I say.

"Cool!" She has always wanted to go to England, she says. "Why are you here?"

"To drive down the road to Mexico slowly and"—I hesitate—"have a good look at what's there."

She frowns. "*Which* road?"

"This road here." I gesture sideways toward the south. "Highway 83."

She looks puzzled.

"Route 83," I say. "It goes south through the states all the way to the Texas border with Mexico."

"I know the road, 83. I live here."

"Have you been down it?"

"Sure. I been into the States. We went to Bismarck." She speaks slowly, as if trying to remember. "We went on a boat trip there, on the Missouri. That was cool." She smiles. "But I don't know where the road goes after that."

"Well, that same road goes all the way to Brownsville, Texas, and you can cross a bridge there over into Mexico."

"I didn't know that." Her mouth is open. She bites her lip and I notice the whiteness of her teeth. "So cool you're from England. I really want to go there. I almost did—with my cousins—and then I went to California instead, with my school. That was fun, though."

She has one hand on the table, and I wonder whether to ask her to sit down—the other customers have left—but I think that might be awkward for her. "You should go to England, to Europe, when you can, if you can."

"I'd like to go, but it'd be expensive, wouldn't it? Would it take long to get there by boat?"

"A week or so, I think. That would be *very* expensive."

"*Really!* I thought it was much nearer than that."

"It's about three thousand miles from the east coast. The planes are fairly cheap if you book ahead."

"Oh. I'd *love* to go." She twists on her feet and giggles, as if in anticipation. "I'd like to see the Eiffel Tower, the Blarney Stone, Stonehenge, and... er, Buckingham Palace and Big Ben." She gazes east, at the pine-slatted wall. "I'm part Irish... and part Ukrainian." She smiles.

I ask her name.

"Brenna."

And I think how I've never been to Ireland, never seen the Blarney Stone.

ELEGANT WOMEN

COLD DRIZZLE SLANTS ACROSS the car park. I sling my bags into the boot of the red Prius, a hybrid car that I have just about learned to drive since collecting it from the rental office in Winnipeg. It is a replacement for a small car I drove from Chicago to Winnipeg, where a window was smashed by a kind thief who stole a bottle of water, but left me the ten CDs I had brought from home and the *Michelin Road Atlas of North America.*

Next to the Prius is a dirty white pickup, the back strewn with a glutinous mélange of grimy plastic containers, collapsed cardboard boxes, and a filthy oil drum with a sinister blue rubber hose sprouting from it. This flotsam looks so frightful that I stand in the rain and photograph it.

You don't start a Prius: you switch it on by pushing a button. Icons and graphs appear on the dashboard. You move the gearstick into drive and listen to the silence as Prius glides slowly away.

As I accelerate, the gas engine kicks in. I drive west along Main Street, turn left onto Centennial Drive, pass the 83 shield, and soon I'm among fields, green and golden, broken by occasional clumps of trees. To my right, five or so miles off, is a low ridge called Thunder Hill where locals ski in winter. At the top, the border between Manitoba and Saskatchewan is marked by a small obelisk hidden among trees. The road is smooth, wide, two-lane tarmac. I see just three other vehicles as I drive the twenty miles to Durban, the town, half a mile south of 83, where my grandfather lived.

Through the raindrops on the windshield Durban looks dismal. Several buildings seem to have disappeared since I was last here. Only two or three houses have cars outside. The post office, a modern single-story building, is lit but locked. Eleven years ago, when I first visited, the little grid of streets with wood-framed houses scattered among grass and trees had a church, a curling rink, the grain elevator by the railroad track, and an air of community. Now it seems on its way to becoming a ghost town.

I stop the car by a well-kept house with mown grass and neat trees. Close by are three worn, white-painted wooden shacks that I have gazed at on previous visits. One of those shacks could—just *could*—be where my grandfather lived. It is unlikely, almost certainly a romantic fantasy; wooden buildings rarely last *that* long, though these shacks *are* in the part of Durban where the bachelors once had their little board cabins.

Back then, at the beginning of the twentieth century, Durban was a boomtown. There were two hotels, two dance halls, a pool hall, a curling rink, a doctor, a drugstore, a barber, a blacksmith, a cobbler (Thomas Reynolds), a livery stable, two butcher's shops, three groceries, two hardware stores, two banks, a school, a church, and a Chinese café. About four hundred people lived there. Every day except Sunday, a train arrived at the station, and several wagons, pulled by teams of horses, came into town. Every night, the hotels were filled with farmers, traders, and teamsters—and, behind John McCauley's livery stable, men, the cobbler among them, gathered to break the law by drinking alcohol.

I sit in the car beside the well-kept house and the three shacks, and remember meeting a man in Dale's bookshop a few years ago; he wore a blue baseball cap and was leaning on a stick. He had read the book I had written about my search for the story of my grandfather and said, to my astonishment, that he had known him. I thought perhaps he was a little crazy. He looked as if he were in his seventies. My grandfather had been dead for ninety-two years.

But I was wrong. He *had* known my grandfather—just. He was ninety-four years old, and he had been born here in Durban in 1908. His name was Elgin Ostrum (rhymes with post room). He, his parents, and siblings had lived next door to Tom Reynolds, the shoemaker—perhaps where the well-kept house is now. Though he didn't remember my grandfather directly, he remembered his parents talking about him. For some years Elgin's father had worn a pair of boots made by Tom Reynolds. After my grandfather died, Elgin's parents acquired his sewing machine. It had been an excellent machine, Elgin told me, capable of stitching leather; he had inherited it from his parents and had used it to make his own clothes. He couldn't remember what had happened to it. It might still be around, somewhere. His brother would have known, but his brother no longer remembered much; he was ninety-six.

Elgin told me that he too had written a book, the story of his life. Would I like to read it?

I'd love to, I said.

Despite my offering to collect it the next day, he drove home—a forty-mile round-trip—to fetch a copy. "Forty miles is nothing," he said. "And it's a nice day."

I remembered watching through the shop window as he drove off in a red pickup truck—and thinking that my grandfather must have looked at this old man when the man was a baby. Perhaps he had held him in his arms. I had shaken Elgin's hand, a hand that perhaps had gripped my grandfather's.

An hour later Elgin handed me forty-three photocopied sheets that he had typed himself and bound in orange cardboard. On the first page the words "MEMORIES OF THE GOOD OLD DAYS BY ELGIN OSTRUM" were handwritten in thick black capitals. He sat down and signed the title page, "To David Reynolds from Elgin Ostrum." Then he stood up, said good-bye while shaking my hand, adjusted his baseball cap, and walked out of the shop.

I didn't see him again. He died in 2006, aged ninety-seven. His book, an account of his early life, is vivid and plainly written, as if Hemingway were writing in a hurry. Reading it, I could see him as he was in the 1920s and '30s: a hunter, trapper, fisherman—not for sport, for food; an early radio enthusiast and lover of automobiles, who married young and worked hard at a range of jobs, on farms, in forests, on railroads, as a traveling brush salesman, radio repairman, shop worker.

I leave the car and wander up the road and around the corner by the railroad track. A man drives past on a tractor and waves. I wave back and mutter, "Hallo." It is early in June, but I feel cold. I return to the car and switch it on. I lower the window a little and the miserable drizzle blows in. I drive across the railroad track, back up to 83, and on through the rain.

The slow rhythm of the windshield wipers settles inside my head until a slick black pickup roars past showering spray. I switch the wipers to double time, shifting the rhythm to a rapid bebop. I can see the fields beside me and not much else. I pass a farm and, beside it, a tall cylinder that I know is a grain bin; these huge corrugated tubes now contain dryers, which means that farmers can keep their grain at an ideal temperature while they use the internet to see where and when prices are best.

Farmers have more power now. Not long ago, they took their grain to the nearest grain elevator and had to accept the price offered.

I REACH A small town called Benito. 83 runs along its western edge. I turn left and find Main Street, a handful of shops, and some parked cars. A sign swinging outside a low, white concrete building reads M and M's Café and Lounge.

There are plenty of customers: a table with five men in baseball caps who look like farmers; three elegantly dressed women, earnestly chatting; two old couples at a table together. Everyone is having lunch. A waitress, young middle-aged, with the edge of a tattoo showing above her right breast, smiles, puts a menu in front of me, and rushes off. I'm not hungry—I have come in out of curiosity and have brought the sports pages of a Winnipeg newspaper which carry news of the forthcoming football World Cup. I have to order something, so ask for a cup of tea and a muffin. After a while, I realize that people are helping themselves to tea and coffee from a table in the corner. One of the elegant women is there and shows me that I can take a teapot and a tea bag and make my own tea.

The elegant women appear to be in their late thirties. They are well dressed, but not chic or glamorous. Two wear trousers, but not jeans. Trouble, but not too much, has been taken over their hair—subtle dyes, careful cutting. Makeup has been used in a restrained way—a little lipstick. At a glance they seem to be visitors from a big city passing through. But they clearly belong here. They know this café, and everyone in it except me; they are at home in this small town, two hundred miles north of the United States border (90 percent of Canadians famously live within fifty miles of the border). Who and what are they? They could be schoolteachers, but with all that elegance they would have to be headmistresses, all three of them, and there is only one school here. Could they be wealthy farmers or ranchers, or the wives of farmers or ranchers, who do some farming or ranching while managing tribes of teenage children? I'd like to ask them, but I sense that, if I address anyone other than the waitress, the whole place will stop talking and listen.

The waitress brings a hot blueberry muffin. The part of her tattoo that I can see appears to be the wing of a bird. She rushes off to another table. It's the wrong time to start a conversation with her, or with anyone else. I pour a second cup of tea, feel warm and comfortable, and read profiles of footballers.

NOT SO ELEGANT WOMEN

THE ROAD IS ALMOST empty of traffic. The next town, Roblin, is fifty-one miles south. The rain has stopped and the country is green and beautiful, rising and falling, with many trees. To my left, a few miles away, are the wooded slopes of Duck Mountain.

I stop to admire a line of aspen. A lowering gray sky covers the land and curves down to the horizon that encircles it—a disk with me and Prius at its center.

The road enters Duck Mountain Provincial Forest. I pass a turning to the right: Route 57 to Madge Lake. Yesterday in Chicken Chef, Stuart told me that he remembered when 83 was built from here, the Madge Lake turning, to Roblin in the 1930s. Until then 83 didn't reach this far north, and traveling from Benito to Roblin meant looping many miles west past Madge Lake. Getting around this far north and west in Manitoba was difficult before 83 was built. In his *Memories of the Good Old Days,* on a page headed "The Durban to Roblin Road," Elgin Ostrum wrote:

> About 1928 [he would have been nineteen years old] the Dominion Forestry and also the Manitoban government decided that

a road between Durban and Roblin would save a lot of miles and money.

I was asked to find a feasible route across the mountain... I packed a kit bag with some potatoes, onions, flour, salt, baking powder, coffee, sugar, etc., and set out. Took a 22 rifle, frying pan, can to make tea, and another pan for making stew. One blanket and a 4 x 7 silk pup tent was living quarters. I had an axe but no compass. The whole trip took well over a week as I had to backtrack many times when I hit a slough or bog...

The present road follows almost my exact trail right down to where the road branches off 83.

A lumberman in Durban told me last year [Elgin was writing in 1987] that he had found a lot of very old blaze marks and my initials carved in a tree. He thought it was some old Hudson's Bay men years ago.

I would shoot a couple of partridges and toward evening I would boil them good with some onions and potatoes and then thicken it a bit with flour. While it was cooking I would mix up a cup of flour, baking powder, and salt, and cook a bannock [flat bread] on the coals.

The horse never went over a few yards from the fire all night. It was afraid of bears. There seemed to be lots of them, but they were very wild and fat so they were not dangerous. I also had my 45 Colt automatic pistol with me, so did not worry if they did get mad.

In the morning I would boil a pot of coffee, warm up the rest of the partridge stew, and get going.

On smooth, gray tarmac, I drive slowly, pass a pair of deer to my left, and realize that I've never driven like this before: unhurried, giving myself as much time as I fancy to look and think. In the hour after I leave Benito, I stop the car and turn back three or four times to take photographs—a derelict shack, a lake surrounded by graceful aspens, a line of rusting pickups in a field, the road ahead. Could I drive like this all the way? Will it be possible on busier roads?

SOON AFTER THREE o'clock I reach Roblin, and wander down Main Street, three blocks of it with shops either side. I go into the creatively misspelled Caspuccino's Flowers and Gifts Café and am served at a counter by a lady with a sepulchral expression who finds it hard to understand why I want milk in my coffee—but goes to much trouble to find some in a cavernous fridge. Later I understand her puzzlement when I spot a carton of half-and-half cream on a side table, clearly provided for those who like their coffee white.

Three elderly women sit at a round table in the window discussing skin cancer—one of them might have it, but isn't sure yet; and kidney problems—one of their husbands definitely has them. There is loud rock music playing as I eat my second muffin of the day—and the women move on to pneumonia.

I got her wrong, the sepulchral lady. She beams when she discovers that I am from England—something I mention to explain why I am peering so closely at my Canadian coins. So I tell her about my trip down Highway 83.

"Not many people know what is down there on Route 83," she says. She thinks I should call in at the newspaper office—it's round the corner—because they will be interested in my arrival in their town and in what I am doing.

I'm not keen on this idea—suffering, as I do, from what is sometimes called an English reserve—but I straighten my collar and walk off the street into a large office with several desks. Inside are two people, both women: one rather slim, the other not at all slim. They both look up.

I say, "Hi. I'm from England."

The unslim one points at the door I've just walked through. "England's that way." They both explode with hoots and cackles—then calm down, shake my hand, and listen to me explaining my travels. I find myself asking whether they have heard of the Highway 83 Association. They haven't, but suggest I ask at the local council offices next door.

I'm not fond of approaching strangers, but it usually works out all right once I say something—and clearly I am going to have to say something many times during this trip. So, again, I check my collar and walk off the street into a large room. This one contains four women. One of them gets up from her desk and greets me at a counter. I tell her I'm from England, that I'm driving the length of Highway 83, and is she, by any chance, aware of the Highway 83 Association? She isn't, but all four women want to help. Two scour the internet. The other two make phone calls. This goes on for about ten minutes, during which I apologize several times for interrupting the work of Roblin Town Council.

"It's no problem. In fact it's fun," the first woman says.

Eventually I am handed a small piece of paper with a man's name, Leonard, his telephone number, and his hometown, Cranberry Portage. He is said to know a lot about the road and perhaps the association.

Back in the car, I look for Cranberry Portage in my road atlas, hoping it will be on Highway 83 and that perhaps I can visit Leonard. I find it, two hundred miles *north* of Swan River on Highway 10, south of Flin Flon.

I DRIVE ON, slowly, at around 50 or 55 mph, heading for Russell, thirty-three miles on, where I'll likely stop for the night. Cars and pickups pass me, but I don't care.

Here there are fields of cows with black calves, some so small, keeping so close to their mothers, that I wonder if they were born today, or perhaps yesterday. I stop frequently, usually parking where a dirt road leads off at right angles into farmland. There are many such turnings, relics of the land's division into square, 160-acre homesteads. Some of these roads have grown over, returned to grass, or been planted with crops as farms and fields have grown larger; all that remains is a stony break in the grass verge, ideal for parking.

As I get close to Russell, 83 surprises me by transforming into a four-lane highway with a barrier in the middle. It turns out that this change is paving the way for the confluence of 83 and Trans-Canada Highway 16, also known as the Yellowhead Route, a road that runs for seventeen hundred miles northwest from Winnipeg to the Pacific Ocean. This mighty highway smashes its way along the southern edge of Russell, and 83 widens as if to maintain its self-esteem. Which it has to because, for twenty-four miles south of Russell, it is required to share the tarmac with Trans-Canada 16—a damned cheek and a tangling of routes that I would have to unravel the next day.

For now, I drive up and down the four-lane highway and see that there are two motels almost opposite one another. One looks newish and pretentious; the other is called The Jolly Lodger. I go for the latter, which proves to be a conventional motel in all but name: a long, low building where every room has its own front door with a parking space outside.

I sit at a small table beside the bed making phone calls to people Stuart suggested I contact. Some are away, some don't answer, some suggest I phone someone else, some talk and give me interesting information and then suggest I phone someone else.

No one suggests meeting—which is in some ways a relief, what with my English reserve and my feeling that it'd be fun to move quickly south tomorrow.

THE JOLLY LODGER has no restaurant or bar, so I set out to walk the fifty yards or so to the Russell Inn. It seems likely that I am the first person to have made this trip, which includes crossing Trans-Canada 16/Highway 83, on foot. There are no pavements, so I balance on overstuffed grass verges where I wobble as if standing on a pile of mattresses, wait for gaps between fast-moving trucks, and sprint. The swanky sprawl of the Russell Inn embraces Pizza Hut, Tim Hortons, Subway, the Russell Inn Dining Room, and Kristie's Neighborhood Pub.

Kristie's is dark, noisy, crowded, and filled with mirrors that make it hard to see where the walls are. I go to an empty table, high off the floor, and sit on a bar stool with a back. To my left are four lean young men, three of them wearing what I think of as "soft" baseball hats, the type that fit close to the head. A cheerful waitress appears with a menu.

I shout that I would like a Rickard's Red.

"Large or small?" She gestures with her hands.

"Large," I yell and copy her gesture.

Down in front of me ten or twelve people are celebrating the birthday of a beefy middle-aged man whose bare arms are decorated with tattoos. Behind me a group of young women are discussing boyfriends and husbands, and using the expression "I'm like" to mean "I think" or "I feel" or "I say," just as people do in England. Facing me are screens showing baseball, basketball, ice hockey, and what looks like a soap. Across the room two lines of gambling machines wink and blink at a couple of customers whose hands are full of coins.

The waitress returns with the beer and I order spaghetti with meatballs. A large woman emerges from the table behind me and heads across the carpet toward the far corner of the room and a dim neon sign. I squint and adjust my glasses and decide that it says Restrooms. A minute later another large woman sets off.

From behind me I hear the phrase "marijuana milkshake," followed by licentious cackling.

Then a voice says, "I love a milkshake with a Long Island muff dive."

"What that?" another voice says.

"Just a sprinkling of marijuana."

Am I understanding this properly?

The spaghetti arrives and, by the time I have eaten a quarter of it with garlic bread, much melted cheese, and tomato sauce, six women have brushed past me and tacked across the floor to the restrooms. So far, five have come back. I've been able to have a good look at them from both sides. Two are tall. Four are short. All are large.

I watch baseball and find it hard to follow. I must find out about it, especially why the pitchers do that funny thing with their legs, lifting them up—their left legs, if they throw right-handed—across their knees. I am surprised when a pair of baseball pundits are interrupted by news of World Cup football—especially when the news is merely that a Dutch player may miss his country's first match owing to a hamstring injury. The World Cup does not begin for three days, and do the Canadians care? Canada did not qualify, though the United States did and will play England this coming Saturday.

More women squeeze past me from behind. Some of them must be making the trip for a second time. It'll be my turn soon. The conversation back there gets louder. They are talking about penises and boobs, and I hear about someone, evidently not present, who had a child at the age of eleven. Can this be someone local? Or was it national news? I wonder whether there is more sex in small towns than in cities, while on TV an ice hockey player called Chris Pronger is interviewed. Behind me a voice says, "Guys won't wake up for wake-up sex," pauses for a moment, and continues, "so I'll drink a bottle of wine."

I RUN ACROSS the four-lane highway in the dark and make it back to The Jolly Lodger, which is a no-ballpoint motel.

I've discovered that Canadians and Americans do not use the word "biro." I explained to a polite hotel receptionist in

Winnipeg a few days ago: "Laszlo Biro was a Hungarian who invented the ballpoint pen—so in Europe we call them biros."

"Cool," she said and smiled—briefly.

I have been collecting ballpoints from motel rooms since I landed in Chicago. A ballpoint in a motel room is a small sign that someone cares—about advertising the motel's name, address, and phone number.

7

GHOSTS AND GRAIN ELEVATORS

IT WAS A GRAY day, cold, a streak of blue on the horizon. Sharing the tarmac with Trans-Canada 16 meant traffic and speeding trucks. It was impossible to follow my new, slow approach to driving. To see anything except the back of a truck, I had to overtake them. If I drove slowly and let a truck pass me, another would race up behind, its radiator grille a chromium cathedral in my rearview mirror until it swerved past in a whirlwind of noise and smoke.

I was yawning and I found myself looking forward to getting to the USA. This part of Manitoba seemed dull and gray. At last, I came to a junction where 16 headed east, taking almost all the traffic, while 83 headed on south, alone again. And once more I drove slowly.

The road made a turn to the left and dropped into a valley. A bridge and a small town came into view, and then the road beyond, climbing upward. It was a pretty sight, and my faith in Manitoba returned. The town was Birtle, and 83 went right through it, for a while becoming Main Street. I glimpsed a stone chapel, a Chinese café, and a few shops.

Chinese cafés are common in Canadian prairie towns; many were opened in the early years of the twentieth century when

Chinese men came to work as cooks on the burgeoning railroad, preparing food for the navvies. Often they would stop off after the railroad moved on to start a café, and it would be the only one in town. From what I could see of Birtle this one still was.

I TURNED WEST at a sign to Birdtail Sioux, guessing that it was an Indian reservation. A couple of miles off 83, along a new, dead-end road, I found a school, a council building, several homes, and a supermarket—all built of new yellow timber. I drove through and back again, feeling that I was gawping at other people's lives—though there wasn't much to see: buildings, a few pickups, and two men at the door of the supermarket. The place looked unfinished—as if its people were yet to move in.

Later I found out about the Birdtail Sioux. Their reservation covers roughly seven thousand acres and about 640 people live there. Along with other First Nations from southwestern Manitoba, the Birdtail Sioux First Nation is a member of the Dakota Ojibway Tribal Council. (Dakota is another name for the Santee Sioux, a long-established branch of the Sioux Nation. The Ojibway, also known as the Chippewa, is one of the larger groups of First Nations in Canada, and there are Ojibway south of the border too.)

Recently the Birdtail Sioux fell out with the tribal council because, led by their then chief, Ken Chalmers, they formed partnerships with the federal government of Canada and with corporations, such as the Canadian National Railway and gas distribution corporation Enbridge, to fund building projects on their land. The tribal council objected to these deals on the grounds that they will weaken its continuing claims to ownership of land—claims that go back to 1870 (the year that Manitoba became a province of Canada).

In response, Chief Chalmers stated that the only way he can improve the living standards of his people is "by partnering, not fighting."

To this, one of the Dakota Ojibway chiefs, Frank Brown, replied: "Divide and conquer is a game Indian Affairs plays all of the time... When you challenge Canada in court or when you challenge for your rights, they take one of your people and give them money to convince them otherwise. The job creation is a good thing, but it's not fixing nothing; it's just a little Band-Aid, whereas we're working for the future of our people."

The contrasting strategies of the two chiefs echo the tactics that Indian chiefs have used since the Europeans arrived five hundred years ago (while the tactics of government and business have changed perhaps only by degree). Some chiefs signed treaties and made compromises in the hope of peace and prosperity. Others resisted—sometimes forfeiting their lives—insisting that the land belonged to their people and their ancestors, and often that the white men's promises would not be kept anyway.

In the past, Canadian First Nations fared better than their cousins in the United States, in the crucial sense that a lot less of their blood was shed. This is held to be because the colonizers—first the French and then the British—were more interested in furs than in land. Carl Waldman, author of *Atlas of the North American Indian,* writes that the colonizers of Canada "wanted to buy from, sell to, and employ Native Americans, not displace them." After Canada became a Dominion in 1867, the peaceful stance was preserved because the immigrant population remained low—about 10 percent of that of the U.S.—and because many reserves for Native people in the West were set up before, rather than after, the arrival of European settlers. A third factor, says Waldman, was the "Northwest Mounted Police's level-headed approach to relations with the First Nations" right from its foundation in 1873. However, despite relatively few outbreaks of violence, "the same long-term repercussions of U.S. expansion—diseases, liquor, land cessions, and reservations—are as much a part of the Canadian Indian story."

I LOOPED NORTH on a dirt road and eventually rejoined 83 a few miles north of where I'd left it. Soon it plunged steeply into another valley, crossed the fast-flowing Assiniboine River, and rose again to travel in a straight line across farmland. Fifteen miles on, after zigzagging across the five-thousand-mile coast-to-coast Trans-Canada Highway, it reached Virden, the oldest and largest town on 83 so far.

I drove around and found that, instead of Main Street, Virden has King Street with shops at one end and old, brick-built family homes at the other. One of these is now the Virden Pioneer Home Museum, a two-story, late Victorian, red-brick house with an octagonal turret to one side, set in a spacious, grassy garden. I paid a few dollars and was shown around by a teenage girl with a pretty face, wearing black. She was a volunteer guide working during her holidays from school, and was a lot better than those guides who deliver a lecture in every room while you stare around trying to look interested, desperate for them to finish so that you can walk about unhindered. She knew some stuff and I guessed at other stuff, and together we made sense of the house and some of its beautiful, old, locally made furniture.

In a room at the back, among old carts, plowshares, and bicycles, was a four-person sled. Sleek and inviting with stuffed seats, it would have been pulled across the snow-covered prairies by a horse. I stared at it and told my companion about my grandfather writing home to London from Swan River more than one hundred years before—how he described traveling twenty miles by sled to a dance, and sledding home hours later by moonlight.

My guide showed me early photos of Virden and said that there were no trees when the pioneers arrived around 1880. As I drove on south through flat country, I saw that there are very few now.

I turned off 83 and drove on empty dirt roads in search of a ghost town called Ryerson. Among the crops and the grazing cattle, curious metal contraptions rocked up and down. About the size and shape of a donkey, they seemed to be in perpetual motion, to be some kind of pump—perhaps, I thought, pulling up water for irrigation.

I came to a wide dirt road with a sign, Ryerson Road. Promising, but should I turn north or south? I chose south and, a couple of miles on, came across a bunch of bulldozers, earthmovers, and backhoes, their necks raised and mouths gaping like a herd of angry dinosaurs, tearing at the earth, throwing out clouds of dust. I sat at a red light in a traffic jam, squirting the windshield washer to clear the dun-colored dirt. Prius's red paint was already coated with mud, yet he seemed feminine as he waited among deep-voiced, smoke-belching tractors, and pickups whose drivers sat, high up and looking at me, on wheels that could ford the Assiniboine. But when, at last, we began to jolt over earth pitted with holes and strewn with boulders, he rocked and rolled with the rest of them.

I gave up looking for Ryerson—perhaps, like many ghosts, it wasn't there. Had I been wasting my time? Or was I learning something by looking, smelling the air, and listening to the cattle, the birds, the wind in the grass. When I planned this trip, I decided that I would explore *around* 83 as well as drive every yard of it. I gave myself two rules:

Rule 1: If I leave the highway, I must return to the place where I left it or farther back, so I travel all of it.

Rule 2: I will not stray more than ninety miles from the road, ninety miles being, on average, half the distance between 83 and the neighboring north-south highways, 81 and 85. Neither of those goes north into Canada, or is as complete within the United States as 83, but they are there and, on average, are roughly 180 miles to the east and west. My territory therefore is an imaginary Corridor 83: 180 miles wide, ninety miles either side of 83.

In a village called Maryfield I took photographs of a row of rusting fifty-year-old cars and trucks, and approached an elderly man in dungarees—in a classic Western he would have been called "old-timer"—to ask the way. He didn't say much, but he pointed. I went that way and, in half an hour, was back on 83, north of where I'd left it.

I was heading for Melita, thirty-five miles south, and the only place before the U.S. border where there might be a motel. The country was flat, the light dull, and there were few trees. I drove faster than usual on an empty road.

LATE IN THE day the sun appears, throwing a sharp light across the land. Clouds rush east, streaming low above me and putting on a light show in blues and grays and whites that curves to the horizons. I am at the center of a multidimensional cinema in the round, even as I travel at 60 mph. I stop, leave the car, stand, and stare. Could this be filmed? Only with a fish-eye lens, and that would distort the beauty only my eyes can see. Millennia ago this sight must have filled the Assiniboine Indians with wonder—and then enchanted the pioneers from Europe, in their turn.

Melita tumbles down a hill with 83 at its center. At the bottom I drive into a gas station and a blond lad fills the tank with gas. I ask about motels.

"There's only one." He points back up the hill, at a rectangular building to the left.

"Can I eat there?"

"Yep." He grins. "That's where everyone goes. The only place in town."

The gas is still pumping and I ask about the town. "Busy," he says. "Oil people, more of them every day."

AT THE MELITA INN I am greeted by a gruff, middle-aged woman who gives me a room key and tells me I can eat in the dining room or the bar.

In the bar a man called Dan, who wears a black eye-patch over his right eye, says, "83 is a boring, dull road, all the way to Texas." And then admits that he hasn't been down it; his father told him.

Later he tells me a joke. A group of Indians (he uses that word) are repeatedly told by their chief that the next winter is going to be very cold, so they spend much time chopping and storing logs. The chief is getting his information from a friend who is a meteorologist. After a few weeks the chief asks his friend how he can be so sure about the coming winter. His friend replies, "Well... those Indians are storing logs big-time."

When Dan goes outside for a cigarette, a neat, blond woman called Charlotte tells me about him. "He's a good man. A bit wild. He lost his eye when he was nineteen; was cleaning a gun and it went off. Lucky to be alive."

I go for a walk in the dark. The town has a frontier, plonked-down air about it: commercial buildings dumped along a couple of roads at the bottom of a hill, with narrow, lumpy, street-lit roads climbing the slope above. Small white houses and bungalows seem too close together, though each stands in its own patch of grass. All are different, many with a home-made feel: a curious gable, an ungainly cantilever, an eccentric afterthought stuck on the side, or the back, or the roof.

Two men walk downhill in front of me, twenty yards apart. In the semidarkness they seem sinister. Where can they be going this late?

Only to the gas station, which is still open, lit up, selling food and cigarettes.

I gaze up at a white-painted grain elevator beside the railway lines. It might be one hundred years old, but is almost certainly much younger, the average lifespan of these towering, wooden structures being forty years. Far taller than any local church or chapel, they have a simple, stark beauty. Often they stand, apparently alone in the vastness of the prairie, visible for miles in every direction, the only sign that humans exist in the emptiness. This one has the common boxy design, with sloping roofs and a gable at the top, that was used from the 1900s to the 1980s. There is another, similar one farther along the road. Melita is an unusual town—perhaps because there is oil here, as well as heaps of wheat: enough, it seems, to fill two elevators.

FRACKING IN GATSBY COUNTRY

I ATE BREAKFAST AT THE Melita Inn in the company of twenty-five people. Sixteen of them were wearing baseball caps. Ten elderly men—spectacles, short gray hair, modest paunches—shared a large oval table and gave the impression that they had sat there many times before: if not every morning, then at least every Thursday morning. Nine of them wore high-fronted baseball caps in an assortment of colors. The maverick tenth wore a floppy cotton sunhat in dark blue and a vacant expression. Younger men, some wearing low-fronted, close-fitting baseball caps, sat in small groups and were perhaps oil workers. There were two female customers: one young, with a man and two nice-looking children; the other, at the table next to mine, an older woman with a man whose long gray hair straggled from beneath a red baseball cap which was pushed to the back of his head so that the peak pointed toward the ceiling, giving him a raffish, devil-may-care air—in contrast with everyone else.

The waitress was the gruff woman who had welcomed me the previous evening. She was wearing blue jeans and a blouse with yellow checks. She wasn't thin, nor was she fat. This morning her gruffness was tempered by short smiles, quips, and an almost-warm familiarity with everyone. She addressed me, but not just me, as "darling." She brought coffee, eggs, bacon, hash browns—real hash browns, not the cardboard kind that come out of a packet—and toast, with strawberry jam and peanut butter in little boxes. All this on a very small plate, so I had to dig the eggs out from under the toast.

"Fishing is a dirty job but someone has to do it." The old man in the red baseball hat looked glumly at the woman I had assumed to be his wife, and put a forkful of egg into his mouth.

Would a man say that at breakfast to a woman he knew well? Perhaps. At any rate, the woman just murmured agreement, as if she had heard this before. This woman and the other women I had seen in the past few days—the waitress, the women in the bar last night, the women in the pub in Russell, the journalists in Roblin, the elegant women of Benito, my friend Dale in Swan River—had a noticeable toughness and self-reliance. Might this come from living on the prairies, on ground that was homesteaded and broken with plows and pickaxes little more than a hundred years ago?

I wondered how relations between the genders worked. Why were there so few women in here? Where were the wives of the ten old men at the oval table? Where were they eating their breakfasts? Those men couldn't all be widowers or bachelors.

I looked out of the window at the street, the valley, and the gas station. A man in jeans and baseball hat walked by leading a small white dog with a fancy curled-up tail. The dog looked cute and expensive—and incongruous in this thrown-together town full of oilmen and farmers. (The paper table mat underneath my plate carried five advertisements for agricultural supplies and five for oil-drilling products.) Was it only the dog, or was the man mincing just a little? Might the dog belong to the man's wife? Might the man be gay? Could a man be openly gay in a masculine kind of town like this?

The waitress came round offering coffee. She put her hand on red baseball cap's shoulder—as much to keep her balance while she poured, as out of affection, perhaps—and she complimented him, flirtatiously, on his fitness.

He smiled. "I walk a lot and I eat small proportions—not too much carbohydrate," he said.

The old men were leaving slowly together. I watched through the window as they raised their hands to one another and climbed into SUVs and pickup trucks. And I remembered an important distinction that I'd picked up from William Least Heat-Moon. In *Blue Highways* he lamented the loss of "old hotels to the motel business. The hotel was once where things coalesced, where you could meet townspeople and travelers. Not so in a motel. No matter how you build it, the motel remains a haunt of the quick and dirty, where the only locals are Chamber of Commerce boys every fourth Thursday."

I stood behind red baseball cap as I waited to pay. He turned and looked into my eyes for a second and nodded, "Hi." His eyes were rheumy and he had an old man's nose, blotchy with deep pores. With his long gray hair, he reminded me of a friend in England, another lean philosopher of small proportions.

"Hi," I said.

He smiled and turned away to hand over his money.

The gruff waitress smiled at him—and me. The Melita Inn was a hotel.

THE SKY WAS dull and a light drizzle plipped onto the windshield as I drove south. I turned on the radio. A man was talking about his son, how he couldn't control him. The boy insisted on climbing aboard his new mower and starting the engine. "I told him, 'You get your legs cut off in that lawn mower, don't come running to me.'"

I was getting close to the border. Friends from Toronto and Vancouver had warned that crossing from Canada to the U.S.

would be tiresome and time-consuming, with queues of traffic as customs officers searched cars, examined documents, and asked awkward questions. But I wondered about this: 83 seemed to be an insignificant two-lane road—and there was no traffic in either direction. I came around a bend and saw signs and a brick building. The U.S. border post had come on me suddenly—in part because there had been no Canadian border post. It seemed that in this remote place, at least, the Canadians rely on the Americans to look out for Canadians who are on the run.

A man in uniform signaled me to stop and wind down the window; he was on the passenger side of the car—in some cars I would have had to lean across the seat and literally wind it down. Unsmiling, he took my passport and fired questions: When, where, how long, where does this car come from, why are you here?

All these questions except the last were easy to answer. But I had been advised by friends *not* to say that I was writing a book about driving down this very road. I was driving this road to Texas, I said, because my grandfather had lived farther north, he used to drive down south for the winter, and I wanted to see where he went.

The latter part of this was not true; my grandfather died before 83 was built, and he didn't have a car. The man just stared at me. Did he know I was lying?

I said that I had a ticket for a flight back to London from Houston.

He pointed to a customs shed, told me to drive into it, and walked off with my passport.

In the shed I was met by another customs officer who took me into an office. There he asked me to empty my pockets and fill in a form. As I did this, he—clearly the good cop—smiled a lot and chatted: about my route, my job, and even my wife and her job. Then he asked me to wait while he searched the car.

Soon bad cop came in, told me my passport was "on the dash," and went away again.

Good cop came back. "That's fine. You're free to go, but let me show you how to get to the Black Hills."

He spread out a map and we leaned over it together. He thought that to drive straight down 83 wouldn't be enough fun. After Minot I should cross over to Route 85—he traced it on the map with a ballpoint—and head "through more interesting country." On the way I should stop at a place called Medora where I could see a show in an amphitheatre—he'd seen it with his wife and kids: a great show, with fireworks, horses, singing, and dancing. Knowing that I wouldn't be making this detour, I nonetheless fetched my road atlas from the car so that he could show me the way on my own map. I suppose I wanted to repay his friendship with my enthusiasm. Besides, one day I *might* take his route to the Black Hills and be glad to stop off at Medora.

He walked with me to the car. I said, "I guess you have to do this. A middle-aged Englishman could be a bomber..."

"Yes," he said. "Since 9/11."

"I understand. I appreciate it," I said.

THE DRIZZLE HAD turned into a dense mist. Hunched behind the windshield wipers I couldn't see much of North Dakota. What I could see seemed flat, like southern Manitoba.

I came to a town called Westhope, a small, square place, laid out on a grid. I drove up a street, crossed over a block, and drove down a street, Main Street. There was a bar, a bank, a post office, and a few shops—a very neat town, unlike Melita, yet apparently thriving on the same fare: farming and oil.

The rain grew heavier, and it became the kind of day when a booger flicked out of a car window comes back in and sticks to your shirt. I turned on the radio and heard what seemed like the saddest song of all time: "If Tomorrow Never Comes" sung by Garth Brooks. Then came Alan Jackson's "She's Got the Rhythm (And I Got the Blues)," which was much more jolly. I was tuned to Farm Radio. Country music was cut into with information for farmers about such things as wheat futures, hog prices, and the likelihood of the coming days' weather being suitable for crop spraying. I was interested to hear these things and there were good songs and singers: Dolly Parton, Johnny Cash, Willie Nelson, Emmylou Harris, Vince Gill. But, as the rain drummed ever harder on the roof, there were some terrible, mawkish songs about sunny weather and bountiful harvests.

I switched the wipers to top speed, but the manic arm-waving, inches from my face, gave me the jimjams. I turned them back to French-art-movie speed. Once again, I could see better sideways than straight ahead. The land seemed almost featureless: no ruined shacks or barns as there were in Canada. Broad fields held few trees; those that there were, had been planted long ago in lines, perhaps as windbreaks or as boundaries between homesteads that have merged into larger farms. I spotted a couple of the curious rocking, pumping mechanisms, the donkeys that dipped their heads to the ground, that I had seen the day before.

Despite the rain, I felt exhilarated at the thought of the days of driving that lay ahead. At last I was on the road, alone and free to go wherever I wanted in this vast country. But sticking close to 83 was the plan and a good one. Traveling the length of the United States on a north–south route meant, obviously, that I would cross every east–west route: historic roads like the Lincoln Highway, railroads like the Union Pacific, and the pioneer trails that came before them and spread westward during the nineteenth century: the Oregon and Mormon trails through Nebraska, and the Santa Fe Trail across Kansas. But first, not far beyond the next city, Minot, I would go further back into history and cross the route of Lewis and Clark, the boldest pioneers of all.

I STOPPED AT a convenience store beside a gas station, ran in through the rain, and bought a packet of biscuits (Nature Valley Oats 'n Honey granola bars) from a smiling woman and her small smiling daughter. We moaned about the weather, and I asked about the rocking, pumping donkeys.

She raised her eyebrows and went on smiling, as if I were a small, stupid, but lovable child. "Oil. They're pulling up oil."

"Oh!" I had thought that oil wells were like factories, shrouded in smoke and chimneys, always with a flame burning from the tallest chimney. I'd seen photographs and I'd seen them on TV, in the Middle East, and on platforms off the coast of Scotland. "Oh—so it's sort of small scale?"

"Maybe, but not to the farmers. Some of them make more out of that than they do from their regular work. They do deals with the oil company, get a percentage."

There is, indeed, oil on a large—in fact, massive—scale. North Dakota, I soon learned, sits on the largest pool of oil in the original forty-eight states, and is producing more of the stuff than many OPEC nations and almost as much as Texas. The source is a rock formation named the Bakken, after a farmer on whose land oil was first found in 1951. Back then it was hard to extract. So nothing much happened until 2008, when new methods—horizontal drilling and fracking—brought almost half a million barrels to the surface every day. Now the state attracts migrant workers from all over the country and has the lowest rate of unemployment in the U.S. Once-sleepy farm towns, around fifty to a hundred miles west of 83, have turned into booming cities that struggle to manage swollen populations and the vice that feeds on new money.

I drove on through the rain and flatness, and remembered that this place, North Dakota, was where James Gatz lived as a child, "the son of shiftless and unsuccessful farm people," before he changed his name to Jay Gatsby, moved east, and succeeded, for a while, as a fraudster.

There are fewer farm people in North Dakota now than there were in the distant, World War I time of the Gatzes. In fact, there are fewer now than there were in 1980. Advances in techniques, technology, herbicides, and seed genetics mean that fewer workers are needed. At the same time, at least until the recent recession, farm workers have been drawn away from the land, enticed by higher wages in cities.

Meanwhile farms have become larger. Neighbors have been buying the farms of neighbors, who often go off to live in nearby towns, since homesteading began—and they're still at it. Arable farms of fewer than six hundred acres were common thirty years ago in the Great Plains from North Dakota to Kansas; now most are at least eleven hundred acres, and some are ten times that size. But a high proportion of the larger farms are still family owned, even if the family members are directors of a corporation. Since 2000, a drive in the other, hippier direction has occurred—toward farms of fewer than fifty acres run by people who work part time at another job or are retired. There are now more large farms and more small farms, but fewer middle-sized, hundred- to five-hundred-acre farms.

9

TURKEY DINNER IN A GLASS

THE RAIN EASED; THE road widened to four lanes and began to drop downhill; long, low houses appeared on both sides, a yellow sign on a concrete pillar announced Super 8 Motel, then a Burger King, then traffic lights. This was Minot.

I drove across the Souris, or Mouse, River and uphill again on a busy road lined with motels, eating houses, strip malls, and gas stations. Minot was bigger than I'd imagined. On the southern edge of town I turned into Walmart's car park. I've visited Walmarts in other parts of the U.S. and Canada; they are all the same: concrete blockhouses filled with cheap food and other stuff, standing in car parks as big as Los Angeles. They appeal to me because of their enormity, in both senses. It took me ten minutes to find a tin of almonds and pay for it.

I checked into a small motel, then headed downtown where a few blocks of small shops, cafés, and bars are grouped around South Main Street. It was mid-afternoon: gray, and a little cold. I wandered into Main Street Books and soon found myself telling the proprietor about my trip. She introduced me to another customer, a man called Andy, who is a professor at the University of Minot. (I hadn't realized there was one but, of course, didn't say so.)

Andy knows 83 well and is an enthusiast. "It's a nice highway. It's enjoyable. It joins many great cities—smaller cities, where you don't get lost in the metropolitan hustle and bustle. They have character. People are predictable, open, and friendly." Every summer Andy and a group of friends used to ride down 83 on motorbikes as far as North Platte, Nebraska, and then head west to Denver and the Rockies.

Andy tells me that he has a friend called Mark, another professor, who has written a history of Minot, and that I should meet him because he will be able to tell me some of the history of 83. Andy leads me across the shop and shows me Mark's book, *The Last Hurrah: An Account of Life in the Mouse River Valley, Bone Town, Little Chicago, and the Magic City* (the last three are old nicknames for Minot).

Andy pulls out his mobile, phones Mark, and soon hands the phone to me. Mark suggests we meet on campus at nine the next morning.

Andy is a very nice man. So nice that, if we were in London, I would be suspicious. Could he be plotting to steal Prius? We English aren't so friendly... Or are we? Andy tells me that he has just been to England with his daughter and that everyone there was charming and helpful. After he had bought tickets for *We Will Rock You* at the Dominion Theatre, he asked the box-office clerk if he knew of anywhere they could stay; he didn't, but he fetched a young woman who did, and she brought a map and directed them to a hotel, which was friendly and cheap and they had to share a bathroom down the corridor, but who cared about that.

Andy gives more examples of English helpfulness, and we have a discussion about how to pronounce Tottenham, as in Tottenham Court Road where the Dominion Theatre is. However many times I say "Tottenum," Andy and the bookshop owner say "Totting-ham," as if the word denotes a type of smoked meat. It's as if they can't hear me. I tell them about the football club Tottenham Hotspur and the great Argentinian footballer Ossie Ardiles, who played for it in the 1980s; for years Ossie called the club "Totting-ham" to the great amusement of English football fans. In the end I write the pronunciation down as I have here. Then they understand and say it the English way.

I wander the streets again and come to a bar, an old, single-story, red-brick building standing alone beside a car park in a side street. The bar is small, the size of a garage intended for a single car, and looks warm and inviting. It's 7 PM. I go in and find a richly decorated room, with pictures all over the walls and colorful furniture, and two people: a young woman behind the bar and another sitting in front of it. Both of them say hello in a restrained way. Blackboards behind the bar list many strangely named beers; none is familiar to me, but one is something "bock." I order it. I remember drinking a beer that ended in "bock" and liking it—though the word means "goat" in German.

The woman behind the bar has lush, dark hair and is called Chris; she's standing in for the regular barman who is late. She and her friend, Wendy, explain that Chris's father owns the bar. He bought the building, which is more than one hundred years old, fifteen years ago to save it from demolition. He's an artist and professor of art at the university, and he renamed the bar The Blue Rider after a group of expressionist artists, centered on Wassily Kandinsky and Franz Marc, who named themselves *Der Blaue Reiter* in Munich before World War I. (Writing about *Der Blaue Reiter* years later, Kandinsky explained that Marc loved horses, and he, Kandinsky, loved riders—and both of them loved the color blue. Indeed, Kandinsky held that blue—the darker the better—is the color of spirituality.)

A youngish man with a short beard and a baseball cap has come in and is sitting at the bar next to me with a beer. He nods in my direction, we get talking, and he tells me that I should visit a place in South Dakota called Bullhead where Sitting Bull was born. He turns away, back to his beer, unaware of the effect of his casual mention of the great Sioux leader. I have only ever *read about* Indian chiefs and their people and their struggles to save their ways of life and their lands. Now I am *there,* on the land where those Indians lived—and I will be *there* all the way as I drive south.

In his book *Great Plains,* Ian Frazier says: "Highway 83 runs from Mexico to Canada and is like the Main Street of the Great Plains." The plains extend perhaps a hundred miles east of the road and farther than that west into states I won't be visiting: Montana, Wyoming, New Mexico. In the 1980s Frazier drove all over the plains. Twice, with great difficulty, he visited a patch of land at the bottom of a steep hill beside a creek not far from the place the man sitting next to me has just mentioned, Bullhead, because this is where Sitting Bull, chief of the Hunkpapa Sioux and scourge of General Custer at the Little Bighorn, spent his final years—living in a log cabin.

Frazier's book has plenty to say about the Indians—for example: "In former times Indians thought the white men's custom of shaking hands was comical. Sometimes two Indians would approach each other, shake hands, and then fall on the ground laughing."

I become friendly with the man on the next stool. In fact, over the next few hours, maybe he and I get a little drunk together. His name is Joe. My guess is that he is in his late twenties; perhaps he is thirty. He has an easy way of talking, engaged and sympathetic, quietly American, like James Stewart. He plays bass in more than one band—bass, because, when he was growing up, the rest of his family played instruments and they needed a bass player—and, for a day job, he looks after disabled people.

Joe knows all the beers, so he orders for both of us, and we listen to hints from the barman, Eli. We drink two pints each of Summit Red, a beautiful honey-flavored drink: ambrosia with hops. Then a bottle of Summit pale ale. We move on to Grain Belt Beer Premium, which Joe says is "like turkey dinner in a glass"; then Moose Drool, from Montana; and then Sierra Nevada Torpedo, which is a little on the strong side. I think we have two of them, but I'm not sure. Sometime—about the time we order the Grain Belt, I think—we share a pizza. The Blue Rider has a stock of pizzas bought from somewhere swanky and Eli heats them in a big oven so that the cheese melts. Joe is vegetarian, so we choose plain cheese that drips from the points of the triangles as I lift them.

The television at the end of the bar is showing baseball. Just recently Joe has decided to support the Minnesota Twins—the nearest Major League baseball team to Minot, despite it being on the other side of the next state—because "I kinda need an interest in life." He smiles and points to his cap, which carries the word "Twins" in small letters low down. "Minnesota Twins hate Chicago White Sox," he hollers, and waves a fist. Joe and Eli know that the USA will play England in the football World Cup in two days' time; they are going to watch the game right here in this bar, and they are expecting their team to lose. They invite me to join them. And I am tempted. The game will be played in the evening in South Africa—lunchtime in Minot. Can I hang around here that long?

Joe is telling me that he wants to get away from Minot. It's too conservative. He'd like to move to Colorado, a liberal state, or even better Austin, Texas. "Austin is cooler than San Francisco now," he says. As he speaks I notice a moose's head on the wall beside the television, huge, bigger than the screen. I think about Britain. Are some parts cooler than others? Yes—to some people sometimes. But we don't have the choice that

Americans have—with their huge land and a tradition of migration across and within it.

I tell Joe about the strange, right-wing politics that I'd heard amid the country music on the car radio that morning. He says I should listen to a program called *Democracy Now*, with Amy Goodman—and that he likes Nancy Pelosi, the Speaker of the House of Representatives and an Obama supporter.

Eli has round glasses and a blue woolen hat that Joe says is a beanie; reddish hair blooms from beneath it.

I ask about the high-fronted baseball hats that seem popular with old men.

"Trucker hats," Joe twiddles his glass on the bar and smiles. "They were given away to truck drivers by people with stuff to advertise. Grain companies, John Deere, people like that."

Joe has to go. I have to go. It's half-past midnight. Again Eli mentions the World Cup game on Saturday; he would enjoy watching it with an Englishman. He will be opening the bar earlier than usual, at noon.

The glass eyes of a bear gaze down from close to the ceiling. Below the bear is a painting of a green bird and below that a piano. The room feels like the warmest place on earth. I swallow the last of my beer, say good-bye to them, and tell them I'll be back.

BUFFALO HOOVES

IN THE MORNING I feel grungy and would rather not have to meet an academic whom I don't know at 9 AM. But I have to, and I will learn something.

A trim, gray-haired man, wearing a black cord jacket and blue jeans as he had said he would, stands in the drizzle where we had agreed to meet.

"David!"

"Mark!"

Mark leads me through an atrium to a space with white walls, Scandinavian-style furniture, and lots of light. We sit on soft brown chairs and between us is a soft brown cube, a pouf.

I learn that the first white man known to have traveled in what was to become North Dakota was a French Canadian fur trader named La Vérendrye, who arrived in 1738. At that time many Indian trails met at the crossing on the Mouse River around which Minot would eventually grow, and the Mouse Valley was popular for hunting, with plenty of antelope, deer, and beaver. The Dakota (Santee Sioux), Cheyenne, Mandan, Hidatsa, and Arikara Indians were all in the region, while the Assiniboine lived and hunted along the Mouse, which flows south to Minot from its source in Saskatchewan and then turns back north into Manitoba.

Mark hands me a map dated 1885, four years before North Dakota became a state, and points to a spot southeast of a fork in the Mouse River. This is where Minot will be, he says, once it has been officially founded two years later. He runs his finger down the map, south for about fifty miles, to a point on the north bank of the Missouri River marked Fort Stevenson. "The city founders all used this trail to Stevenson; they went down there to get supplies, flour, sugar, and things like that, that were coming upriver. It was just an old Indian trail, but it pretty much follows the exact route of 83 today." Then he shows me a map dated 1924 and points to a road running north–south through Minot, marked Highway 6. When the national U.S. Highways were built a few years later, North Dakota 6 became U.S. 83.

Route 6 went north into Canada and carried trade across the border, mainly wheat and cattle—but also illegal alcohol. After Dakota Territory was created by an Act of Congress in 1861, most of its counties—peopled predominantly by European protestants—passed laws banning liquor. And when the territory became two states (North and South) in 1889, North Dakota remained dry. Route 6 is known to have been used for bootlegging in the early 1900s, when the border was poorly guarded, but the trade likely began earlier than that.

From 1920, when Federal Prohibition was instituted, Route 6 (soon to become 83) was packed with bootleggers, especially at night south of Minot, as the city became a hub for the distribution of alcohol. Again it came in from Canada, while also being produced illegally in local stills. It was stockpiled in Minot and sent south to thirteen cities, as far away as Sioux City, Iowa—and this is why Minot came to be known as Little Chicago.

Later I discovered in the State Historical Society of North Dakota in Bismarck that the route of 83 and its number were decided by a board in Washington in the fall of 1925. By the spring of 1927, grading and surfacing were complete and U.S. Highway shields were put up.

A buffalo trail became an Indian trail which became a pioneer trail and then a road providing a route for trade, legal and illegal. Then, in little more than one year, 1926, the road became Highway 83 and continued, until Prohibition ended in 1933, to be laden with booze.

AS MARK WALKED with me to the car park, he told me that he used to be "in the military." Then, as if to show another side of himself, he said with a laugh: "You know Minot had a communist party until 1954, but they don't talk about that now."

I drove away, keen to find a cup of coffee and something to eat. The rain had stopped but the sky was still lowering gray. On the road out of town, there were plenty of fast-food chains and no other options. I chose McDonald's because its car park was easy to reach.

The place was large and warm; people sat munching behind plate glass, staring out at rows of cars. I stood in a queue with my mind in neutral until a good-looking man in a neat cotton suit came in from outside. He was trying to lean on a stick. The stick and his legs and arms were shaking severely. A cashier glanced at him from behind the till, turned, and shouted something. Immediately a man in a tie appeared, hurried over, helped the man to sit down at the nearest table, and beckoned a "crew member," who took his order. The man's shakes began to subside. He put a newspaper on the table, smoothed it, and started to read. I suspected—and, in a way, hoped—that this happened every day.

I knew that I couldn't manage an Egg McMuffin or anything involving bacon or sausage. I ordered coffee and "hotcakes."

It was a dismal meal, served in plastic and Styrofoam. As I ate, I opened Mark's book and read about the intercourse between the North Dakota Socialist Party, the Industrial Workers of the World (aka the Wobblies), and the Minot Socialist Local in the early years of the twentieth century.

Further on I found this, and liked it:

> Prior to 1886, the Mouse River Valley held a true treasure of the Northern Plains. The Creator had aptly decorated the area with giant silver-leafed cottonwood, stands of burr oak, and American elm... Here and there old trails, shallow grooves several feet wide, swooped down into the valley. They had been formed over time by buffalo hooves as they meandered across the landscape down into the valley for water and shelter. Other trails crisscrossed the valley and were remnants of old Native American trails that headed north to the Assiniboine, Ojibwa, and Hudson Bay fur traders and to the south to the Mandan, Hidatsa, and Arikara.

As I left Minot I saw a stretch of the old 83—steep, narrow, and long-ago abandoned in favor of the smooth, wide, gently graded, and cambered modern road. Mark had told me to look for it "in a little valley" that he called a "coulee." The old road was cracked and potholed and sprouting grass and weeds. I drove onto it and bumped downhill into the valley. It didn't look like much, but it was possible to imagine a two-lane highway that, in the 1920s, bootleggers had sped along on moonless nights in six-cylinder Buicks and eight-cylinder Cadillacs—cars chosen for their strength and speed and known as "whiskey sixes" and "whiskey eights."

The rain fell again as I returned to the highway. The wipers thrashed and I was deep in fog, peering ahead at a pair of taillights that kept sliding into the murk. Occasionally, looking sideways, I saw a windmill—the modern turbine type. Otherwise I was alone with the radio for thirty miles, sighing as Willie Nelson kept Georgia on his mind. But country music had its price; for every decent song there was a five-minute rant from a nutcase who believes that Europe is governed by communists and that Obama is a Muslim. (Why would it matter if he were? I wondered.)

11

LEWIS AND CLARK AND SACAGAWEA

THE RAIN WAS EASING as I drove onto the mile-long causeway that crosses Lake Sakakawea, one of the largest man-made lakes in the U.S., formed by damming the Missouri. The road was charcoal-black, the lake was gray and choppy, and the sky was turning silver.

A few miles on I came to a building that commemorated two of the most celebrated Americans in history: Captain Meriwether Lewis and Lieutenant William Clark were the first Americans to travel overland to the West Coast. The Lewis and Clark Interpretive Center is here because it is close to the place on the bank of the Missouri where Lewis and Clark spent the five-month-long winter of 1804–5.

How Lewis and Clark and their party traveled this far is quite a story. How they reached the Pacific and managed to get back again is even more thrilling.

When Thomas Jefferson became the third U.S. president in 1801, he was keen to expand the United States beyond what was then its western border, the Mississippi, and to find a river route to the Pacific. A Scotsman, Alexander Mackenzie, had crossed the Rockies in Canada in 1793 and, finding the Fraser

River impassable, had reached the Pacific by land. Publication of his journals in 1801 inspired and energized Jefferson; if the Americans didn't cross the continent soon, the West Coast might end up British. In the spring of 1803 Jefferson persuaded Congress to fund an expedition and appointed Captain Lewis, who not only was his private secretary but actually lived with him in the White House, to command what he called "the Corps of Discovery." Lewis, in a letter which has been described by the American historian Donald Jackson as "one of the most famous invitations to greatness the nation's archives can provide," invited his former army comrade William Clark to join him as coleader of the expedition.

As well as finding a way to the Pacific, Lewis and Clark's brief from Jefferson included mapping the interior of the continent, researching its plants and wildlife, and establishing diplomatic and trading relations with the many Indian tribes they would encounter.

Lewis spent much of 1803 studying relevant subjects, such as botany, zoology, medicine, and navigation, with scientists in Philadelphia. Then he moved to Pittsburgh where he supervised the building of a boat, fifty-five feet long and eight feet wide, with a thirty-two-foot mast, a keel, a hold that could carry twelve tons of supplies, and a cabin at the back. He bought a dog for twenty dollars, a large, black Newfoundland which he named Seaman. On August 31, with eleven men, the dog, and another boat, a rowing boat with a sail called a pirogue, Lewis set off in the keelboat down the Ohio River on the 980-mile voyage to the junction of the Ohio and the Mississippi. On the way, at Clarksville, Indiana, Lewis picked up Clark, with a group of men—later known as "the nine young men from Kentucky"—whom Clark had recruited. Clark's slave, York, also came aboard. He was the only slave and the only African American on the expedition. He was about the same age, thirty-three, as Clark, and had been his slave since they were both children; York's father had been Clark's father's personal slave. In his book *Undaunted Courage: Meriwether Lewis, Thomas Jefferson, and the Opening of the American West*, Stephen E. Ambrose describes York as "big, very dark, strong, agile, a natural athlete."

On November 20 the expedition—now comprising the keelboat, two pirogues, and about twenty men—turned into the Mississippi and headed upstream toward St. Louis. Progress was so slow and the strain on the men so great that Lewis and Clark decided they needed at least to double the size of their party. They recruited more men from an army post—Jefferson had arranged that they could second any U.S. soldiers whom they considered appropriate—and made it to St. Louis, where they set up camp for the winter close to the mouth of the Missouri. There they collected plants, animals, and insects, drew maps, wrote in their journals, made connections with the locals—Native Americans, Americans, French, French Canadians, and Spanish—and trained and selected men for the voyage up the Missouri.

Lewis and Clark knew that the Missouri flowed north and west from St. Louis, and they hoped that it would eventually arrive at the fabled Pacific coast which, at that time, Europeans—most of them Spanish, but including the Englishman Sir Francis Drake—had reached only by sea.

They left St. Louis in May 1804 with more than forty men, and rowed, towed, punted, pulled, pushed, paddled, and sailed their flotilla—the fifty-five-foot keelboat and two pirogues—upstream from St. Louis for more than five months, crossing the present-day states of Missouri, Nebraska, South Dakota, and much of North Dakota. On the way they hunted and fished, studied flora and fauna, drew more maps, and drank whiskey almost daily. Charles Floyd, a popular sergeant, died of peritonitis during this stage of the journey—the only fatal casualty of the entire trip.

The two leaders were generally good-natured, but for indiscipline they approved harsh punishments, shocking to us today but commonplace in a world of slavery and among the American military at that time. A man who outraged the whole party by stealing more than his share of whiskey was sentenced by a court of his peers, presided over by a sergeant, to one hundred lashes on his bare back. Another man was tried for insubordination and given seventy-five lashes; and another, who lay down and slept while on guard duty, an offence punishable by death, was tried and sentenced to one hundred lashes a day for four days.

On their way upriver, the party encountered a few European fur traders, and several bands of Indians, all of them friendly except one. Some of the chiefs of a large band of Teton Sioux were unimpressed by the presents offered—peace medals featuring Jefferson's head in relief, a red coat, and a cocked hat. Jefferson had instructed Lewis to remain cool and avoid conflict with Indians. But hostile words led to hostile actions, perhaps exacerbated by whiskey given to the chiefs in an attempt to improve matters. Three Teton warriors grabbed the towline of one of the pirogues while another held on to the mast. An overbearing chief staggered into Clark, saying he hadn't received enough presents and he would not allow the expedition to move upriver. Clark drew his sword. The men loaded rifles, blunderbusses, and their deadliest weapon, a swivel gun mounted on the keelboat. The Teton responded by stringing their bows, pulling arrows from quivers, and cocking shotguns. Lewis, on the boat, held a lighted taper close to the fuse of the swivel gun, now loaded with sixteen musket balls.

Stephen E. Ambrose takes the view that the history of North America might have been very different but for a Teton Sioux chief called Black Buffalo, who did manage to keep his cool: he broke the tension by taking the towline from the three warriors and telling the fourth to let go of the boat's mast. Had the guns been fired, many Sioux would have died. But the far greater numbers of Sioux—there were hundreds on the bank of the Missouri—and their ability to fire arrows more quickly than the soldiers could reload, would have won them the battle and the treasure of the soldiers' weapons. With those weapons, and incensed by the deaths of a large number of their tribesmen, the Sioux would have fought off many future explorers who attempted to sail up the Missouri. A way to the Pacific might not have been found for many years and the expansion of the United States into the West might have been halted.

The flotilla continued upstream and arrived close to this place, one thousand miles north of St. Louis, at what were then known as the Mandan villages, after the Mandan Indians who lived here, in late October. Back in Washington, Lewis had been given a specially drawn map of the West. Just three places were marked with certainty, at known latitudes and longitudes: St. Louis, the Mandan villages, and the unnamed place on the coast of Oregon where the Columbia River flows into the Pacific. Between here and the Pacific, the map was vague, filled with guesses at the position and extent of the Rocky Mountains, and at the course of the Columbia River which, it was hoped, connected with the Missouri.

Close to the Mandan villages was a village lived in by Hidatsa Indians, a tribe closely allied to the Mandan. There Lewis and Clark met a forty-five-year-old French Canadian trapper, Toussaint Charbonneau, and his teenage Hidatsa wife, Sacagawea (historians differ on Sacagawea's age as between fourteen and seventeen; Ambrose says she "was about fifteen"). Spelled "Sakakawea" in North Dakota only, for arcane reasons, her name is thought to mean "bird woman" in Hidatsa. Both Sacagawea and Charbonneau joined the party as interpreters, with Sacagawea considered especially useful because she had been born into the Shoshone, a tribe that the expedition expected to encounter in the mountains of present-day Montana; though kidnapped by the Hidatsa, Sacagawea could still speak and understand the language she had grown up with.

THE INTERPRETIVE CENTER focuses on the expedition's time in North Dakota, in particular on the five months when they lived near here in a fort that they built themselves and named Fort Mandan. I spent more than an hour at the center, poring over maps, paintings, letters, journals, and lists, and looking at moccasins, arrowheads, military uniforms, muskets, and a canoe dug out of a tree trunk.

Then I drove about a mile to Fort Mandan itself and was shown round with two American couples by a bright, laid-back boy from a local high school. The fort is a compact stockade, built from the branches of cottonwood trees sharpened to a point—the kind of place, only smaller, from which the U.S. cavalry rides out at great speed, led by a flag bearer, in the movies. Rooms—cookhouse, smithy, officers' quarters, stores—line the walls inside. A waxwork replica of Meriwether Lewis, in bright military uniform and cocked hat, sits on a stool beside a bed covered in buffalo hide. William Clark leans against a post nearby. Through glass eyes and with startled expressions, both look across at us tourists as if to say: "Yes! And what do *you* want?"

There weren't many beds on view, so I asked our guide where the rest of the men slept. He pointed to a ladder and invited me to climb it. Poking my head through a hole in the ceiling, I found thin mattresses in a dark loft. A room was set aside for Charbonneau and Sacagawea—and on February 11, 1805, right there in the fort, Sacagawea gave birth to a baby son, who was named Jean-Baptiste.

Despite the waxworks, the fort seemed old and authentic. So I was disappointed when our guide told us that it's a replica.

The original stood about ten miles upstream and—had it not burned down while Lewis and Clark were away in search of the ocean—would long ago have been submerged beneath the Missouri when it was dammed and widened.

THE CORPS OF Discovery headed upstream from Fort Mandan on April 7, 1805, in the two pirogues and six dugout canoes. Its numbers had been reduced to thirty-three people, twenty-eight of whom, including the two leaders, were soldiers. Then there was Clark's slave, York, and three civilians classed as interpreters: Sacagawea, Toussaint Charbonneau, and the half-Shawnee, half-French Canadian George Drouillard, a master of sign language, tracking, and hunting, who had joined the expedition on the Mississippi in November 1803. The fifty-five-day-old Jean-Baptiste Charbonneau was swaddled on his mother's back. And Seaman, the dog, was on board.

Lewis had bought a large buffalo-hide teepee from the Mandan and, in this, he and Clark, Sacagawea, Charbonneau, the baby, and Drouillard slept at night, while the men slept outdoors. The idea was that this arrangement would forestall any awkwardness that might arise from the presence of a woman among a squad of soldiers. It worked and this is how the party spent their nights for sixteen months. Sacagawea, helped it is thought by York, put the tepee up and took it down in the morning.

On the same day, April 7, the keelboat headed back downstream to St. Louis carrying about twelve men, a few of whom their leaders were happy to dispense with. The boat was loaded with plants, five live animals including a prairie dog, animal skins and skeletons, Indian artifacts, reports, maps, and journals—all to be sent to Jefferson—as well as letters from members of the corps to their families.

Over the next seven months, the corps survived many difficulties including near starvation. The Missouri did not connect directly with the Columbia River—far from it. It contained forks, which sometimes took many days to explore, and waterfalls. After the Great Falls of the Missouri, which Lewis described as "the grandest sight I ever beheld," came a chain of four more waterfalls which took eighteen days of portage to negotiate. On August 12, Lewis climbed toward the top of the Continental Divide, found "the most distant fountain of the waters of the Mighty Missouri in search of which we have spent so many toilsome days and restless nights," walked on up to the top where he expected to see a vast plain leading down to the Pacific, and saw only range upon range of mountains. The Rocky Mountains were a much higher, denser, snowier barrier than they had anticipated; even their eccentric Shoshone guide, whom they called Old Toby, got lost.

On the way, they encountered and marveled at birds and wildlife that they had never seen before. Clark was amazed by herds of as many as ten thousand buffalo. Several of the men were chased by grizzly bears. They were cautious when meeting Indians, but two tribes were especially helpful. When they met the Shoshone, Sacagawea recognized her own brother, by then chief of the band. From them Lewis and Clark acquired twenty-nine horses and the help of Old Toby, who did, eventually, lead them through the Bitterroot Range of the Rockies. Arriving on the west side of the mountains, sick, cold, and starving, they were befriended and fed so much salmon and camas root by the Nez Percé that many of the men became ill. A chief of that tribe showed them how to make canoes by burning hollows into pine trees, and on October 7, 1805, they sped down the Clearwater River in five new canoes with the current behind them for the first time since they'd entered the Mississippi in the summer of 1803.

The Clearwater led to the Snake River, which led to the Columbia River, which took them, through falls and a deep gorge, out of the semi-arid desert of eastern Oregon and into the rain forest. On November 7, Clark wrote in his diary, "Ocian [*sic*] in view! O! the joy." Delayed by storms and winds, they reached the shore on November 18 and strolled on the sand fronting the Pacific. Clark estimated by dead reckoning that, in those months, they had traveled 4,162 miles (modern methods of measurement suggest that he was correct to within forty miles). On November 24, in a free vote, the party chose a site for their winter camp on the south side of the Columbia.

Everyone had played a part—and Sacagawea, always level-headed and resourceful, had played a bigger role than many. When a boat overturned and others were in a state of panic, she calmly retrieved vital pieces of equipment from the river including Lewis's and Clark's journals. As the expedition approached the Rockies, she recognized landmarks and became its guide. She used sign language to communicate with Indians whose languages she couldn't speak—and at the first meeting with the Shoshone, when Lewis and Clark traded with her brother for horses, she was at one end of a chain of interpreters, translating Shoshone into Hidatsa, which her husband, Charbonneau, translated into French, and which Private Francis Labiche translated into English, to which Lewis or Clark would reply, setting the chain into reverse. Of course, she carried and cared for her son, Jean-Baptiste—and he became popular with the party, especially with William Clark, who nicknamed him Pomp because of his pompous "little dancing boy" antics.

The slow return journey, against the current to the Rockies, began on March 22. The party became short of food, found that the Indians had no horses to sell, and instead bought dogs, which all of them are said to have enjoyed eating. Snow, and the advice of the helpful Nez Percé, delayed their crossing of the Bitterroot Range of the Rockies, but, after a foolish false start without Nez Percé guides, they crossed with five guides and seventeen horses in six days, arriving on June 27 at the campsite of the previous year, which they called Traveler's Rest.

There the party split into two groups, both of which explored regions and rivers they had not traveled before. Clark, finding the way with the help of Sacagawea, took a party down the Yellowstone River, while Lewis traveled up the Blackfoot River. Having split his party again and leading just three men, Lewis came across eight Blackfoot Indians on a remote northern tributary of the Missouri. The Blackfeet were known to be the most aggressive of the tribes of the northwest; all the other Indians feared them. Indians and Americans camped together for the night, but in the morning the Blackfeet tried to steal the Americans' horses and rifles. In the struggle that followed, two Blackfeet were shot dead. The others escaped, and Lewis knew that large numbers of their fellows were nearby. Lewis and his men rode away, and kept riding until two o'clock the following morning, by which time they were a hundred miles away.

Given the Blackfeet's notoriety, it was foolish of Lewis to lead such a small squad into their territory. He was a strong leader and a very hard worker, but he was occasionally hot-headed and sometimes moody. Jefferson suspected that he suffered from depression; historians, including Ambrose, think that he suffered bipolar disorder. Clark was more steady and an equally good leader.

The two officers and their men met up again on August 12, a little south of the confluence of the Yellowstone and the Missouri. On August 14 they reached the Mandan villages, where they parted from Sacagawea, Charbonneau, and the now eighteen-month-old Jean-Baptiste. Speeding south with the current, they got back to St. Louis on September 23.

DESPITE THE SENSE of achievement and the fame and acclaim he received following the success of the expedition, Lewis's euphoria did not last. Jefferson made him governor of the new and vast Louisiana Territory, a job he found difficult and in which he was undermined by his deputy; he began to drink heavily; his debts grew larger; he found it hard to prepare his journals for publication and was under huge pressure to publish them; he failed in various attempts to find and woo a wife. On October 10, 1809, on his way to Washington from St. Louis, Lewis stopped for the night in a small log-built inn, some miles south of Nashville on the route known as the Natchez Trace. In the early hours of the morning he shot himself twice, cut himself with his razor, and, in the presence of his servant, a free black man named John Pernier, who could do nothing except give him water, died.

CLARK MARRIED HIS cousin Julia (Judith) Hancock, whom he had known since she was a child and after whom he had named a particularly attractive tributary of the Missouri in Montana. They lived in St. Louis and had five children, the eldest of whom was named Meriwether Lewis Clark. Another member of the Clark household was the little boy whom he had called Pomp; during the expedition Clark grew so fond of him that he offered to have him to live in his home and to pay for his education. In 1809, Sacagawea and Charbonneau accepted his offer, and Jean-Baptiste went to school in St. Louis until 1822. In 1807 Clark became brigadier-general of militia and superintendent of Indian affairs for the territory of Upper Louisiana, and in 1813 governor of the Missouri Territory (later the state of Missouri). He died in St. Louis in 1838, aged sixty-eight, much respected, especially by Indians and fur trappers.

I DAWDLE ON the path outside the replica Fort Mandan and gaze at a line of trees a little way off. They are not quite like any that we have in England. One of my fellow tourists, a big man, not at all slim, with a large—but not wobbly—belly, is standing nearby. I ask him if they are cottonwoods.

"Yep," he says, "just like what they used to build the fort."

This man and his wife said nothing during our visit to the fort; I'd put them down as retired people passing time on a day out, people who perhaps weren't really interested in the fort or in Lewis and Clark. But I am wrong. They have visited the place many times and are entranced, perhaps obsessed, by Lewis and Clark. Once they start, it is hard to stop them talking. The man waves his hands and tells me that this was one of the most exciting adventures ever undertaken.

I say good-bye to the friendly couple and wander over to the line of cottonwoods. Only when I get among them do I realize that they are on a riverbank and that the broad, slow-moving stretch of water in front of me is the Missouri. Well, of course it is! Where else would a replica of Fort Mandan have been built? Memories float into my mind: my father, now long-dead, telling me that the Mississippi–Missouri is the third-longest river in the world; Paul Robeson singing "cross the wide Missouri" on the radio; lying on my bed, aged about ten, reading *Tom Sawyer*—and, later, *Huckleberry Finn;* much later, scrambling up a steep bank with my wife to stare at the southern end of this river, the Mississippi at New Orleans; later still, listening to Pat Metheny and Charlie Haden on one of my favorite jazz albums, *Beyond the Missouri Sky*. I have that album in the car.

As there often is, there was a thread of melancholy woven into this nostalgia. I was alone, up to my knees in bright wild grass. The sky was a dirty gray-white, and the water matched it. The river, of course, was flat and the farther shore, save for a line of trees to the north, was featureless; some mudflats and long, low, reedy islands were flat too. I thought about the length of this river: how, with the Mississippi, it bisects this immense country from northwest to southeast, rising in the Rocky Mountains of western Montana and flowing on down some four thousand miles to New Orleans and out into the Gulf of Mexico. As I stared and wondered, two white pelicans, their beaks angled toward the water, floated serenely downstream. Pelicans winter on the Gulf Coast and spend the summer up here, breeding, raising their chicks, and feasting on the local fish.

Perhaps Lewis and Clark and Sacagawea and Pomp had seen the ancestors of these strange birds. The expedition and its discovery of a route to the Pacific seemed very recent—little more than two hundred years ago. But then much American history seems recent: the Homestead Act, handing out land to those prepared to trek across the continent, and leading to the settling of the West, 1862; the adoption of the Thirteenth Amendment, abolishing slavery, 1865; the Wounded Knee Massacre, seen by many as the end of the centuries-long Indian Wars, 1890. But what do I mean by recent? In his novel about slavery, *The Confessions of Nat Turner,* William Styron wrote: "The relativity of time allows us elastic definitions: the year 1831 [the year of "the only effective, sustained revolt" by American slaves] was, simultaneously, a long time ago and only yesterday."

Recent or not, I had come upon a layer of history, deeper down than that of the pioneers who had come from the east and from Europe to found places like Minot and Swan River in the years around 1900. I was one hundred years deeper, pondering a pivotal part of American and world history. Lewis and Clark made Thomas Jefferson's dream, of building a country that would stretch from ocean to ocean, seem real. In July 1803, shortly before Lewis left Washington on his way to Philadelphia, Jefferson, on behalf of the American people, bought the vast tract of land that the French called Louisiana from Napoleon for fifteen million dollars. At that time Louisiana reached north from New Orleans right up into Canada, and from the west bank of the Mississippi to the Rocky Mountains. The deal and the land came to be known as the Louisiana Purchase—and Highway 83 runs north-south right through its middle.

KNIFE RIVER

I DROVE OFF, AND SOON arrived at a place and time long before Jefferson and his purchase, a grassy place on the bank of a narrow tributary of the Missouri, where Hidatsa and Mandan Indians lived in adjoining villages for more than five hundred years before the arrival of Lewis and Clark. Back then the Knife River was to the Missouri as a residential side street is to a main road—with the junction of the two not far away, perhaps a mile. Maybe then, as now, it was safer and quieter to live on a side street. The villages were clusters of homes—up to 120 in each village. Each home housed a family of between ten and thirty people. In the comics that I read as a child, and in the films and television series that I watched, Indians appeared as nomadic people, living in tepees and dependent on horses and on hunting buffalo. These people didn't live like that. They were farmers and market gardeners who traded among themselves and with other bands of Indians—and, eventually, with white fur traders. Their homes were permanent and their villages lasted for hundreds of years, and were abandoned only after a catastrophic smallpox epidemic in the 1830s—a disease brought by white men. If the white men had stayed away, perhaps they would be there now, in their stout circular houses built of cottonwood logs and mud, a style of building that, but for the shape, reminded me of the wattle and daub of Elizabethan cottages that survive in England.

Jefferson had a vision of an America stretching to the Pacific, peopled by farmers, living on their own 160-acre homesteads, all the way across. His solution to the so-called Indian problem was that they should be farmers too, just like Americans: families owning, tilling, and living off their own soil. Americans, Jefferson thought, would teach Indians how to farm. Jefferson didn't know that, owing to the dry climate, 160 acres weren't enough to support a family of any kind west of the 100th meridian. But perhaps a bigger irony is that many Indians were already skilled farmers and vegetable gardeners: for example, the Cherokee in the southeast, the Pueblo in what is now New Mexico, the Mandan and the Hidatsa in the north. These peoples had centuries of knowledge of what would grow in their soil. And they farmed collectively. Whole villages participated and everyone got something to eat.

Not only were these Indians farmers, but they had no horses! There were horses in North America in prehistory, but they died out nine thousand years ago, along with the woolly mammoth; after that there were no horses until Cortez and his Conquistadores brought just fifteen from Spain to Mexico in 1519. Very slowly horses filtered north into what is now the U.S.

In the seventeenth century, Pueblo Indians working for the Spanish along the Rio Grande learned to handle horses, though they weren't allowed to own them. Then, in 1680, they rebelled and managed to push the Spanish out. Many horses were left behind, but the Pueblo were farmers and didn't want horses. Instead they rounded up the Spaniards' sheep, leaving the horses to be taken by the Apache, the Ute, and the Comanche, the last of whom would become the most admired horsemen of all the Indians. Another hundred years would pass before horses reached all of the Plains and Rocky Mountain Indians, including the Sioux in the north. Once they had horses, some tribes—but not the Hidatsa or Mandan—gave up farming and became nomadic, charging around the plains hunting and gathering.

No one told me this when I was a kid. I thought Indians and horses went together, like cowboys and hats.

Exploring the villages, starting from the Knife River Villages Visitor Center, was like taking a pleasant country walk, though the sky still loomed low and gray. A path led through a flowery meadow where small dark birds flitted about, with a come-hither patch of yellow on the backs of their heads. Then the path pushed through trees to a grassy space of about an acre where there were numerous circular depressions in the ground, the foundations of the homes of the Hidatsa, all the same size and close against one other like the impressions of wine bottles in the bottom of a cardboard box. I wandered between the circles, as if I were respecting the privacy of those who lived inside them. And it occurred to me that the passages and crevices between the houses would have made perfect, after-dark meeting places for blushing teenagers.

I walked on and soon reached another village, similar to the first and set on the bank of the Knife River. A painting dating from 1810 shows children swimming across, while others splash in the shallows and a small group paddles by in a canoe. On the bank the circular houses have domed roofs where people stand and sit in groups. Lances with feathers decorate the village, and a man on horseback looks down at the water. This is the Hidatsa village where Sacagawea lived.

AS I DROVE back to Minot, I turned on the radio—and the car was invaded by a man shouting, ranting, close to losing control.

He was disturbed by Obama's plans to improve Medicare, the system that provides free medical care to the poor. After a while, he stopped yelling and, instead, played part of a speech made by Ronald Reagan forty years ago. At that time Reagan was famous as an actor who played cowboys and was campaigning to be elected governor of California; his message from beyond the grave was that even the tiniest Band-Aid of state-funded medical care would lead to communism. The stingy, ranting man was called Glenn Beck. I switched him off and entered a better world by sliding Pat Metheny and Charlie Haden into the CD player.

THERE WAS NO internet connection at my motel that night. The young man on reception rolled his Rs. "Go to Arrr Bees," he said. "Arrr Bees on South Broadway. It's a fast-food place with free Wi-Fi."

I knew South Broadway; it was also Highway 83. I drove up one side—about a mile—and down the other. I couldn't see RBs. I drove round again, saying the name over in my head and rolling my Rs, until I saw an illuminated sign forty feet in the air—a sign in an avenue of signs: Arby's.

Arby's specializes in hot beef sandwiches. I ordered one with horse—horseradish—and took it to a table. I found I was asking myself whether anyone would play Reagan's pal Margaret Thatcher's old speeches, now, on the radio, in the U.K.—for anything more than historical interest. The answer, surely and mercifully, was "No."

13

COWBOY PICTURE LIBRARY

NEXT MORNING I WENT to Denny's—and stared at a menu filled with lurid, life-size photographs of burgers, chips, salad, and so on. A small, dark-haired young woman called Lisa waited on me. She took my order and returned instantly with coffee. Thirty seconds later she came back with a wide smile and said, "You doin' OK here?"

I had managed to take one sip of coffee while she'd been away. "Fine, thank you."

Soon she returned again. "You doin' OK here?"

And then again, "You doin' OK here?" I was drinking coffee and trying to read a book. Perhaps I didn't look well. But I felt OK, as I kept telling her. Then she brought the two-egg breakfast and placed it carefully in front of me. "OK?"

"Yes. Great, thanks."

"Anythin' else you need?"

"No thanks. That's great."

A minute later, when I had a forkful of egg in midair, she appeared again—with a more sinister question: "Doin' OK so far?"

I told her I was doin' OK, pushed the egg into my mouth, nodded, and tried to smile while keeping my mouth shut. I was thinking about the "so far." Was she expecting something to go wrong? Did she know something that I didn't? Perhaps the two-egg breakfast was a mistake. Perhaps it attracted more complaints than the other breakfasts. Perhaps it provoked merriment among the staff: "Hey guys! Guess what! There's a sucker out there who wants the two-egg breakfast!"

I maintained my *sangfroid,* and carried on munching and reading and letting Lisa know that I was doin' OK. The two-egg breakfast turned out fine. I did OK. And so did Lisa.

ELI WAS ALREADY at the Blue Rider, turning on lights and tuning the television. In fifteen minutes the pundits would begin their warm-up prattle for the big football game in Johannesburg.

"Fun," Eli said, "to be watching it with an Englishman." He pulled down a glass and poured me an orange juice.

While we waited for football, he gave the bar a thorough wipe-over. I sat on a bar stool and talked about Lewis and Clark, and the Indian villages. I asked him how he felt about the Indians.

He carried on wiping and didn't look up. "The genocide, you mean?" He spoke almost matter-of-factly.

"That's a strong word," I said.

He stared at me through small rectangular glasses. "Well, that's what it was." He squatted down close to the floor and began to fill the cold shelves with bottles.

I told him that I hadn't heard an American use that word to describe what happened to the Indians.

"Maybe not many do," he said. Then he stood up, leaned his hands on the bar, and told me that his father was orphaned as a child and adopted by Native Americans, so he, Eli, grew up with Native American grandparents. Perhaps, he said, this made him especially sensitive to the fate of the Indians. His grandparents came from different villages, both of which had been submerged beneath the widened Missouri when the Oahe dam was built south of Bismarck in the 1950s. His grandparents had been hugely resentful and had protested. Both were proud of their heritage and had campaigned for the rights of Indians, and his grandfather had worked hard to preserve the Mandan and Hidatsa languages. Eli remembered stories of his grandfather's youth in the 1920s—in particular that he rode bareback with his friends and that they were herded around by police simply because they were Indians.

By now Joe had arrived and was sitting next to me—and a handful of others had come to watch the football. We all, including Eli, turned to the television and discussed football. I expected England to win. The Americans expected the USA to lose.

England scored a good goal after four minutes. Not much happened in the next thirty-five minutes, but then, not long before halftime, the England goalkeeper, Robert Green, let a limp shot run through his hands and into the goal—a mistake that would have embarrassed a ten-year-old. In the second half the USA looked the more likely to score a winning goal, but, disappointingly, no one did. The English striker Wayne Rooney, thought by many to be the team's best player, did little except whine, curse, and scowl. He is not the most attractive of men, and the Americans noticed that. I told Joe that the British magazine *Private Eye* calls him "the spud-faced nipper."

"Spud-faced. Yes." He chuckled. Then he leaned closer. "What's a nipper?"

Eli announced that England should have won—and he wished that the Americans' equalizer had been their own creation and not an English cock-up. It was time to leave. I wanted to drive slowly and reach Bismarck, the state capital, today. Eli presented me with a Blue Rider T-shirt—white with a blue rider on a blue horse—and then there were handshakes and promises to meet again.

ON THE WAY out of town, I stop at Walmart.

As I am leaving, I see a bent, elderly woman in the car park pushing—perhaps being held upright by—a well-filled trolley. She is moving slowly, her head low, her far-from-slim backside and legs providing gradual forward momentum. She rolls the trolley into the side of a mountainous two-tone, brown-and-cream, four-wheel-drive vehicle. Orange indicator lights flash and it is clear that this SUV is hers, her means of moving from home to shops and wherever else she wants to go. She leans her weight against it and, pushing the trolley in front of her, slides along its side, past several doors and windows, until eventually she reaches the corner and turns the trolley and herself around to the back. There she lowers the tailgate and heaves bags from the trolley; she moves farther around the car and lifts more bags onto the back seat. She lets the empty trolley roll away, and holds onto the vehicle to maneuver herself from the rear passenger door on the off-side all around via the back and along the other side to the driver's seat. I am reluctantly reminded of a snail working its way around the end of a brick.

She drives away calmly, and I—by now I am sitting in Prius—follow, thinking there must be a better way for an elderly, overweight woman to obtain groceries. Could it be that, despite the full trolley and the swanky car, she is short of money—and this is the cheapest way? There are a lot of poor people in the world's richest country; Barbara Ehrenreich discovered that some of them work in Walmart and wrote about them in her book *Nickel and Dimed*. If they work there, they likely shop there too. Of course, this elderly lady may not be poor. Rather, perhaps, like many elderly people, she wants to look after herself, however difficult that might be.

I HIT THE road to Bismarck, a little over a hundred miles south—or about two hours' slow driving. I drove seventy of these miles yesterday before turning back, so I don't dawdle, though the sky is clearer and I stop to photograph forests of wind turbines. They are scattered across the empty landscape, turning slowly beneath a silver sky. They seem graceful and statuesque, like something created by Antony Gormley with help from R.J. Mitchell, the designer of the Spitfire. To remove oaks or cottonwoods or Indian villages to make space for them would have been vandalism; but here, a few miles east of the Missouri, there are almost no trees, and a deal, albeit unfair, establishing a form of status quo was long ago struck with, or imposed on, the Indians.

When I was a child, I saw Indians on TV who were subservient friends, almost pets, of the white man. And I saw other Indians, usually in large numbers and on horseback, who were presented as a threat to life and civilization: uncouth, unholy, sometimes barely human—their image not unlike that accorded by most people to members of al-Qaeda these days. (It is surely significant that Osama bin Laden was code-named Geronimo by the U.S. Navy Seals who killed him.)

Two or three years after those evenings when I kept guns beside my dinner plate, my friend Richard and I discovered Cowboy Picture Library. Every month there were four new sixty-four-page comics, each with a series character. Somehow—we must have been seven or eight years old—we managed between us to buy all four. Richard bought *Buck Jones* and *Davy Crockett,* while I went for *Kit Carson* and *The Kansas Kid*. Sometimes a story featuring Buffalo Bill was included in the *Davy Crockett* comic, and we came to like him almost as much as Carson and Crockett. We spent hours reading, swapping, and, though unaware of the concept, role-playing.

Soon we both had cowboy outfits, with gun belts and holsters. Then my sympathy with the Indians, kindled by Tonto, caught fire when my father gave me a tepee, a small, conical brown tent with feathers and strange markings painted on it. Then, utter joy: the local toy shop began to sell small plastic models of Indians! They already stocked plastic cowboys, but the range of Indians was greater and the Indians themselves were colorful and beautifully clothed. They had long hair, feather headdresses, and bows and arrows, and came in many poses: standing, kneeling, crouching, and, for an extra sixpence, on horseback.

Richard and I were inventive. We had already devised a game with complex rules where we raced model Formula One cars on the concrete path that led to my front door. But, as our collections of model Indians grew, we forgot the cars and came up with an Indian war game that we played on the floor in Richard's parents' sitting room. At first we had about ten Indians each. Richard was the Apaches and I was the Comanches. We lined up our Indians at either end of the Axminster carpet and took it in turns to move one Indian at a time a hand's length toward the other's tribe. I could kill one of Richard's Indians—and knock him over, dead—by getting close enough to move one of mine into the space where Richard's stood.

We knew enough from television, comics, and, by then, the cinema to give names to some of our Indians. Richard's Apaches were led, of course, by Geronimo, and the chief of my Comanches was Quanah Parker. My father, ever keen to look things up in the *Encyclopaedia Britannica,* explained that Quanah had had a white American mother called Parker; to Richard and me, this was a minor and passing curiosity. As we spent our pocket money, and as Christmases and birthdays came around, the Apaches and the Comanches grew in number. Then the Apaches gained a tribe of allies, the Cheyenne, who assembled on another corner of the carpet, and the Arapaho arrived to support the Comanches at my end of the room.

More than fifty years later I am driving south on what was probably once an Indian trail. I can't pretend that the

Comanches or Apaches rode this way because they were never this far north (not after the arrival of horses, anyway), but other tribes—in particular the Mandan, Hidatsa, and Arikara—would have traveled this road.

Richard and I got it right insofar as, in the first half of the eighteenth century, the Apaches and Comanches fought each other for territory in Kansas and Texas; in the end the Comanches won and the Apaches moved off south and west. We were also correct to ally the Arapaho with the Comanches. But teaming the Cheyenne with the Apaches was a mistake. In fact, in the second half of the nineteenth century, when the Indians were struggling for survival against the U.S. Army and the U.S. government, the Cheyenne and the Arapaho were close allies, and, indeed, members of both tribes fought alongside the Comanches against the U.S. military during the Red River War of 1874–75.

Only recently, as I prepared to make this journey—and now, as I drive and meet people and read and learn—have I appreciated how ignorant Richard and I were. The Indian Wars lasted for four hundred years, from 1493 when the Spanish fought the Arawak on the island of Hispaniola (now Haiti and the Dominican Republic), until 1890, when almost three hundred Sioux were massacred at Wounded Knee. Gradually, during those four hundred years, the Indians were either killed or moved on from their homelands, generally in a westerly direction—and ultimately forced onto reservations. This happened right across what is now the United States and Canada. Richard and I, innocent, ignorant boys in small-town England, were fed references mainly from the last thirty of those four hundred years, and from a single north–south slice of the United States: the Great Plains that lie between the Mississippi and the Rocky Mountains, the north–south slice that just happens to be bisected by Highway 83. We didn't know it, but we were focused on the events and years immediately before the near extinction of traditional Indian ways of living.

Now, I can see that much of what we thought we knew came from the *Kit Carson* comics which made a hero of a handsome man with flowing blond hair and a fringed, buckskin jacket. The comic-book Kit Carson knew Indians, considered many of them to be his friends, and defended them with both words and actions against brutish U.S. soldiers. In one story, titled "The Man Who Hated Redskins," an army colonel snarls at Carson, "The only good Indians are dead ones"—a statement that I now know to be a corruption of a remark attributed to General Philip H. Sheridan, the man whose job was to subdue the Indians of the Great Plains during the 1860s and '70s.

I know now, too, that the Kit Carson of our comics was created by writers and artists employed by Fleetway Publications of Farringdon Street, London EC4, a division of Amalgamated Press, a company founded by Lord Northcliffe, who also founded the *Daily Mail* (a paper that supported Hitler and the British fascists in the 1930s and is still known for its reactionary views on such topics as immigration and women's right to work). The real Kit Carson was less handsome and more morally ambivalent than his comic-book counterpart. He was a brave man who had many exciting adventures, and he did know and like Indians—indeed, he married two of them in succession: Singing Grass, an Arapaho, and Making-Our-Road, a Cheyenne. But later he took orders from a U.S. general who was hell-bent on wiping out the Navajo of New Mexico or, if he couldn't kill *all* of them, on forcing the survivors onto a reservation. Carson led a force that for six months undertook a scorched-earth policy, destroying Navajo cattle and farms. He is said to have tried to avoid killing Indians, but in some accounts is held responsible for the deaths of many Navajo.

Richard and I saw the Indians as both good and bad. We didn't fully appreciate that the "bad" ones were frequently goaded into aggression by the actions of white men. We would have been surprised by the truth—as put, for example, by Carl

Waldman, author of *Atlas of the North American Indian:* "Since Indians were generally protecting their people, culture, and lands from invasions and exploitation by outsiders who, more often than not, were white supremacists with the attitude that Native peoples were incidental to human destiny, Indian violence is now regarded in hindsight more sympathetically than white violence."

Richard and I and thousands, perhaps millions, of other little British boys saw and enjoyed films about World War II as well as Westerns, many of them starring thoroughly British actors like John Mills (Corporal Binns in *Dunkirk*), Kenneth More (Douglas Bader in *Reach for the Sky*), Richard Todd (Guy Gibson in *The Dam Busters*), and Jack Hawkins (George Ericson in *The Cruel Sea*). And we boys read World War II comics, in particular a series about a character called Battler Britton, who had fistfights with Germans while mouthing expletives like "Take that, Fritz." But those war heroes didn't excite us in the way that cowboys and Indians did. Perhaps in the late 1950s World War II was too recent and raw and local a memory for its heroes, real or imaginary, to sustain the tough-guy-devil-may-care appeal of Carson, Crockett, and Buffalo Bill.

AS IT ENTERS Bismarck, 83 turns east to avoid the city. I swoop straight on and down into the state capital, a city that seems to slope southward. A multilane road curves through a park and leads into streets where homes with spacious verandas slumber in the shade of tall trees.

That night I looked for mean streets, but didn't find any. Instead I went into a bar called Paradise Alley, sat at a small table against a bare-brick wall, and ate walleye, a fish so named because its eyes reflect white light enabling it to see and feed in the dark; it was panfried in pecans and looked and tasted better than it sounded. The place seemed to be a hangout for talkative, smart-casual men and women in their thirties. Some tables were mixed gender, some weren't, and there was flamboyant table-hopping by men in clean, pressed shirts.

High up, on a TV, Joe's and Eli's team, the Minnesota Twins, was playing the Atlanta Braves. I couldn't hear the commentary and had little clue what was going on but, in an ad break, learned that a shop called Menards was offering an adventure playground as a flat pack for $599. Eventually Atlanta won 3–2. Reading subtitles, I saw one of the pundits praise the Twins for playing well.

But not well enough, darn it! I realized that I had been supporting the Twins, that I had a team—even though I didn't understand the game.

An ad for some kind of rugged outdoor clothing appeared on the screen, and I remembered a notion that had come to me earlier in the day while driving behind a shiny black Jeep Grand Cherokee. Why, I'd wondered, do so many American cars—and helicopters and missiles—have Indian names? Presumably because the Indians—of the past, at least—are now seen as attractive, tough, carefree, self-reliant, cool, hip: everything that people require in a car. Yet, my mind meandered on, no marketing guru seems to have realized that the same words can be applied to the African tribes from which the slaves were kidnapped. So why not the Pontiac Mandinka, the Chevy Chamba, the Mbundu helicopter, the Wolof missile, and the Jeep Grand Yoruba?

IN THE LAND OF THE SIOUX

FROM THE WINDOW OF my fifth-floor room at Bismarck's Expressway Inn I can see Prius, some way off, neatly parked between white lines. This means that I'm in a hotel, rather than a motel. It's a ballpoint hotel, a clicking-ballpoint-that-doesn't-need-a-lid hotel—and there's a coffee maker with which I can make not just coffee but tea; I boil water in the glass jug and pour it onto a tea bag that I brought from England, because tea, when you can get it in the USA, is usually Lipton's, bland and fit only for drinking with lemon.

When I leave the room in the morning, a tall, lean man in a black cowboy hat is walking along the corridor toward me. Together we wait for the elevator and travel down to the ground floor. I linger behind him as we cross the lobby so that I can have a closer look at this dude whom my sideways glances have identified as a very clean cowboy. His Wrangler jeans are ironed, his shirt with mock-mother-of-pearl press-stud pocket flaps is pressed, and he even has a packet of Marlboro (original, not light) in his hip pocket. I wonder what happens when he sits down. In the car park he is joined by an ordinary-looking woman in a white T-shirt, whom I take to be his wife, and then by a large couple. All four climb into a small, beaten-up red car.

The larger people sit in the back, and my man lights a Marlboro before getting into the driver's seat while still wearing his hat. As they chug off, I see that the car is a Nissan Stanza.

I guess that this man is one of the cowboys whom Stuart and Garry described, the ones who "don't have any cattle," for whom cowboyhood is "a way of life," who "wear the clothes" and are "not armed totally, but they'll have a gun around." Stuart and Garry said this with no disrespect. However, this cowboy is so clean, ironed, and immaculate that the snide aphorism "all hat and no cattle" comes into my mind. Of course, I could be wrong: he might be a real cowboy who is driving his Nissan to wherever he left his horse.

IN 1872 THE executives of the Northern Pacific Railway named the new town that would become Bismarck, Edwinton, after their chief engineer. A year later they took a more Reaganite-Thatcherite approach, eschewing sentiment and going for the money, and renamed it in honor of the German chancellor in an attempt to attract investment from Germany. Bismarck has an austere air with grand, gray public buildings, an unforgiving traffic system, and a tight beltway around its circumference.

I take a turn around the art deco skyscraper of the state capitol. High on a rough stone plinth stands a life-size bronze sculpture of a young woman in a flowing robe with a baby peeping over her shoulder—at least, he would be peeping if he weren't asleep. The position of the baby and the woman's resolute gaze make clear that this is not the Virgin Mary but Sacagawea and her son, Jean-Baptiste Charbonneau, who was nicknamed Pomp. The same image, plainly a North Dakotan icon, is printed in dark blue on the business cards handed to me by several people who work at the State Historical Society of North Dakota.

IN 1960, ACCOMPANIED by his dog, Charley, John Steinbeck drove around the United States in a customized van that he named Rocinante, after Don Quixote's horse. In *Travels with Charley,* he wrote:

> Someone must have told me about the Missouri River at Bismarck, North Dakota, or I must have read about it. In either case, I hadn't paid attention. I came on it in amazement. Here is where the map should fold. Here is the boundary between east and west. On the Bismarck side it is eastern landscape, eastern grass, with the look and smell of eastern America. Across the Missouri on the Mandan side, it is pure west, with brown grass and water scorings and small outcrops. The two sides of the river might well be a thousand miles apart.

Looking forward to seeing the pure west, I drive out of Bismarck and across the Missouri on a long, unexciting bridge, from which there is no view of the water, and arrive in Mandan, the town on the other side. It seems a dull place, enlivened only by a sign that announces Big Willies outside a closed-up, white-painted building.

Beyond Mandan, I see a lot of *green* grass—but I am driving south, whereas Steinbeck struck out west and was soon describing the North Dakota Badlands, one hundred miles away. My plan is to follow the west bank of the Missouri, as closely as possible, south for some hundred miles to a bluff overlooking the river where Sitting Bull is buried—and then to return to Bismarck.

Steinbeck doesn't mention Highway 83; he probably didn't notice that he crossed it as he drove into Bismarck from the east. Nor does he have anything to say about the 100th meridian west, a line of longitude 100 degrees west of Greenwich that runs down the middle of the United States and Canada, cutting the continent into two almost-equal halves.

John Wesley Powell, on the other hand, had plenty to say. Powell was a much-respected man of action, described by Simon Schama in *The American Future: A History from the Founding Fathers to Barack Obama,* as "an all-American hero, soldier, explorer, and scientist." A team led by Powell, then the director of the United States Geological Survey, wrote *Report on the Lands of the Arid Region of the United States,* which was published by order of Congress in 1878 and made much of the 100th meridian as a line that marks the border between climate zones. The report warned that most of the land west of the meridian did not get enough rain to sustain agriculture—by which Powell meant arable farming; some parts of the dry west were good for ranching, he conceded, but almost none of it for farming. However, despite Powell's authority and popularity, the railroad companies ignored him and persuaded gullible homesteaders, eager for their own free 160-acre farm, of the nonsensical doctrine that "water follows the plow," a notion—promulgated by a misguided professor named Cyrus Thomas—that merely plowing up land causes rain.

Of course, Powell was right and much suffering would have been avoided had his advice been taken. In his book *Bad Land: An American Romance,* Jonathan Raban describes the desperate struggles of homesteaders west of the 100th meridian in Montana and North Dakota in the early years of the twentieth century.

The 100th meridian does indeed roughly divide the moist East from the arid West, and mark where the West begins. And the same can be said of 83. Until it reaches the citrus groves on the Texas border with Mexico—where it turns southeast to follow the Rio Grande—83 stays close to the 100th meridian and crosses almost the very center of North America. For most of its length, the road lies a few miles to the west of the meridian. South of Bismarck it crosses the meridian and keeps to its east for about a hundred miles before crossing back close to the South Dakota border; it crosses from west to east again north of Abilene, Texas, this time staying to the east until the end of the road in Brownsville.

It can fairly be said, then, that Highway 83 marks, roughly, where the West begins. West of 83 and of the meridian, the Great Plains become the drier High Plains and rise gradually toward the Rocky Mountains two hundred miles or so west.

THE DAY IS sunny, blue sky, big white clouds—and, as soon as we leave Mandan, Prius and I bowl along, windows down, on a two-lane road through open grassland. This is State Highway 1806—a piffling strip of tarmac compared to U.S. Highway 83. The Missouri is nearby to my left, though I can't see it.

I turn left at a sign to Fort Rice Camping Ground and find a car park containing three or four recreational vehicles (RVs) and a shiny black pickup. I stroll up a slope and get a glimpse of Lake Oahe, the reservoir created by the damming of the river 230 miles to the south, close to Pierre, South Dakota. It is a quarter of a mile away: a gray puddle between flat meadows. Then, from beneath my eyebrows and at a distance, I watch as the man from the shiny pickup, big, bald, and wearing a tight blue T-shirt, rummages through a line of evenly spaced rubbish bins. He is picking out drink cans and putting them in the back of his truck. Can this be an altruistic exercise in recycling, or is he paid by the can like hobos in New York City?

He doesn't look like a hobo. I stroll past nonchalantly, say something about the weather, and tell him that I appreciate his efforts at recycling.

For a moment he looks puzzled. "Recycling?" He scratches his head. "No, no. I remove these to prevent bobcats. I'm paid to do that." He turns away and reaches into a bin.

"Oh!" I say—and walk on.

Bobcats are wild cats common in much of North America, but rarely seen because they are nocturnal. About twice the size of domestic cats, with pointed ears and short tails, they steal up on hares, rabbits, rodents, and even deer, and leap on them from several feet away. There are websites that encourage the preservation of bobcats and their habitat, while others show photographs of smiling men and boys holding dead bobcats by their necks or forelegs. For $350 a day, an Arizona-based company offers the shooting of bobcats and other "critters"; your guide will coax the "varmints" with a mouth call or electronic caller. "AR-15 and other semi-auto rifles" may be used, but by law the magazine may not hold more than five rounds. It is suggested that punters wear "camo."

I DRIVE ON. Despite the blue sky and green grass and rolling countryside, the region seems desolate, perhaps because that is all there is: blue sky and green grass. There isn't even much traffic.

I come to a sign: You are entering Standing Rock Indian Reservation. It has several bullet holes in it; otherwise it is a conventional U.S. road sign, with rounded white letters on a green background. A few yards on, another sign: Welcome to the Standing Rock Nation, tasteful white letters on dark blue with a message underneath, dark blue on cream: Take good care of the land, your family, and your life.

I am in one of the largest Indian reservations in the U.S., in the land of the Hunkpapa, or Standing Rock, Sioux—the grouping of which Sitting Bull was chief. Long blue-green grass rises to the tops of hills to my right, and, as I drive south, the hills grow gradually more angular and majestic.

I turn left into the small town of Fort Yates, headquarters of the Standing Rock Sioux. Here there is a new-looking school, a well-maintained administrative building, a smart health center, a low red-brick courthouse. In a car park on the edge of the lake is the standing rock itself: small, curiously shaped, and sacred to the Sioux. It is said to be the petrified body of a young woman sitting on the ground with a baby on her back. After her tribe moved on she stayed behind, upset that her husband had taken a second wife (not uncommon among the traditional Sioux). When her husband's brothers came back to look for her, she and her baby had turned to stone. Thereafter the band of Sioux took the stone with them wherever they traveled and revered it as holy. Now mother and child sit on a plinth of beige bricks, and a brass plaque tells their story.

On a road away from the lake are small wooden homes: some are well maintained, others look abandoned, a few are boarded up. I stop at a small supermarket. Inside, an Indian woman is shopping with her teenage son and daughter. The boy wears a red hoodie; he swings his arms—clearly bored with shopping—rubs his eyes, spins slowly on one foot, and lopes off behind mother and sister. An Indian woman in a green overall is mopping the floor; the place is very clean. I find dried apricots and a box of Nature Valley Oats 'n Honey granola bars. A small woman, also wearing a green overall, smiles as she takes my money and offers me a plastic bag.

I RETURN TO 1806 and head on south. For miles there are no houses, no sign of man, save for wire fences and the road, which sweeps on, dipping and swerving. Flat-topped hills, mesas, with no rocks, just grass, appear faraway—and then closer. Are these Steinbeck's "water scorings and small outcrops"? A group of horses—eight or ten of them, tiny to my distant eye, chestnut brown and somehow perfect—stand against the sky, high above me, gazing west; they look wild and ready to be ridden by Indians, bareback and fast.

There is a fork in the road, and a sign: 1806 is closed ten miles on. Arrows point to the right, to a diversion away from the Missouri. I stay on the country road; I want to reach the cliff above the river where Sitting Bull is buried; perhaps I can get through.

Still there are no houses, no cars, just hills in random folds like a rumpled blanket, empty fields—and then a crowd of black cows, way off in the lee of a line of trees. From the crest of a hill I look down at the Missouri, wide and blue.

The road *is* blocked; it is being resurfaced. I must drive back the way I have come. But I will get to Sitting Bull—tomorrow, or perhaps the day after, from the south.

Later, in mid-afternoon, there are pickups on the road and SUVs up close in the rearview mirror, black and intimidating. In an essay called "The View from Mrs. Thompson's," about the impact of 9/11 on the inhabitants of Bloomington, Illinois, David Foster Wallace mentioned "the town's two basic classes and cultures, so well and truly symbolized by the SUV and the pickup truck." Those classes and their vehicles seem to be all over North America. And SUV drivers, despite being posh or at least aspirational, are probably friendly and harmless. Many are women, not that that means they are friendly or harmless.

The sun is high to my left, the air is warm, mirages—pools of water that aren't there—somehow reflect the lights of oncoming cars. Many of these all-terrain vehicles keep their headlights on in daylight, perhaps to make sure that the cows can see them—a twenty-first-century adaptation of shooting in the air and yelling, "Yeeee-eeee-eeee-haaaaah!"

15

CUSTER: THE MAN WHO DIED LAUGHING

A FEW MILES NORTH OF Fort Yates, I turn onto a wide and dusty road following a sign to Walker Bottoms RV Park. A yellow cloud trails high behind Prius. From the brow of a hill, I see another cloud coming toward me. In the valley bottom, I pass a large man driving a silver pickup; he glances across, raises his index finger from the steering wheel, and is gone. I am ready for this greeting and return it. In fact, I was hoping for it and would have been disappointed to have left North Dakota without it; in his history of Minot, Mark Timbrook describes this tiny gesture as "the North Dakota hello."

A burly man, an Indian, presumably Sioux, looks down at me from a kiosk high above the road at the entrance to the RV park.

"I came to go for a walk and eat a biscuit." It sounds silly.

He smiles a big smile. "Go right ahead." He leans down from the window and waves me through.

Lake Oahe spreads northward for miles, forming a distant horizon against blue hills. A few feet from the bank, aspens stand waist-high in the water. An electricity pylon looms on an artificial island, a giant praying mantis carrying power to a line of comrades marching away from the farther bank; colored balls mark the dipping curve of the uppermost cable. It's a nice-enough place: litter bins; restrooms; a few people by a jetty; a man pootling in a speedboat.

LATER, AS I came close to Mandan, I turned off to Fort Abraham Lincoln State Park. It was half-past five. Guided tours were finished for the day. I didn't mind. I preferred to look alone. I paid a few dollars and was handed a map.

The park contains the remains of an Indian village established by the Mandan in the late sixteenth century, and two distinct parts of the long-disused Fort Abraham Lincoln, an infantry post and a cavalry post.

The fort was built in 1872—by then the Mandan had moved on after suffering a severe outbreak of smallpox—as a base, one of many from which the U.S. Army would sally forth to protect settlers and travelers from Indians. And sometimes, if so ordered, simply to attack Indians with a view to their extermination. Custer, in charge here from 1873, sometimes didn't wait for orders.

Again it seemed so recent, 1872: just nineteen years before my father was born. My grandfather, the one who emigrated to Canada, would have been thirteen.

Walking in that place and seeing the remains of the elaborate fort and the beautifully designed cavalry quarters, including what the map called "the Custer house," and thinking about the U.S. Army and the Indians in the 1870s and '80s, heightened my understanding of the seriousness of what happened. No wonder Sitting Bull, Crazy Horse, and others are seen as heroes. They were fighting for the survival of their people, fighting against—Eli was right—genocide. A tiny remnant survived—great-grandparents, perhaps, of the boy in the red hoodie—but a way of life and much of a rich culture didn't.

Standing on a replica of the veranda where Custer would have stood with his wife and his fellow officers and their wives gazing at the barracks that housed his cavalrymen, I looked to my right, to a gap in the hills. In the spring of 1876 Custer led his Seventh U.S. Cavalry out through there on their way to the Little Bighorn River, 250 miles away in eastern Montana. There, on June 25, Custer and every one of his 265 cavalrymen were annihilated by Sioux warriors, led by Crazy Horse, Sitting Bull, and Gall. The lesser-known Gall—an orphan whose prowess as a young warrior had, years before, prompted Sitting Bull to adopt him as a younger brother—has to be mentioned, because he, more than anyone, by correctly anticipating Custer's tactics and acting quickly, brought about this greatest of victories and defeats. Gall was indeed a hero—and one who had plenty of motivation: both his wives and most of his many children had been killed when a detachment of Custer's Seventh Cavalry started the battle with a surprise attack on the Sioux encampment.

What about Custer? My schoolboy knowledge of him, drawn from comics, movies, and the phrase that carries a legend, "Custer's Last Stand," led me to see him as courageous—perhaps in the way that foolish people, like Evel Knievel, or Clyde Barrow, or Lord Raglan who led the Light Brigade, can be seen as courageous. However, having found out more about him, I see that he can't be characterized quite so simply. For one thing, his guiding light was to have fun. In *Great Plains* Ian Frazier writes: "In the field he sometimes traveled with his own cook, a cast-iron cookstove, a sixteen-piece Army band, and a pack of staghounds... Whenever buffalo crossed the line of march, Custer was liable to forget everything and take off after them."

I tried to imagine him on that spring day in 1876, blond hair rippling, mustache resplendent, kissing his wife Elizabeth good-bye for what was to be the last time. Elizabeth adored him and he adored her. After his death she wrote in a book called *Boots and Saddles:* "My husband used to tell me that he believed he was the happiest man on earth, and I cannot help thinking that he was."

Frazier calls Custer "the happiest man ever to ride the plains." He quotes "an account of Custer's death which Sitting Bull gave to a newspaper reporter. 'He killed a man when he fell. He laughed,' Sitting Bull said." Frazier continues: "Although Sitting Bull did not see that himself, I like to believe it. I like to believe Custer even had fun dying." A page or so later, Frazier writes: "Custer's life demonstrates the power of a person having fun. Why, for example, were his superiors never able to restrain him successfully, or to keep this repeat offender away from important command? Maybe because they secretly looked up to him; maybe because a career of cavalry charges and danger and glory was something they dreamed about as boys."

The idea of fun giving people power over authority is appealing, and brings to mind the Situationists, the Yippies in the USA in the 1960s, and Richard Neville's book *Playpower* of the same period. However, had Custer curbed his enthusiasm on June 25, 1876, and waited for a day, instead of immediately attacking thousands of Indians with a small force of cavalrymen, he and his men might have lived a lot longer. A much-larger force was a few hours away. The Indians too might have benefited. In *Bury My Heart at Wounded Knee,* Dee Brown describes the reaction of the U.S. government: "When the white men in the East heard of the Long Hair's [Custer's] defeat, they called it a massacre and went crazy with anger. They wanted to punish all the Indians in the West. Because they could not punish Sitting Bull and the war chiefs, the Great Council in Washington decided to punish the Indians they could find—those who remained on the reservations and had taken no part in the fighting."

In *The Lost Continent* Bill Bryson writes: "Custer was an idiot and a brute and he deserved his fate." True—but, at least, according to Sitting Bull, he died laughing.

MY CAR WAS alone in the car park. As I approached it, an SUV drove in and a handsome couple climbed out. They were actors, come to rehearse roles they would be playing for audiences of tourists the next day. The man had been doing this every day for weeks; among other roles he played Custer. The woman, though, was a beginner. She smiled and said, "And I'm Elizabeth Custer—*if* I can learn the lines."

The Custers suggested that I eat some German food while I was in this part of North Dakota. The region had been homesteaded primarily by Germans. Why else was their city called Bismarck? If you knew where to go, you could find good traditional food, Custer said. He recommended a restaurant in Mandan called Dakota Farms. It served German and Russian food—he named a couple of German-sounding dishes, and added that many of the German homesteaders had escaped from Russia where they had been persecuted for their Catholicism.

Would I be able to understand the menu? I asked.

"Oh yes," he said. And I could always ask the waiter to translate.

LATER, AS I looked at the menu, I tried to remember whether Elizabeth Custer had also suggested this place. I was beginning to suspect a windup. There was no sign of German or Russian food—and the place didn't look anything other than American: a square single-story building on a main road, with a car park at the front and to the side. The menu had all the usual American stuff: breakfast, umpteen sandwiches, burgers, steak, chicken.

Had I been sent here as a joke? I thought back a couple of hours. The young woman actress *did* know this restaurant; she had nodded and said something positive about it. It was a well-coordinated joke—*if* it was a joke. The place seemed strangely empty: lots of tables, but very few customers. The strangeness was intensified by an off-hand young waitress who couldn't understand what I said, while I couldn't grasp much of what she said. But this wasn't because she had a German accent, just a slurred American way of speaking.

I asked for beer—and said the word three times before she understood.

"No." She shook her head. "No alcohol."

Country music was playing at medium volume on a loop. Alternately: a whiney female voice caterwauling something unintelligible but obviously sad; then a male voice singing fatuous lyrics to a tedious rhythm. It wasn't good; it wasn't Emmylou Harris or Johnny Cash, and it certainly wasn't German or Russian.

I asked about the soup of the day.

She said something that sounded like "nefla."

So it wasn't a joke. The actor had used that word; he'd said it was a soup served with dumplings; he'd suggested I try it. So I ordered "nefla," to be followed by steak and mash.

It was served in a very small bowl and came with very small dumplings. It was green and tasted perhaps of peas and, possibly, bacon. It was OK, but nothing to make a fuss about. The steak and mash came with gravy, mushrooms, and green peppers that perhaps came out of a tin. The fork bent when I pushed it into the steak.

The waitress appeared. "How's that tasting so far?"

That ominous "so far" again. I nodded and spluttered, and she retreated.

I looked around. Some way off, almost in another room, a woman with brown hair was sitting with a child. Closer to me, a few feet away, a middle-aged couple sat opposite one another. I could see his face, a little pouchy, and the back of her head. Both had dyed their hair the same shade of black, a blue-black, like anthracite.

The dessert menu listed something called kuchen. The waitress said this was "a German pie pudden." I hadn't room for pie. Belatedly, I noticed a small blackboard with specials of the day. KNOEPHLA. PORK CHOPS.

I paid and drove back across the Missouri to Bismarck.

I SAT DOWN, pulled off my shoes, and turned on a television news channel. A potential Republican presidential candidate wanted U.S. troops withdrawn from Afghanistan sooner than the deadline set by President Obama.

My attention wavered and I thought about the past. I saw Mandan Indians walking, talking, and playing in their village. Then, in the present, Sioux Indians on the Standing Rock Reservation: a boy in a red hoodie mooching in a supermarket and a beaming hulk welcoming me into an RV park. Then, something else from the past: American soldiers, Custer and his men, invading someone else's country. And there, on the TV, were American soldiers doing just that.

16

THE NIGHT I FOUND CHRIST

FOR TWENTY-THREE MILES OUT of Bismarck 83 travels east. Some people might think that, for that short distance, 83 is following Interstate 94; in fact, Interstate 94 is following the route of 83, which lay there, coated in tarmac, for some thirty years before I-94 was even thought of (by a committee set up by President Eisenhower in the 1950s). I elbowed my way along, remembering the Yellowhead Route back in Manitoba and driving faster than usual to keep ahead of trucks and bring the tedium to an end as soon as possible. But I was on I-94 long enough to appreciate William Least Heat-Moon's observation: "Life doesn't happen along interstates. It's against the law."

When it parts from I-94 and turns south, 83 becomes two lanes for the first time since it approached Minot, some 150 miles back. More than that, it becomes a hick country road—a pleasure to drive on: straight; rising and falling in a switchback; with almost no traffic. Within a mile I had passed a tiny one-pump gas station and a farm with its own grain elevator. The sky was blue with swirling white cloud. I sat back in the seat, steadied the wheel with thumb and finger, sighed, and smiled.

This was it: the American road that Europeans dream of, stretching ahead, empty and forever.

Beneath the usual 83 shield on its narrow metal pole was a sign, OLD WEST TRAIL, in wanted-poster lettering over an image of a Colt revolver crossed with what seemed to be a lance with a feather tied to it—all of this superimposed on the outline of a buffalo's head. I had arrived again on a stretch of 83 that was as it should be: worn, rutted, with occasional bumps, the surface a yellowish-brown color. It followed a straight line between fields and past isolated farms. At a village called Moffit there was a big wake-up kink—right and then left. The road was skirting a lake, and thereafter it went straight on south. I drove at 60 mph and noticed a big empty truck following me at a distance. A mad right-winger came on the radio: Glenn Beck again, this time standing in for the better-known Rush Limbaugh (sounds like limbo, rhymes with bimbo). I put a CD in the slot, cutting him off midsnarl, and soon Van Morrison's bluesy voice filled the car with "How can a poor boy get this message to you?"

We stayed together, the truck and I, for forty miles or so. Then I turned left onto a dirt road at a sign to Temvik. This place was a mile or so off the road and on the list of ghost towns that I had compiled. But it wasn't quite a ghost town. A farm with several grain stores and barns lolloped along what had perhaps been Main Street. Pickups were parked outside two or three bungalows, a wooded field was filled with rusting cars and tractors, and an old Dutch barn was painted with the usual maroon paint. Back close to 83, a wire fence enclosed Temvik cemetery. New-looking graves with fresh flowers were grouped at the western end, and a notice suggested that the Cemetery Board was still active. A ghost town would need a well-run cemetery. Most of the people who had lived and been born here must now live and die somewhere else—but perhaps some came home for burial. I walked among the graves and read the names: Heyne, Pfeifer, Keller. The descendants, perhaps, of the German Catholics who fled Russia in the 1890s and found themselves on the Great Plains of North Dakota.

I was drawn to a particular grave. Perhaps by the name: Lauri Lynne Silbernagel—to an English sensibility a strange surname, evoking something tough and romantic a century or so ago: new lives in a new country, and hard lives spent breaking the sod on an empty plain. Or it might have been the photograph: a young woman with dark hair falling over one shoulder. There were fresh flowers. Lauri Lynne had died aged forty-two on December 31, 2005. I lingered, wondering pointlessly what had happened to end her life so early. No traffic passed. Nothing moved except two small birds. I thought of my wife and children, and that, if one of them should die, I would like to have somewhere to take flowers and think.

83 SLID ON south, curving a little. Prius bounced as the road rose and fell. Mozart's 9th Piano Concerto came from the CD player—and life had rarely been so good. At 6 PM I reached Linton. I parked at the uphill end of a sloping three-block main street called The Broadway, left the car, and walked. A very unslim, very wide-bottomed young woman came out of a shop in front of me, climbed into a car, and drove off in a hurry. I walked on a block, about fifty yards, and the same young woman was walking from her car across the pavement in front of me. Her bottom, in stretchy red trousers, seemed wider still.

The street was lined with low-rise buildings, some with squared-off false fronts like saloons and livery stables in Westerns. I counted five bars, all announced by large neon advertisements for beer. Four had opaque windows and closed doors. The door of the fifth was open, and inside were beer, jollity, and old men in baseball caps. It would have been good to stay in a small town like this, but it was too early to stop.

The countryside became flatter, less lumpy, with occasional cottonwoods, lone and in clumps and lines. The big sky was there again, and traffic: people coming home from work, or moving kids around, in small black jeeps that, glimpsed sideways, looked like Model-T Fords.

I crossed the border into South Dakota. Nothing changed. Miles of rich green grass, a delicate blue sky washed with clouds. Very small towns, villages perhaps, their nameplates announcing their populations, where I must slow the car to 25 mph. Herreid (pop 432), a neat and tidy place with Stars and Stripes beside the road and rusty trucks in a field. Mound City (pop 89)—slow down, five houses and a crossroads. I leaned back, one hand on the wheel. Alfred Brendel and the orchestra moved on to Mozart's 25th.

And then Selby, a bigger place: Main Street, cross streets, shops. And a motel. Inside people are eating steaks—I smell them as I go in—and they're drinking beer. A smiling woman shakes her head; they are fully booked. She talks to a man at the bar. There are two other hotels. A second man shakes his head: they're full too. He knows; he was at one of them earlier. They talk together and suggest I drive to Mobridge—not far, twenty miles to the west. There are plenty of motels there.

IT'S NEARLY 8 PM and beginning to rain. Mobridge is on the east bank of the Missouri; I was trying to get there yesterday when I was thwarted by the closed road. The rain falls harder and the road grows more hilly as I get closer to the river. I drive down a long hill into the town. There are two, three motels. I drive past peering into the murk, trying to decide which looks best. At the far end of town there is another, the Wrangler Inn, a big place, its car park packed with SUVs, some of them towing boats. I stop close to the entrance and run through sluicing rain. A woman sitting at a desk says they have no vacancies—nor do any of the other hotels in town. This is a popular week for fishing in Lake Oahe; people come from all over. She sucks her pen. "There's one possibility. New Evarts, about eighteen miles south. I can ring them for you."

"Yes. Please." What a wonderful woman!

They have a room. She tells me how to get there.

I frown.

She smiles. "You'll find it. Don't worry. As long as you stay on that road—right at the top of the hill by the radio masts—and don't turn left or right. You'll see it when you get there."

By now it's almost dark and the rain is still heavy. I get on to the road. It's narrow with no white lines; it dips and curves and rises, crossing hills and tracking streams which must run into the Missouri. I pass the lights of two or three houses, and meet a tractor, lights blazing as it comes toward me.

Then, on a bend at the bottom of a hill, a spotlit sign: New Evarts Lodge. A track leads off to the left. I drive through darkness for perhaps half a mile, staring at a solitary light, watching it come closer. The light is on a pole in a car park. The rain has stopped. I see dim shapes of caravans, trailers, cars—and a low building with a door—but no light comes from there.

The air is cool, almost cold. I walk through the shadows to the door and push on it. Inside: lights, noise, music, and at least fifty people, every one of whom, it seems, turns to look—and is overjoyed to see me! Greetings, handshakes. "You from England? I went there once." Within two minutes I register as a guest of the motel and have a large whiskey thrust into my hand and paid for by a stranger. Once again, I seem to have fetched up in heaven.

The whiskey is Crown Royal Black bourbon, my benefactor's favorite. It's new to me, and has that pungent sweetness that tells me it's bourbon and not Scotch. My new friend gives me his card. His name is Dallas M. Christ. Dallas is a middle-aged man wearing a baseball hat and a bit of a gut; he is smiling and looking for my reaction to his name.

My brain cycles through the options. He's a practical joker; a religious maniac; or he really is the son of a couple called Christ who named him Dallas. I look down at the card; Dallas Christ is the owner of a Sears Roebuck Store in a town called Beatrice, Nebraska.

He is still watching me, with a strange grin, seeking a response. "Great name!" I smile and suck in bourbon.

Dallas has a friend beside him at the bar. He is not slim, but he's slimmer than Dallas. He leans toward me. "Dallas's name rhymes with kissed." He has clearly taken pity on me. "Nothing to do with Jesus." He laughs.

"Or pissed." I don't say that, of course. I exclaim, "Oh! I see!"—and am aware of how English I sound.

Dallas's friend introduces himself. "Daryl. Daryl Drewes." He doesn't have a card, but he writes his name in my notebook. Daryl is an engineer. He designs grain stores, grain elevators, things—unlike Sears Roebuck stores—that I know a little bit about, from talking to Stuart Harris.

I sit at the bar next to Dallas. He pushes his stool back and Daryl edges his across, so we form a triangle and can hear what each other has to say. It's nine o'clock. I want some food. I take their advice and order tilapia and chips.

Dallas and Daryl are on a fishing trip. They come every year, towing a boat north, from their hometown, Plymouth, Nebraska, which is a small town (pop 400) and they are proud of that, proud to be part of "small-town America." They come up here because the Missouri is cleaner. "There is good grass which stops filth getting into the water," Dallas says. "In Nebraska it's much drier." He shrugs, and I am left to infer that the grass is poorer and the water less clean. This place, a motel surrounded by an RV park, is for people who have come for the fishing.

I've finished the bourbon. I try to get the barman's attention; I'd like a beer. Dallas intervenes, calls the barman by name, orders me a beer and Crown Blacks for the three of us.

I wonder—silently, of course—if he would be as generous to every stranger.

As if he has heard my thoughts, he grabs my shoulder and says, "England is America's first ally."

Neither of them likes Obama. He is too much of a dictator; he pushes things through without agreement. Bush was better. Even some of Obama's own people, Dallas says, are fed up with him. Daryl likes Sarah Palin. Dallas is keen on Newt Gingrich. "He's educated and he understands history." Both of them liked Tony Blair because of the support he gave after 9/11, but they were against the war in Iraq.

Dallas tells me that all he watches on television are political programs. "*Fox News,*" he almost shouts. Meanwhile his wife watches English comedies, but he doesn't know which ones. I suggest a few—*Monty Python*, *Fawlty Towers*—but he still doesn't know. I mention Rush Limbaugh and they both smile. They like him. Daryl says, "We're different from the people on the coasts. This is the *real* America."

Dallas nods vigorously. "You can say that again!"

They have always lived in the middle of America, in Nebraska. Daryl tells me that he lives on land that was homesteaded by his great-grandfather, a Lutheran who came from Germany. The original one-room house, put up on the empty prairie by this devout pioneer, is now Daryl's dining room. He sold 153 of the 160 acres that made up the original homestead; he has kept seven acres, so he can have a few animals.

I don't share the opinions of these men—to me Sarah Palin, Newt Gingrich and Rush Limbaugh are tiny-minded bigots—but I like their friendliness and openness. They speak as if they know that I might not agree with them, but it doesn't matter.

My tilapia arrives. I dig my fork into the crisp breadcrumbs and say something about the Indians. Daryl immediately says, "It was wrong, what happened to them." Dallas agrees—and after some discussion they say that most Americans, conservative or liberal, Republican or Democrat, would agree.

Then, for some reason, I bring up Ireland—and find that I have to explain the difference between Northern Ireland and the Republic. I say that it's wonderful that there is now a solution in Ireland—and also in South Africa. "If there's an answer in those places, you'd think even the Arab-Israeli problem might eventually be solved."

Dallas says nothing. Daryl is frowning. He says, "That problem—South Africa—it's as old as Cain and Abel."

Now I say nothing. I guess that there is racism behind Daryl's remark.

Perhaps I look confused or awkward, because Daryl says, "We, you, can say anything here; there's no problem with that." As if to say that he knows that there are other points of view, and that he respects those who hold them.

I don't follow up. Instead I get on with eating my fish and chips—and the bar begins to empty. Dallas and Daryl are yawning. Fishermen, they tell me, have to be up early. Dallas is keen, very keen, that I go and visit them in Plymouth, Nebraska—and it would be fine if I want to bring my wife. "I want to show you the real America." And he repeats what Daryl said a few minutes before: "We're different from the people on the coasts, and we're proud of that." Daryl nods agreement.

I thank them—for the invitation and their hospitality.

They clamber down from their bar stools and say good-bye with bear hugs and big fat-handed handshakes.

17

SITTING BULL—AND THE PLASTIC INDIANS

THE SUN BEATS DOWN and the glistening grass all around is bluish-green like jade. I'm driving toward Mobridge under a deep blue sky. I'm thinking about Dallas and Daryl—and whether people have an obligation to understand as much of the world as they can, or whether it is enough for them to keep to their own, to be what Barry Lopez calls "geniuses of local landscape"—like Stuart Harris in the Swan River Valley. I don't know whether Dallas's and Daryl's knowledge of their part of Nebraska would qualify them as geniuses, but I do know that Stuart knows about the rest of the world too, that he has broad concerns and sympathies. For Lopez local knowledge, much as he reveres it, is not enough. He cites a survey that "found Americans woefully ignorant of world geography. Three out of four couldn't locate the Persian Gulf."

NORTH MAIN STREET, Mobridge, is smart and tidy with some proud old buildings—one hundred years old or more, two-story, flat-fronted with tall, arched windows and intricate brickwork beneath their flat roofs. At the northern end of the street, a few steps beyond the delicate, white-painted Chamber of

Commerce building, "established 1906," I stand on the bank of the Missouri and gaze across blue water to the low green hills on the other side. Sitting Bull was born over there, in 1831 or 1834 according to different accounts, in a village called Many-Caches on the bank of the Grand River, a tributary that enters the Missouri just here, opposite Mobridge. He died on December 15, 1890, not far from where he was born, shot outside his log cabin by two of the forty-three Indian policemen sent to arrest him by Major James McLaughlin, the government's agent at the Standing Rock Reservation.

One hundred and twenty years later on Main Street, Mobridge, tasteful burgundy-colored banners hang from antique lampposts and coax passersby with soothing white typography: Quality LIVING: MAKE IT MOBRIDGE; Start a BUSINESS: MAKE IT MOBRIDGE; Raise a FAMILY: MAKE IT MOBRIDGE. The message seems to be getting through. Plenty of smart-casual people are striding about, necks pushed forward, faces full of purpose, while their shiny cars point diagonally at the pavement and wait.

I drive to the western edge of town, toward the bridge that crosses the Missouri, and stop at the Klein Museum. Inside, a whole wall is devoted to photographs of Sitting Bull, and I spend some minutes studying his face, the face of a man who wouldn't compromise—and who eventually came to be admired across America by white people as well as Natives for his bravery, determination, and integrity—and also, I sense as I look at him, for some hard-to-define charismatic, perhaps shamanistic, power; he was a medicine man, given to privation and trances, as well as the leader of his people in peace and war. His face is broad, with a strong jaw and a wide mouth with well-defined, slightly downturned lips. In some pictures he wears a hat or a many-feathered headdress. In others he wears two feathers, or just one, at the back of his head. His hair is parted in the middle and tied, sometimes with beads, in two plaits that fall forward over his chest almost to his waist. When he looks at the camera he seems stern, and when he looks away or down he seems sad, reflective.

The museum curator is called Diane. She's bright-eyed, con-
genial, about my age, and we get to talking about politics. She is a liberal who votes Democrat and thinks Obama is a good thing. I must seem surprised, because she smiles and says, "Well. We're in a minority around here—but, in the state as a whole, not such a minority as you might think." South Dakota, she tells me, has two senators, one Democrat and one Republican. She has two sisters who are Republican, though her father is a Democrat. "I have friends who are Republican." She frowns and shrugs. "But we get on."

I describe Dallas and Daryl and their outlook and opinions, and she says that she knows the type. They might or might not be antiblack. There is racism; there are people who believe that blacks are somehow not as good as whites. "You'll get a sports commentator who'll praise a black man for his basketball skills, while thinking he's less than a white in other ways. It's one reason for the reaction against Obama."

Almost everyone is sympathetic to the Indians, Diane says. However, the welfare payments that some of them get can, she thinks, be a hindrance to them as well as a source of bad feeling toward them. She tells me about some Indian schoolchildren who came to the museum and gathered around the old post office which has been reconstructed outside. She asked an eight- or nine-year-old boy if he knew what the post office was for. "Oh yes," he said, "that's where we go once a month to get our check from the government."

I CROSS THE Missouri on a long, flat bridge. For the second time in three days I am heading for the place where Sitting Bull is buried.

In 1889, government agents called together a group of Hunkpapa and Blackfoot Sioux chiefs at Standing Rock and talked them into selling much of their remaining land. Sitting Bull, their most powerful and respected chief, was not told of the meeting because he was known to be opposed to the sale of any land at any price. He found out what was going on, but arrived too late to prevent the others signing the agreement. In *Bury My Heart at Wounded Knee* Dee Brown writes:

> It was all over. The Great Sioux Reservation was broken into small islands around which would rise the flood of white immigration. Before Sitting Bull could get away from the grounds, a newspaperman asked him how the Indians felt about giving up their lands.
>
> "Indians!" Sitting Bull shouted. "There are no Indians left but me!"

I follow a narrow road that winds between fields for three miles or so. At the end, on a low grassy mound overlooking the Missouri, I find two monuments to the great man. One, at the foot of the mound, is in the shape of a tombstone and shows Sitting Bull's face in relief looking out from a halo draped in feathers. His plaits frame part of the inscription, his eyes swivel left toward the river, and he has a mischievous downturned smile. The story of the site is told in the inscription:

> Sitting Bull was originally buried at Fort Yates, ND. On April 8, 1953, surviving relatives with the aid of the Dakota Memorial Association moved his remains to the present location and dedicated the Memorial Burial Site April 11, 1953.

This place, high above the river, close to where the chief was born and to where he died, must be more appropriate than

Fort Yates, the headquarters of the Hunkpapa but some forty miles away. On top of the mound, a few feet from the gravestone, a bust of Sitting Bull rests on a granite plinth. Here he looks imperious. His eyes are narrowed and his mouth is again downturned, as if he dislikes what he sees—as well he might: the Missouri dammed to form a lake that drowned several Indian villages.

The sun beats down, coarse grass grows through cracks in the tarmac, and, overhead, squadrons of clouds lumber past on their way north. It's one thirty. There is no one else here. I sit on the grass eating almonds, apricots, and granola bars.

For much of his life Sitting Bull was either fighting or evading U.S. soldiers. After the battle of Little Bighorn and Custer's demise, he evaded the U.S. Army and escaped to Canada, the country that the Indians called the land of the Grandmother (Queen Victoria), where he lived for four years with around three thousand followers. But life was hard. The British tolerated rather than welcomed the Sioux. In 1881 the U.S. promised him a pardon and said that he could live on the Hunkpapa Sioux reservation at Standing Rock. He returned. The promise was broken, and he was imprisoned for two years. However, by then, he was famous. Until his return he had been one of only two living chiefs—the Apache Geronimo was still free in Mexico—who had not capitulated, not signed a treaty, not agreed to live on a reservation. After his release in 1883, he went to the reservation, lived beside the Grand River, and again led his people, determined to resist the white man's attempts to extract more land from the Hunkpapa with devious treaties.

From then on his fame grew. He made a fifteen-city lecture tour with an interpreter, toured the United States and Canada with Buffalo Bill Cody's Wild West Show, and met two U.S. presidents, Ulysses S. Grant and Grover Cleveland. Like the Black Panthers who, in the 1960s, were invited to parties by wealthy socialites like Felicia and Leonard Bernstein, and Gail and Sidney Lumet—a trend exquisitely lampooned by Tom Wolfe in his essay "Radical Chic"—Sitting Bull attracted the attentions of wealthy, white liberal sympathizers. One in particular, a rich widow from Brooklyn, went further than Bernstein and friends by traveling west, living in Sitting Bull's camp, and becoming his secretary; she left only when Sitting Bull proposed marriage.

The focus on him was like that directed at A-list celebrities in the twenty-first century. In *Great Plains* Ian Frazier describes matters neatly:

> He received fan letters in English, French, and German, hate mail and letters from lunatics. He not only had an Indian agent, he had a booking agent. He sold his autograph for a dollar each. Fame made him a lot of money, but his colleague Annie Oakley remembered that he gave all the money away to ragged little boys.

Through it all, he held firm to his belief in the rights of his people and of all Indians, and his anger at how they had been treated. He appeared fearless while displaying, what must have been to the authorities, an infuriating sense of fun and of the ridiculous. Perhaps more deliberately than his enemy Custer, Sitting Bull used fun as a weapon and as a conduit for his emotions.

In 1883 he accepted an invitation to speak at a ceremony in Bismarck arranged to celebrate the completion of the Northern Pacific Railroad, an event that was to be attended by President Grant. A young Sioux-speaking army officer was provided to help him write the speech. The plan was that Sitting Bull would speak in Sioux and the officer would translate. In *Bury My Heart at Wounded Knee* Dee Brown describes what happened:

> When Sitting Bull was introduced, he arose and began delivering his speech in Sioux. The young officer listened in dismay. Sitting Bull had changed the flowery text of welcome. "I hate all the white people," he was saying. "You are thieves and liars. You have taken away our land and made us outcasts." Knowing that only the army officer could understand what he was saying, Sitting Bull paused occasionally for applause; he bowed, smiled, and then uttered a few more insults.

The horrified interpreter improvised a friendly speech so convincingly that the audience stood up and cheered—and the railroad company invited Sitting Bull to another ceremony in St. Paul.

I drive away, back across the Missouri and through Mobridge. How far was all this from the plastic Indians of my childhood, from the brown cotton tepee standing in our small garden, from dear old Tonto forever smiling and rescuing the Lone Ranger!

I STOP AT Mr. Bob's Drive-Inn, an irresistible red-and-white-painted eating place at the side of 83 in Selby. Opposite Mr. Bob's, three or four trucks are parked outside Shorty's Truck Stop. Shorty's looks all right, but it reminds me of a passage in *Blue Highways* where William Least Heat-Moon, who showed plenty of nerve as he drove around the USA, explained why he tried to avoid truck stops and truck drivers, or "teamsters": "When I hear teamster cant about being the self-professed 'sons-of-a-bitches of the highway'... and witness their ludicrous attempts to be folk heroes, I get very nervous the next time I see one pushing forty tons seventy miles an hour at me."

At Mr. Bob's I order a root beer float with vanilla ice cream from a girl dressed in red-and-white stripes who stands inside a window. Being English, I've not had a float before and I'm not sure about root beer either. But it is refreshing and exactly what it sounds like: vanilla ice cream floating about, and slowly melting in, a lake of root beer—which tastes like cough medicine.

The girl in stripes asks about my accent, and soon I am asking her whether she knows that 83, which is about ten feet away, goes all the way to Texas and the Mexican border.

She doesn't, but seems pleased to find out. She lives here. "Small town," she says, and giggles.

I drive on, heading for Pierre (pronounced peer), capital of South Dakota—and again feel the thrill of being on the American road: the one seen in movies, imagined in songs, read about in books: John Steinbeck's road—not the one in *Travels with Charley*—the one in *The Grapes of Wrath,* along which Okies with jalopies and handcarts scrabbled to escape the dustbowl. Jack Kerouac's road, Woody Guthrie's, Bob Dylan's. It goes on and on and on, between fields, past small herds of black or brown cattle, under a blue sky filled with fluffy, pillow-shaped clouds, across a relentless flatness—or perhaps curvedness because, again, I seem able to see beyond the horizon, way out into hazy space. And, as I drive this straight road slowly, at a constant speed, mesmerized by a rhythmic rush of telegraph poles, I feel exhilarated. It is as if I have traveled it before, as if I have seen it and dreamed about it.

18

"ONE, ONE THOUSAND, TWO"

IN PIERRE I WALK in a well-kept park, downstream from a bridge that carries 83 across the Missouri and out of town. It is past seven. A few people are idling with dogs and children. *All* of them raise a hand and say hello. A woman on a bike calls out, "Isn't it a lovely evening?"

"Yes. Isn't it?" I croak.

And it is: sunny and balmy. The river is deep blue beneath an almost clear sky and ripples softly in the wind as it bends and flows around a low tree-covered island.

Pierre is small, quiet, walkable—the second-smallest state capital in terms of population (after Montpelier, Vermont). I walk the streets and find an Italian restaurant called La Minestra where I sit in an airy room that was a speakeasy in the 1920s and eat luscious pasta—the chef's special: rigatoni with homemade Italian sausage, sun-dried tomatoes, olives, and roasted red peppers. Perhaps I have been deprived of late—the carpet, the walls, even the cutlery, look good. A print that in England is so commonplace as to be almost invisible, Jack Vettriano's painting of a couple dancing on a beach while a butler holds a tray of drinks, somehow seems right in this place where real jazz, Miles Davis, Herbie Hancock, comes through speakers quietly, as if those geniuses are in the next room.

A family of immensely unslim people is sitting some distance away, at a table to my right—a mountainous couple and a child about twelve years old, a large hillock whom I guess to be a boy from his haircut. All of them are wearing shorts. I try not to stare, while wondering how they got in; the door from the street is of average size. They drink two Cokes each and then the parents tell their boy that he must drink water. He isn't happy about that. The parents eat steaks; the boy has a burger—and they all have chips and bread on the side.

The waitress, who is dark and pretty and looks like one of my daughters' best friends, tells me that there was once a mortuary downstairs—a mortuary below a speakeasy. I order *poire belle Hélène*.

After the boy has eaten tiramisu, which somehow I know is his favorite dessert, the mountainous couple and their hillock waddle away—and leave through the street door sideways.

There are fat people in England but—my impression is—there are not so many as in the U.S. and they are not, on the whole, as fat. However, although the Americans triggered the worldwide explosion of obesity, there are now seven countries where the proportion of overweight adults is higher than in the U.S.: Germany, Greece, Cyprus, Malta, the Czech Republic, Slovakia, and Finland. Several others, including the U.K., are catching up.

How did the Americans prompt the eruption of this growing global fat mountain? The quick answer is with the hamburgers, pizzas, tacos, doughnuts, french fries, sugary drinks, and finger-lickin' slurp that have been sold in fast-food restaurants cheaply and in ever-larger individual portions since the 1950s. And what brought the fast-food chains into existence? In his iconoclastic book *Fast Food Nation,* Eric Schlosser writes: "The fast food industry took root alongside that interstate highway system, as a new form of restaurant sprang up beside the new off-ramps." The conclusion has to be that if the Americans had stuck to the old national highways, most of them would be a lot thinner.

I WALKED THE streets again. The air was still warm. I passed smoked-glass windows lit by neon advertisements for beer. A sign above the windows read Longbranch Bar; perhaps this place was named after the famous Long Branch Saloon in Dodge City. I opened a smoked-glass door. A few steps led down to a darkened cavernous bar with myriad television screens and mirrors, more neon advertisements, pool tables, dart boards, low tables, armchairs, and sofas. And, at the bar, upholstered revolving bar stools with backs. I sat on one with a beer and watched baseball. Again I studied the curious actions of a pitcher, the foot and knee movement, the drawing back of the arm, and the throw. It seemed oddly camp, but then the skipping feet, whirling arms, and twisting wrists of a cricket spin bowler might seem camp to an American.

There were only twenty or so people in this vast space. I moved round the bar. One of the screens was showing CNN. On another a baseball player called Nick Swisher was giving an interview.

I got talking to four men from Wisconsin. Or rather to three of them; the fourth was asleep on his bar stool, head back and mouth open. They had come for the weekend to shoot prairie dogs: sweet-looking, rat-like creatures that live in large groups and make a sound like the bark of a dog. I had seen some standing around on their hind legs near the Knife River. They were found close to the Missouri by Lewis and Clark, who, on September 7, 1804, recorded that they had "discovered a Village of an animal the French call the Prairie Dog." Nowadays, farmers dislike them because they dig extensive burrows and thereby destroy crops and grassland. On the other hand conservationists feel that they are a threatened species and should be protected. Well, they are certainly threatened in this part of South Dakota. Anyone who has a gun license can shoot them—and the men I was speaking to had driven a few hundred miles to do just that, not for money—there is no payment—but for fun. I suppose this is similar to traveling from the south of England to Scotland to shoot grouse—except that in Scotland you have to be either classy or wealthy to gain admittance or pay your host. These men weren't posh or rich. Two of them were retired; another worked for a bank. They were friendly, civilized, and apparently interested in my trip. One of them had read Jonathan Raban's *Old Glory* and admired his writing.

I asked about their guns.

One man owned, "Ooh"—he looked at the ceiling, and back down at me—"thirty." That wasn't that many, he said. He had brought only four for his assault on the prairie dogs.

They left. The place had filled up. There were more people at the bar—a big three-sided bar with a pyramid of bottles in the middle. I watched the barman moving around, shoveling ice, upending bottles into glasses—sometimes four bottles at a time, two in each hand—poking straws into the ice. He limped a little, hauling his right foot behind him as if it were painful to walk on; I guessed he was in his late thirties. I remembered Dustin Hoffman in *Midnight Cowboy,* though Hoffman was younger then. And the barman spoke a little like Hoffman too: deep and nasal. Not that this barman was a hustler; he was smart, confident in what he was doing.

I asked for another beer and he asked where I was from and why I was there. I asked him about guns.

He said he had five or six, as if that were unexceptional; he did a little hunting; he'd shot prairie dogs. His guns were rifles.

Handguns were different, almost a taboo, it seemed. "You can get a handgun only if you pass a lot of checks—no felonies, lots of stuff. I'd pass, but I don't want one. No need for that."

AT ABOUT ELEVEN o'clock, a young woman came in with two friends and sat along the bar from me. She wanted the barman to teach her bartending. "Let me practice with you because you're the real bartender here. How do we... How do we *do it?* Give me a crash course in bartendering right now." Her voice was young, her tone pleading: an innocent appealing for protection.

The barman was bending down, shoveling ice into glasses. He muttered, "Wait a little, Rachel," and went off carrying four glasses.

I hadn't spoken but she turned to me, as if somehow realizing that I would like an explanation. "I... Last summer... I'm used to bar waitressing, but never making the drinks. So this weekend she's making me *bartender* and I'm *'Oh my God!'*"

The barman returned and let Rachel through to his side of the bar. He pointed at a large computer screen above the till. "All the drinks that we have, or 99 percent of them, are built into the system—touch the screen and you see the price. The rest of them—they don't know exactly what's in there—don't even bother to make it unless they can show you the recipe. Then find out the prices. Charge the highest price first and then, for every additional drink that goes in, there's a button on there that says, 'Add twenty-five cents.' So add twenty-five cents for every time you add anything."

"OK." Rachel's voice was sharp, keen to show she understood.

"If it's not a basic liquor—and most of them are top-shelf—start adding fifty cents."

"OK. How do you *do* it though? How do you even *make* the drink?"

The barman grabbed a bottle. "When I pick up a bottle, the first thing is to shake it. When you turn it over"—he put his thumb over the top of the bottle and flicked his wrist—"make sure that you turn it completely over... to about the one-thirty position."

Rachel took a bottle, shook it, and flipped it over.

"Yep. Good," the barman said.

Rachel took a bottle in each hand, as the barman often did, clamped her thumbs over the ends, and tried to flip them both and aim them at a glass. The one in her left hand barely moved. She put the bottles down. "I can't do this thing. I can't do both at the same time." She wiped her upper lip with the back of her hand. Her mouth hung open.

"Then you'll just have to go, 'Asshole, I can't do it that fast.' So you pour one in, pour the full shot, and then add your mixer."

"OK. Maybe on Saturday I'll get good, but not Friday. *Oh my God!*"

"Are you left-handed or right-handed?"

"Right-handed."

"OK. Use this one to pour with."

"OK. Pour first... Got it!"

The barman had a crowd of customers to serve. When he returned, the lesson resumed. "Notice every quirk," the barman told Rachel. "If your customer drinks through a straw, or if they're a stirrer. Or whether they don't use the straw at all. If your person doesn't really stir it and drinks straight from the straw—have your whiskey. Start that first. Do it good. Then start adding your mix. Because what happens when they drink right through the straw without stirring it, then all that booze is on the bottom. "*Wow!*" they go. "*No! No!*" Because they just think you burned their fucking tongue. For them that's a *good drink*—and you get the tips."

"OK," said Rachel.

"If they *don't* drink through the straw and they *don't* stir it, or if they do a little bit, then just bend that straw over and make sure you finish with all your whiskey on top. And they take that first drink, *it burns!*"

"OK," said Rachel.

Next the barman showed Rachel how to make a drink called a Jim Beam cloudy. I said that I would order one. Rachel could make it. I was ready for another drink anyway.

"Did you *want* a bourbon cloudy?" the barman said. "It's bourbon with water and a splash of Coke."

"Sure. I'll try it."

"Jim Beam? Creek is another good bourbon."

"OK. Let's try that. Whatever you recommend. Is your name Johnny?" I thought I'd heard someone call him that.

"John," he said, firmly.

"John?"

"Marso. Used to be French." He spelled it out, "M-a-r-s-e-a-u-x."

"You changed the spelling?"

"My great-grandfather changed it 'cos he had arthritis too bad, and he changed it from M-a-r-s-e-a-u-x to M-a-r-s-o. Sounds the same. Just easier for him to write with arthritis."

Rachel began to make the drink. John told her what to do. It took a while. Eventually Rachel handed me the glass with a straw poking out of it.

"That's three fifty," John said.

"OK? Is that good?" Rachel said.

"That's fine." There was a strong taste of bourbon. "How did you know what I do with my straws?" I pulled the straw out and laid it on the paper napkin. "I'm really impressed."

LATER I HEARD Rachel say, "How do you do it when it's like—there's no pourer?" The pourer, I realized, is the glass bubble stuck in the neck of the bottle that, when filled, measures a shot. The bottles of spirits had pourers; the mixers didn't.

John said, "Just, basically go one, one thousand, two. That's about half a shot. Between half and three-quarters."

"One, one thousand, two? OK. That's good to know. Thanks for teaching me, because I'm going in blind tomorrow. I don't even know what's going to happen tomorrow."

A man leaning on the bar said, "I'm going to come in and order some strange shit."

"No-ooooo!" yelled Rachel. "Don't you do that!"

RACHEL LEFT. MANY people left. I was going to leave. It was after midnight. There were only four or five customers.

Then a man came up to me and asked me to buy him a beer.

John intervened. "If you don't have the money to buy a beer, I've gotta ask you to leave because we don't like people trying to bum drinks from people."

A black man—a rare black man—wearing a suit appeared from somewhere and ushered the man to the door.

"He was a Native American," John said. I wouldn't have known. "There are these younger ones that haven't been off their hometown reservations for very long. He bought a drink earlier. Thought he was going to get drunk on a Shirley Temple." He explained. "A Shirley Temple is what you serve to your kids around here. It's nothing but pop and cherry sugar water." He laughed.

Then he leaned his hands on the bar, looked down at his feet, sighed—and looked up. "A few times I've had to ask people to leave, or get them physically removed. One guy—we had to break up some fighting in here—had actually taken a pool cue and cracked one kid over the head. One of our security guys went in, wrapping him up in a wrestling hold. He still had part of the pool cue. He's trying to hit the security guy. I go running in there and, just mistiming, get cracked across the bridge of the nose, the eye socket. I got eye surgery, lens replacement, on it."

"Oh God! Who was the guy?" I said. "Was this a Native American?" I was hoping it wasn't.

"Yep. Yes. He had enough problems in situations around town, and his name had come up in here *way too often*." He brought his hand down on the bar with a loud slap. "*Ten years!*" he almost shouted the words. "Aggravated assault with a weapon."

"Ten years is a lot. Anyway..."

"She gave him that... Do you want another drink? We don't actually close till one forty. There's still time, if you want, for another drink."

It wasn't quite one o'clock. "OK. If you don't mind. Yeah."

The bourbon with Coke had been too sweet. I asked for Scotch.

"Dewars, Chivas, Johnnie Walker, J&B, Cutty, Glenlivet..." I chose Glenlivet, and John warned that it was their top-shelf Scotch, the most expensive. "That's four seventy-five. That's for a shot with water. If you want Glenlivet on the rocks, which would be two and a half shots, that's seven and a quarter. Second shot is normally half the price."

It sounded like a lot of dollars for one drink, but I paid up and enjoyed it—and John told me another story. A man who was well known in the city came into the bar with a gun, and threatened to kill everyone because he thought they knew that his wife was being unfaithful. All the customers disappeared, as did the security man who was on duty. This left John and another barman to cope, "to talk him down." The irony was that no one had known about his wife's infidelity.

Then John told me about his limp. A spur, an extra piece of bone, had grown in his calf; it caused pain and unbalanced him. There was nothing to be done; surgery wouldn't help. Working as a bartender wasn't ideal—standing up and walking about all the time—but "I'm a career bartender. I've been doing it for twenty years. It's what I know."

He didn't want to be a manager. "I've had several dozen people over the years ask me to come and run their bar, and it's like, '*No,* because, if you want me on that side, you're not even going to be able to pay me the money I can make on this side.'" As it was, he was paid by the hour and made a lot extra from tips. I'd watched him picking up bills left on the bar and tucking them into a glass at the back; there was a good wad in there. On one of his best nights ever, the night before the previous Easter, he had made $425 including tips.

I liked John very much: a straightforward man, open-minded as far as I could see, expert at his job, happy to give what he had learned over twenty years to an ingenue. It had helped that Rachel was bright and switched-on—that, for her, to learn was imperative. I wondered if the unseen boss had noticed her potential and said to her: "*You'll* be all right. Have a word with John. He'll teach you. He knows it all."

A group of six people came in. The Longbranch Bar certainly wasn't closing. John went off to serve them. I sipped at the Glenlivet and crunched on shards of ice. I wouldn't usually dilute a single malt with ice. But this was America.

When John came back, somehow we got talking about age. He would be forty-five next birthday.

I told him truthfully that I would have guessed he was younger. "You're looking OK," I said.

"Yeah? Well, *surprisingly* for a high-stress job. It's a stressful job."

"But you're very good at it. Well, *I* would say."

"I appreciate that."

"It must give you some satisfaction. Not me saying that—but in your own mind. To be good at one thing is the key—one of the keys, anyway—to being content and not kind of screwed up. You know what I mean?"

"Oh yeah." It was an "Oh yeah" of agreement.

I swallowed the rest of my drink. The other customers had left. I *had* to go. John wanted me to take a taxi. "Our local police officers, they don't have a lot to do at night. They have a murder about once every ten years. They watch for people who have been drinking."

He was concerned about me driving. When I told him I was walking, he said that the police also picked up people who were walking, but he wasn't worried about that in my case. "They would probably find you as entertaining as I have and offer you a ride! Not to their place of employment, but to your room."

Good bloke, John Marso.

19

GREAT STORIES OF THE WILD WEST

Pierre seemed to be a pleasant place of parks and friendly people jogging by the river and walking their dogs. I had expected the Great Plains to show some signs of poverty, to see poor farmers barely subsisting, alongside the successful agribusinesses. So far I had seen none of that. Pierre's unemployment rate was 3.2 percent, the same as in the surrounding rural areas, Hughes County and Stanley County.

In December 2013, Pierre's unemployment was down to 2.8 percent. Bismarck, Minot, Valentine, the first town on my route in Nebraska, and North Platte, farther south in Nebraska, had similar levels. Garden City, a Kansas town with several meatpacking plants, had 3.6 percent unemployment; Abilene, Texas, 4.4; Laredo on the Mexican border, 5.6; Brownsville, where 93 percent of the inhabitants are Hispanic, 10.2. Unemployment in Chicago was 9.5; Los Angeles, 9.7; New York, 7.5; Detroit, 14.6.

So there are more opportunities for work on the prairies than there are in the big cities. Yet in Pierre, 10.8 percent are living below the poverty level (defined by the U.S. government in 2013 as an annual income of less than $23,550 for a family of four). In Bismarck, 9.7 percent are below that level; North

Platte, 11 percent; Garden City, 14; Abilene, 18.8; Laredo, 29.8; Brownsville, 34.5. In Chicago 22.1 percent live below the poverty level; Los Angeles, 21.2; New York, 19.9; and Detroit, 38.1. There is poverty everywhere—just more of it in the cities.

A cause of this poverty—alongside the subprime-mortgage-and-collapsing-bank recession—is the dramatic increase in the inequality of incomes over the last thirty years—the Reagan-Thatcher years and onward—in the U.K. as well as the U.S. It's not just me that says this kind of stuff. Barack Obama says it—and there are signs that even some Republicans in Congress are beginning to agree with him. George Packer says it movingly in his excellent book *The Unwinding: An Inner History of the New America*. And Robert B. Reich, former U.S. Labor Secretary, says it and explains it with great clarity in the *Observer* of February 23, 2014: "Widening inequality is making it harder for the poor to escape poverty and thwarting equal opportunity... When almost all the gains from growth go to the top, as they have for the last thirty years, the vast middle class doesn't have the purchasing power necessary to keep the economy growing and generate lots of jobs."

And there are the facts: between 1979 and 2010, real annual wages of the highest earning 1 percent of Americans rose by 130.9 percent (according to the Economic Policy Institute), while the wages of the bottom 90 percent rose by 15.2 percent.

I DRIVE ACROSS the Missouri and out of the city. South of Pierre, the great river flows southeast—and, I like to think, slims itself down and smartens itself up ready for its date with the Mississippi in St. Louis and a life-enhancing sharing of fluids. I've been close to the Missouri ever since I visited Lewis and Clark's Fort Mandan. Now 83 leaves the river and runs due south, a straight, undulating four-lane road made from concrete slabs, with grass in the middle and at both sides. It is good to be back on the road. There are no trees and little traffic, just a few farms away in the distance.

On a grassy rise to the west, four horses stand silhouetted against a flat blue sky; their necks curve in unison as they feed on lush gray-green grass. I stop the car to look, and something—perhaps the horses and the emptiness of the landscape—reminds me of a book that my mother gave me for my ninth birthday, *Great Stories of the Wild West*. I know it was then because I still have the book and she wrote the date inside. It's a hardback, its cover decorated with cowboy hats, Colt 45 revolvers, sheriff's stars, and horses, all wound around with lassos. I loved it and I read it many times. There is no named author, just an editor who wrote a short introduction, in which he says: "If the youngsters of today are anything like my generation, there is no story about the Wild West that they will not devour as hungrily as eggs and bacon." In my experience that was true—and I loved eggs and bacon. As well as me and my friend Richard, most of the boys I was at school with were excited by the Wild West.

Of the five stories in the book, four are about individuals. Three of them were outlaws: Butch Cassidy, Billy the Kid, and Jesse James. The exception is Buffalo Bill, about whom the editor writes: "Buffalo Bill was a champion of the law and the terror of the Redskins"—surely an exaggeration of the truth and only part of it. The fifth story, "California—Here I Come!," is based on the true adventures and miseries of the Donner Party, a group of some eighty men, women, and children who tried to cross the Rocky Mountains in covered wagons in 1846; almost half the party died of cold and starvation while a handful of heroes of both genders emerged. As a boy I liked this story the most because it and the people in it seemed more real. Now, I can see that the writer had the advantage of telling the story of little-known real people, rather than famous men of action whom mythologies had made into caricatures.

Two years or so after she gave me that book, my mother left my father (for good reasons), and she and I went to live with her uncle, a genial old man, whom we both called Uncle Godfrey—and with whom I watched Westerns on television almost every night as he sat in a winged armchair sipping whiskey and soda. *Rawhide* was our favorite—we were much taken by the lean, mean Clint Eastwood in his role as "the ramrod"—but we were also hooked on *Wagon Train, Laramie,* and *Bonanza*. Again, Indians *en masse* were sometimes the enemy, the "baddies," when, if instead we had been given the full story, they might have appeared sympathetic or even as heroes; while individual Indians were often "goodies," friends to the white man and, in my eyes then, dignified men—and occasionally women—who had a special wisdom. Now, I see such Indians as simply—like most people faced with difficult, often impossible, circumstances—willing to compromise. This is not, of course, to belittle the good will and, sometimes life-saving, kindness freely given by many Indians to European settlers over the centuries.

In my early teens, I went to a new school and made friends with a boy called Quentin, who had also been indoctrinated by comics, television, and movies into the myth of the Wild West. He and I took to reading Western novels, *Riders of the Purple Sage* by Zane Grey and a series of books by J.T. Edson featuring characters called Dusty Fog and the Ysabel Kid. When Quentin and I met in the corridors we would reenact scenes from these books, drawing imaginary guns, squinting into a make-believe sunset, and talking in American accents about how we were "kinda hard." Later I learned that neither of those writers had firsthand knowledge of the Wild West. Zane Grey was a dentist who lived in New York. J.T. Edson was an Englishman who worked part time in a fish-and-chip shop in Leicester and had never visited the United States. Their books were constructed from, and promoted, the myth.

HIGHWAY PATROL

THE AIR IS WARM. Long grass ripples in the wind. The smooth sweeps of South Dakota's grassland begin to be disturbed by small hillocks and ditches, and the land becomes more lumpy, like a well-stuffed mattress.

Close to a town called Vivian, 83 comes to a T-junction, turns right, and heads west for twenty miles. For that short distance an interstate, I-90, a road that crosses the United States from Boston to Seattle, imposes its dull uniformities. Then, outside a town called Murdo, 83 lets I-90 go and, liberated, turns south once more.

I drive into Murdo. It's mid-afternoon. I have an idea that I might continue west on the interstate, and I want to think about it; the Black Hills are outside my territory, but the Badlands, another set of hills once dear to the Indians, are within range.

WHILE I'M THINKING, I visit Murdo's much-advertised, and some would say only, attraction: the Pioneer Auto Show and Antique Town, a huge collection of old vehicles—cars, pickups, tractors, trucks, motor homes, motorbikes—housed in a maze of sheds. Many of the cars are tricked out with life-size cutouts, waxwork sculptures, mannequins, and photographs of those who might have driven them or, in some cases, *did* drive them: the likes of Tom Mix, Mickey Rooney, James Dean, and Marilyn Monroe. I don't intend to stay long—I'm not that interested in cars—but many of these are beautiful and there are a lot of them, and they remind me of another consequence of my mother's and my move to live with Uncle Godfrey.

As well as Westerns, my great-uncle was fond of American cop and detective shows. After watching a Western early in the evening, Uncle Godfrey and I would eat dinner with my mother and return to the television in time for the likes of *77 Sunset Strip, Dragnet,* and *Perry Mason*. My favorite of these was *Highway Patrol*. It had an unlikely hero: a brusque, burly police chief called Dan Matthews, played by Broderick Crawford, who drove seemingly enormous distances in a black-and-white patrol car while shouting "ten-four" into a radio telephone. Every week Dan Matthews was involved in a long and thrilling car chase on empty rural, sometimes desert, roads.

Such roads and cars were not to be found in England, and I began to dream of driving a large, flat American car with space for my arm to rest along the back of the bench seat, ideally around the shoulder of a girl, as Kookie, played by Edd Byrnes, often did in *77 Sunset Strip*. Unlike Kookie, though, who was a parking attendant and drove only on the streets of Los Angeles, I longed to whoosh along the kinds of roads that Broderick Crawford patrolled, where almost the only sign of movement came from the rhythmic passing of T-shaped telegraph poles. The idea of driving long distances on another continent, on roads I had never seen, acquired a picaresque romanticism and became a symbol of some kind of freedom—similar to that apparently enjoyed by cowboys.

My attraction to the American road intensified when Uncle Godfrey took my mother and me to the local Classic cinema to see *They Drive by Night,* an old movie from the 1940s with George Raft and Humphrey Bogart playing long-distance truck drivers. I sat terrified, but entranced, as enormous trucks, far larger than any English lorry, chased each other for miles on narrow highways in the dark.

Back then I didn't know that the road movie was a distinct genre—perhaps it wasn't quite yet—or that the American road had a special, almost mythical, significance that I now associate with the American dream. In the past, whoever you were—my grandfather, for example—if life was going badly, you could take a boat west from Europe and begin a new life in North America. More recently, and indeed now, if your life stutters within North America, you can get in a car and drive, often in a westerly direction, in search of a new start. Looked at that way, the American road is just a technological improvement on the American cross-country trail, like the one taken by the Donner Party.

Perhaps the idea—and then the myth—of the American road emerged from the myths of the westward trail—in the 1920s, when cars began to be widely affordable and the U.S. Highway system came into being.

Those who moved in wagon trains along the Oregon Trail wanted a new life—and their stories contributed to a myth. But how different are their stories from, say, that of Jack Kerouac hitchhiking from New York to Denver and on to San Francisco. Kerouac thought he'd go back east some time, and in fact did so, but what was he doing if not escaping from one life and looking for another—and, on the way, passing through long stretches of nothingness, just like those the wagon trains confronted as they rolled across the prairie? No one did more than Kerouac to promote the myth of the American road, except perhaps John Steinbeck whose Joad family in *The Grapes of the Wrath* leaves the Oklahoma dustbowl in the 1930s and sets off in an old

Hudson truck along Route 66 to California. A few years earlier, the Joads would have traveled by wagon.

America, being such a large country and having by the end of the 1920s a good road system, offered, it might be argued, the world's best, longest, wildest, emptiest, often straightest roads. At the same time movies—and, later, television series—were being made in the U.S. and watched all over the world. Many of those movies featured American roads. People in other countries—particularly perhaps in Europe—watched enviously as cars streamed along seemingly endless highways as their occupants sought—and sometimes found—a kind of freedom that seems to come with blue skies, open space, no traffic, and, often, no people except oneself and maybe a friend or lover. Everyone knows these movies, or some of them. *Thelma and Louise, Two-Lane Blacktop, Five Easy Pieces, Easy Rider*, and the recent *Nebraska* come to mind. *The Grapes of Wrath* made a great movie, and Cormac McCarthy's *The Road,* the book and the film, took the American road beyond an apocalypse to a place where there are no cars but there is still a road, at the end of which lies, perhaps, a glimmer of something better.

AFTER THE BEAUTIFUL old cars, I am delayed by a village-sized collection of old buildings, including a homesteader shack; I like to look into these and imagine my grandfather living inside. He was a pioneer, rather than a homesteader, but he built a one-room shack and lived in it.

21

BADLANDS

THE VERY WORD WAS enticing. No good, thieves, murderers, danger, darkness, *mystery*. It would have been foolish not to go. And, if I saw the Badlands, I should get a better idea of what the word really meant: dry, bad for farming—and yet the Indians, Arikara and Oglala Sioux, had lived there in numbers.

On a hot morning, I drove west along I-90. The sky was deep blue, paler toward the edges. There was little traffic. The land was flat and grassy—so flat and so grassy as to be dreary, even boredom-inducing. I was hungry. I looked for an exit that might lead to a café or a filling station, some place where I could get something to eat.

After half an hour, I saw a sign, high on a concrete stalk off to the left: JR's Bar and Grill. I drove off and under the interstate, past a sign announcing the town of Belvidere (pop 49), and into a dirt car park where a solitary pickup stood in front of a low brown building.

Inside: dim daylight; pine floors and pine tables; a dance floor, speakers, microphones on chrome stands; a long wooden bar against the front wall. There seemed to be no one in the room.

Then a voice said, "Howdy. What can I get yer?"

My eyes adjusted to the gloom.

He was a tanned, middle-aged man with a kind face and a short-cut beard. I asked if he had tea—and he did and, yes, I could have it with milk or any other thing I wanted.

Was he doing food?

"What do you want?" he said. "I got eggs, bacon, burgers, steaks."

He handed me a menu. "Stuffed tators." It was ten o'clock in the morning. I wasn't going to eat a potato or a steak—and I wasn't in the mood for eggs. I asked for a burger with salad and no fries.

The man called out to someone. Far away, at the other end of the bar, stood a small boy. He came nearer and the man told him to cook me a hamburger, and to wash his hands first. I watched as the boy did what he was told, while the man made a fine salad with lettuce, tomato, cucumber, carrots, and onion. As he moved around, I saw that he had a limp—the kind where one leg stays straight because the knee won't bend.

The man was John Rogers: JR from the sign outside. The boy was his son. "Second marriage," he said, with a shrug.

John liked Highway 83. He often drove down it to Oklahoma to visit his daughter. He'd had English people in his bar before, a couple who had stopped on their way to the Grand Canyon. He'd liked them so much that he'd invited them to stay on their way back—and they had, "in my camper out the back."

The burger was good. The boy had fried it on a gas-fired hob behind the bar. Now he needed a new lighter for the gas and persuaded his father to give him the money to buy one. John threw him a bunch of car keys, and I watched through the window as the boy—all four feet of him—climbed into the pickup and started the engine.

I asked how old he was.

"Nine," John said. And explained that he wasn't going to drive on a public road. The store was next door and the boy would drive from one parking lot into another. He'd taught all his children to drive when they were young. One daughter had been driving in the fields at the age of five. One day, in snow, when the wheels wouldn't grip, she'd accelerated so fast that John was thrown off the back of the pickup where he'd been throwing out bales of hay for the cattle. The little girl had cried when she'd seen him lying on the ground. "'Oh no! I've killed my daddy!'" John laughed.

He had built the bar and dance hall himself, all of it out of wood, with a springy floor and no concrete, because a doctor had told him to walk on a soft surface—otherwise he'd be in a wheelchair inside five years. This was after he'd been dragged by a horse, damaged his leg, and been forced to give up farming.

He called it farming, but he had kept some cattle. It's hard raising cattle in this region, he said. Low rainfall and lack of water mean that it takes twenty acres to feed one cow, whereas one hundred miles east, where his brother farms, three acres will keep a cow.

"We're on the edge of the Badlands here," he said. "And Badlands means dry land." So they grow wheat and other crops, but only biennially; in alternate years the land lies fallow, often with straw and a thin layer of dirt on top to conserve moisture. The average farm here is twelve thousand acres, John said. And everyone wants to make their farm bigger. One of John's neighbors is ninety-three years old and still buying land.

I remembered Jonathan Raban's descriptions, in his book *Bad Land,* of the lives of homesteaders in eastern Montana—not far from here; how, in the early 1900s, they struggled and failed to make a living growing wheat on their allotted, and arid, 160 acres.

A few years ago the water supply to Belvidere was so unreliable that people traveled to a spring four miles away to fetch drinking-water. By writing endless letters, John had persuaded the authorities to provide an efficient supply. He told me this with modesty—but it was clear he was a man who liked to make things happen. He was proud of his dance hall and the numbers it attracts; people come from a hundred miles around. He hires bands who play "CCR, country and western, and rock 'n' roll in that order." (I didn't like to ask what CCR stood for, but I checked later. Of course! Creedence Clearwater Revival. Duh!) "The farm workers are working hard now," he said. "They're busy haying—fourteen- to sixteen-hour days for four weeks, so no dances."

I had to get moving to see the Badlands. After that, John said that I should visit Wall Drug. "That's something else."

I'd read about Wall Drug, and wasn't so sure.

I STOP AT a gas station. A gale is blowing from the west. Two horses stand nearby on the prairie, heads up and sideways to it. The sky is hazy, smudged with dust. The car rocks as I sit in it, and grit pops against the paintwork. In the service-station shop yet another pair of immensely unslim people are blocking the aisle.

I wrench the car door open against the wind, and pull my foot in before the door slams. I gaze at the brown prairie through the dust on the windshield, and I'm reminded of the Buffalo Commons, the idea that an enormous area—ten or twenty million acres—of the drier part of the Great Plains be restored to native shortgrass prairie, which the buffalo thrived on.

The Buffalo Commons is the brainchild of an academic couple called Frank and Deborah Popper who point to the depopulation of the Great Plains: in places there are fewer than six people per square mile, and in Kansas there are said to be six thousand ghost towns. The Poppers believe that the current use of the land is not sustainable. They suggest that farms and ranches might be turned over to their former wild state—gradually and with the agreement and participation of farmers and ranchers who would be remunerated over a long period and continue to live on their land—and that wild buffalo be brought in.

Others have pointed out that the buffalo and their habit of scratching up the soil would encourage other plant and animal species, including wolves, which are declining in numbers and for which buffalo are a source of food. In turn, boosting the wolf population of North America, in particular in its national parks, would keep down the elk which are currently running rampant, eating and damaging too many trees and shrubs that produce berries, and thereby reducing the bear, beaver, and bird populations. When there are no wolves in wolf country, as there weren't in Yellowstone Park between their extermination in 1926 and their reintroduction in 1995, the natural order collapses—including the shapes of rivers since the roots of the trees, on which elk thrive, hold their banks in place. A study by William Ripple and Robert Beschta of Oregon State University has shown that, since the return of the wolves, the ecosystems of Yellowstone and other national parks have quickly swung back to normal.

It is thought that twenty to thirty million buffalo once lived on the plains from the Gulf Coast to Alaska. In 1889 there were just 1,091 survivors. Now there are thirty thousand wild buffalo in protected herds, of which five thousand roam free, unfenced and, it is said, disease-free. (There are almost five hundred thousand farmed, semidomesticated buffalo, most of which have been crossbred with cattle.) In part this growth is the work of the InterTribal Buffalo Council, which was formed in 1991 when members of nineteen Indian tribes met in the Black Hills of South Dakota. The council now has fifty-six member tribes across nineteen states, and it trains Indians to manage buffalo and to nurture appropriate grassland. In 2009, the tribes were responsible for fifteen thousand buffalo.

A HALF HOUR on, I drive off at a sign to Scenic Overlook. There's space to park, and a path that curls for thirty yards up a shallow slope to a high point. From there I can see for miles to the north, west, and east, but there is little to look at: just long grass blowing in the wind. To the south is the interstate and beyond it some small rocky cliffs.

Two girls, one of them pretty fat, struggle up the path in the wind to look at the view. As they walk back down, a car pulls up and a woman calls out, "Is it worth it?"

"No," they both shout. And the car pulls away and back on to the highway.

I SAT IN a queue of vehicles waiting to get into Badlands National Park. The wind had dropped and once again the sun bore down from a deep blue sky. Prius's four windows were down. Rough conical rocks rose from the prairie to my left. In front of me, a starburst of reflected sun came from the rounded rear of a vehicle that seemed to be made of stainless steel: a mobile home, the size of a small bus—a Winnebago. (*Game for children on long car journeys:* How many names of Native American tribes can you find written on the backs of cars?) We were being admitted to the Badlands in batches. A line of cars drove out and then a line drove in. It was like waiting outside a car park for someone to leave, and finding that ten leave all at once.

Soon I paid fifteen dollars and was given a map and a Badlands visitor guide, both nicely printed in color. Then off I went behind the Winnebago, and gradually the line of vehicles spread out.

The Badlands Loop Road wound between strange, horizontally striped rock formations: mountains and canyons, peaks and gullies, buttes and mesas. Some of the mountains and buttes and mesas rose all alone out of the green prairie; others were clumped together in ranges that stretched for miles.

I stopped in a car park packed with vehicles from all over the United States and beyond. From there I wandered and looked, sometimes up, sometimes down, at the stripes and triangles and curious bulges that made up peaks and ravines and plump grassy rolls of rock. Eons of time were stacked up in unimaginable numbers, like the wages of footballers and film stars. At the base of some of the mountains and mesas was black rock that was seventy-five million years old; above it were layers of many colors—red, gray, brown, yellow—formed by seas and rivers and forests and volcanoes that had come and gone over time. The youngest layer, a rock that was a sort of beige color, was twenty-eight million years old. But the erosion of what had been a flat plain into the shapes that are there now, began more recently, just half a million years ago—and continues every time it rains.

Fossils of animals that lived millions of years ago have been found, and paintings of those creatures were on the page in front of me, as were photographs of animals that live in the Badlands now. Many of them aren't that different. *Leptomeryx* looks like a deer, and, as far as I can see, *Paleolagus* is a rabbit.

Easier to imagine were the humans who once lived around here. The first were mammoth hunters who arrived only eleven thousand years ago. Later came nomadic tribespeople who hunted buffalo, and then the Arikara Indians, who didn't just hunt but lived here, close to the White River in the south of the Badlands.

In the mid-eighteenth century, the Sioux took over and stayed until they finally lost out to the white man on December 29, 1890, at Wounded Knee, a creek some sixty miles south of the Badlands Loop. There 120 Sioux warriors, led by Big Foot, on their way to what they thought would be the safety of the Pine Ridge Reservation, set up camp with 230 women and children. Big Foot and his men were then ordered by a colonel of the Seventh U.S. Cavalry to lay down their weapons. They did so, but there was confusion, possibly caused by a deaf man who held his rifle above his head. A single shot was fired and set off the Massacre of Wounded Knee; the unarmed Sioux were strafed by Hotchkiss guns, early machine guns that fired almost a round a second. Close to three hundred died.

Two weeks earlier Chief Sitting Bull had been shot dead. After Wounded Knee the surviving Sioux and other Plains Indians effectively capitulated, did what they were told, and tried to adapt to life on reservations.

After two and a half hours and forty miles, I left the park and soon entered the town of Wall, named after the Badlands Wall, a sixty-mile line of rock formations, some of which I had just driven through.

WALL IS FAMOUS for a curious reason that has nothing to do with rocks. In 1931 a couple named Ted and Dorothy Hustead bought the only drugstore in the town, which had then a population of 326, all of whom were poor and had become poorer as they struggled to survive the Depression. The Husteads made this move for three reasons: Ted was qualified as a pharmacist and was tired of working for someone else; Ted's father had died and left him three thousand dollars, enough to buy the drugstore; encouraged by two of Dorothy's aunts who were Dominican nuns, Ted and Dorothy and their families prayed together and collectively decided that their taking on the pharmacy in Wall was God's will.

The Husteads soon became popular in Wall, and Ted was pleased with his role as supplier of medicine to the community. But for five years the drugstore made very little profit. Too few people were buying the ice cream and soft drinks that American drugstores sold in those days, and Ted felt that he spent too much time staring out of the window looking for customers, and swatting flies. That year, 1936, the Husteads' second child was born, and Ted worried about the privations he would put his young family through if he carried on with the drugstore.

On a Sunday afternoon that hot summer, Dorothy left Ted in the shop and went off for a nap. An hour later she came back. She hadn't slept. She'd lain awake listening to the traffic on what was then Route 16A (now Interstate 90), and it had occurred to her that the people in those cars must be hot, and that they must want water. "Ice cold water," she said. The Husteads had plenty of water and ice. Dorothy suggested that they put signs on the highway inviting passing motorists to come and get it for free.

The rest of the story is an archetypal example of the fulfillment of the American dream, and should long ago have been made into a film starring Doris Day and Jimmy Stewart. The Husteads acted on Dorothy's idea the following weekend. Ted was skeptical, but before he and a helpful high-school boy had finished putting up signs on the highway, Dorothy was struggling to cope with the rush back at the shop. And, of course and crucially, many of the customers who came in for free water saw that the drugstore sold ice cream.

In 1982 Ted Hustead wrote about that day in 1936:

> When the day was done, Dorothy and I were pooped. We sat in front of the store, watching the sun set, feeling a cool breeze come in off the prairie...
>
> "Well, Ted," Dorothy said to me, "I guess the ice water signs worked."

The next summer, the staff at the store expanded to include eight girls who wore matching gingham-check dresses.

And now Wall Drug, still owned by Husteads, has much in common with a theme park. It has twenty thousand customers on a good day in summer, one million annually. It takes up a complete block on Main Street, sells almost everything, and, as well as a pharmacy, contains a 520-seat café, a museum, a chapel, Ted Hustead's cowboy orchestra, an eighty-foot-long dinosaur, a creature called a jackalope made of fiberglass, the Chuck Wagon Quartet, and a replica of Mount Rushmore.

I parked in the immense and crowded car park and went in. Inside I wandered around, lost among thousands of others, all of us gazing glassily at stuff: lumps of rock, gold bracelets, cowboy hats. I bought some postcards, a chicken burger, and a Hershey bar—and before I left, I pressed a lever on the wall of the café and filled a plastic glass with free ice water.

I DROVE FAST along I-90, slowing a little to pay homage to John Rogers with a wave at the JR's Bar and Grill sign, which rose out of the plain like a giraffe on the savanna. With *Continental Stomp,* a recording of a live concert by The Hot Club of Cowtown, in the CD player and the volume turned up, I covered the sixty miles to the junction with 83 in less than an hour.

ROSEBUD

I AM AWAY FROM THE rhythmic concrete slabs of the interstate, and back on the old brown-washed tarmac of 83. The road is two-lane for the first time since some miles north of Pierre, and here, south of Murdo, there are surprising bends, hills, and valleys, and cottonwoods in clumps and rows. Again the land is uneven, pouchy, like an assembly of giant buttocks. It's seventy miles to the Nebraska border, and not much farther to the town of Valentine.

I pass a sign announcing the Rosebud Sioux Reservation, which means I am on land that belongs to the Brulé Sioux, who are also known as the Sicangu Lakota. The Brulé, led by their chief Spotted Tail, set up permanent camps along the Little White River, close to here, in 1877. In that year, despite their victory over Custer at the Little Bighorn the previous year, several bands of Sioux, including the Brulé, admitted defeat in the War for the Black Hills, surrendered to the U.S. government, and, after negotiation, agreed to live in specific places. The Oglala Sioux, led by the famous warrior Red Cloud, had to settle beside a series of creeks, which included Wounded Knee Creek, at Pine Ridge to the south of the Badlands. The

Hunkpapa Sioux—whose leader, Sitting Bull, had escaped to Canada—were placed at the Standing Rock Reservation.

At first these settlements were agencies within the Great Sioux Reservation that had been established by treaty in 1868 and which spanned all of South Dakota west of the Missouri, as well as parts of Montana and Nebraska. But in 1889, following the agreement to break up the Great Sioux Reservation that so enraged Sitting Bull, Rosebud became a reservation in its own right.

I DIDN'T GET to Valentine that evening. I was crossing open, flat country and the Welcome to Nebraska sign was perhaps three hundred yards ahead when, to my right, I saw a motel, a Quality Inn, alongside the Rosebud Casino.

The lobby was carpeted and high ceilinged, with elevators and a flat-screen television showing CNN. Behind the reception desk, a sign yelled in capital letters that alcohol was not permitted and that anyone breaking this rule would be fined one thousand dollars. I didn't mind, but it seemed strange. Did the Sicangu Lakota disapprove of alcohol? Could abstinence be part of their religion? Perhaps this was a reaction against the white man's ways—after all, the immigrants had made their ancestors weak with whiskey.

I was welcomed by a man with long dark hair, swept back behind his ears and held in place perhaps with a little gel; he wore a badge with his name: Troy. He swiped my credit card and gave me a room key. Then he handed me three printed vouchers and explained that I could use them in the casino: two of them were for five dollars' worth of gambling chips; the other was for five dollars' worth of drinks. "Yes, there is alcohol in the casino," he said. "It is banned only in the hotel."

So the religion was commerce. Anyone who wanted a drink had to go to the casino. And it was very easy to get there. I just had to take my room key and go through the connecting door. Troy pointed across the lobby. I would have to become a member of the casino, but that was free, a formality. And through the same door there was a restaurant and a café.

OF COURSE, I very soon walked through that door. It was eight twenty. The restaurant had just closed, so I went to the café, which took up one-third of a tall, airy room about the size of an indoor tennis court. The rest of the space was hidden behind a low screen. I ordered food at a counter, sat down, and waited; the five other customers were speaking very quietly or not at all. On the other side of the screen a bland male voice was calling out a sequence of random numbers through a microphone.

There was a strong hum of air conditioning. Somewhere, someone whistled intermittently. The solemn recitation of numbers continued—just numbers here, no visual puns: no legs eleven or two-fat-ladies eighty-eight.

After a while, a small voice on the other side of the screen said, "Show."

"This game is closed," the man said quietly and without expression.

Someone had won a game of bingo and presumably some kind of prize, but there was total silence. I noticed then that the man calling the numbers was sitting on a platform close to the ceiling, behind my right shoulder. He was a large Native American with smooth cheeks, a wispy mustache, and glasses.

The bingo began again. My food arrived—chicken and chips—and I broke two plastic forks.

IN THE CASINO two or three hundred slot machines were booping and binging and flashing and winking in two large, dimly lit rooms linked by a broad arch. Perhaps a hundred punters—mostly white, some Indian, no African Americans that I could see—were chatting, drinking, smoking, and dropping coins into slots. At the back of the farther room was a bar and, close to it, two blackjack tables. I used my voucher to buy a beer, and got talking to the bartender. When she heard I was from London, she seemed pleased and asked if I knew Kathy Kapowski, her teacher who had moved to London two years before. How I wished I knew Ms. Kapowski!

I told the bartender that I liked her name. It was printed on a plastic badge: Willene Horse Looking.

She smiled. "It comes from my father and grandfather."

I wandered around. The slot machines had less wondrous names: Crystal Forest, Invaders from the Planet Moolah, Enchanted Kingdom, Dean Martin's Wild Party. At the blackjack tables six players sat on tall chairs, a dealer faced them across a field of baize, and a small crowd watched. As well as a gender divide, there was a gender stereotype divide. At one table all six players were women, all of them giggly and not too bothered if they won or lost. At the other table six men glowered—all hard-faced and cool, as if they were playing poker with Wyatt Earp instead of blackjack against a polite, well-dressed woman called Serena Horse Looking, Willene's older sister.

Eventually one of the women left and, waving my vouchers and membership card, I took her seat facing the dealer, a handsome, open-faced man called Delaine Blue Thunder. I used a voucher to obtain ten fifty-cent chips, and slowly lost them. I handed over my other voucher. Meanwhile the women at the table went off to have fun somewhere else and were replaced by two men: a gaunt, chain-smoking, frowning person in a tight red baseball hat, and a large, young Indian with a wispy beard and a white T-shirt.

The game goes on and on. It has a rhythm set by the dealer. After a while another unsmiling man who smokes joins us. He wears a red polo shirt and sometimes upsets the rhythm by failing to be decisive, failing to say "twist," "stick," or "hit it" as soon as Delaine Blue Thunder looks into his eyes for a decision. This annoys the other two, who grunt and shrug, but red polo shirt doesn't apologize; he just pulls on his Camel Light and narrows his eyes.

Red polo shirt leaves, and then the young Indian. There are just two of us playing. I think about stopping. I've been sitting on this seat for more than an hour. If I quit, I can buy another beer. Delaine Blue Thunder goes off on a break, and Serena Horse Looking takes over. She's in her late twenties, perhaps thirty. She has neat dark hair, gold rings and earrings, subtle not showy. I keep playing, run out of chips, and hand over a ten-dollar bill. Red baseball hat has lost a lot of money. He's playing for higher stakes now; is cursing almost silently and biting his lip. After a while he gives up and tells us he's lost five hundred dollars. He stares at the floor and lights a cigarette as he goes.

Serena relaxes. She tells me that red baseball hat is there almost every night; he's an addict and sometimes gets angry. Then she takes the trouble to explain something that she has guessed I don't understand: the insurance bet, which she says can be made when the bank's first card is an ace. I play for a while longer. I place an insurance bet and save a couple of chips. The games go quickly. I win a few hands, and stop at midnight when I cash in my chips and receive fifty-five dollars.

The place is still very much alive. The slots are taking money, and a room has been opened where a group is playing poker.

I buy another beer. Delaine Blue Thunder is standing nearby watching the crowd. His jacket is buttoned, his tie straight, his hands clasped loosely in front of him; he is young, but he has a confidence about him, as if he owns the place, which in a sense, perhaps, he does, along with twenty-one thousand other Sicangu Lakota who live on the reservation and, maybe, many more who don't. Casually he asks where I'm from, where I'm traveling to; he knows that I haven't come here just to gamble.

He doesn't say "Wow!" or "Cool!" or ask about Prince William and Kate, as some do when I say I'm from London. He's interested in my answers, in what London is like, how big it is, how wide the Thames; he'd like to go there. He's been long distances north and south on 83. I sense both pride in himself and some respect for me.

I ask him how it is to be an Indian in the USA now. (I've learned that Indians have no difficulty with that word.)

He smiles, and raises his thumbs in a tiny shrug. "It's no problem," he says.

I talk about Sitting Bull and Crazy Horse—how I have read about them and admire them—and I mention Spotted Tail, who I think brought the Sicangu Lakota to this place.

Delaine corrects me and says that Sitting Bull did that.

Of course, I don't argue. All that I think I know about the Sioux comes from a few books. There are many ways of looking at the past, and of thinking about place, tribe, nation, and the roles of individuals.

I shake my head and say that what happened 150 years ago wasn't good or right.

Delaine smiles and raises his thumbs again. "I wasn't around then," he says—and he looks away, scanning the room, taking in the flashing lights and the fingers pushing coins into slots. It's as if he's said, "Relax! Let's live here, now."

THE SOURCE OF MANKIND

IT'S 6:30 AM. SUNLIGHT is filtering through the curtains. I stare at the ceiling and remember the previous day: the dim daylight in JR's Bar and Grill, the crowds and noise at Wall Drug, the worn reddish-brown tarmac of 83 south of Murdo, Delaine Blue Thunder calmly watching coins falling into slots. I think about the American dream—the idea that in America even the poorest immigrants can succeed if they try hard enough. John Rogers is living the dream; he's built a successful business with his own hands. And Ted and Dorothy Hustead, their children and grandchildren, have been living it without a break since 1936.

I get up, pour water into the coffee maker, lay a porous paper pouch of ground coffee on grooved plastic, and switch the thing on; maybe the inventor of this ubiquitous contraption patented the idea and made a fortune. Thousands, millions of people must have dreamed the dream—people of all kinds: from would-be inventors, businessmen, and movie producers to the millions who have dreamed of their own homestead, ranch, shop, diner, bar, taxi, hotdog stand—a business that will sustain them and their family. Many have succeeded and many have failed, but it's the dream itself—the possibility, the potential—that seems to matter. Faith in the dream seems to be set in concrete in the minds of many Americans, together with the idea that the dream depends on the freedom to go about one's business with no, or minimal, interference from government. Which is perhaps another way of saying that capitalism must not be restrained.

The fear of government is perhaps why so many Americans have, to European eyes, an almost-crazy belief in individual freedom, typified by their insistence on their right to carry guns, and their apparently neurotic fear of high taxes, welfare schemes, free medicine, and what they see as European socialism—if not communism. I remember Dallas and Daryl, the men from small-town Nebraska, the place that they called "the real America." And I hear again, on the car radio, the hysterical Glenn Beck enlisting the ghost of Ronald Reagan to his cause.

Where do Indians owning and running a casino fit in with the American dream? The Indians' dream, of a life of farming and hunting on land they knew to be their own, was destroyed by dreamers from another place. And they are now, by many common yardsticks, the most deprived ethnic group in the U.S., with the highest rates of teen suicides, teen pregnancies, and high-school dropouts. They also have the lowest per capita income. Of Indians who live on reservations, 39 percent live below the poverty level, compared with 26 percent of Indians who don't live on reservations, 25 percent of blacks, 23 percent of Hispanics, and 9 percent of whites.

Do they hanker after the American dream? Some do, I am sure. But it seems likely that many don't think in that way. First, because they are not primarily American; and, insofar as they are American, that is not by choice. Their ancestors began dreaming their dream in the land that was to become America at least eleven thousand years before anyone in Europe dreamed that there was such a place, let alone found it and gave it a name.

Second, their capacity to prosper—especially on reservations—is curtailed to an extent that must deter all but a few. Reservations were brought into being—at first only in the territory that would later become Oklahoma—by Act of Congress in 1851. The concept, its legalities and ramifications, has developed and been argued over ever since. In 2010 roughly 640,000 of the 2.9 million Native Americans in the United States lived on reservations (data from U.S. Census Bureau). A problem for those 640,000 is that, back in the nineteenth century, non-Native Americans wanted the best land for themselves—the land that was most fertile, mineral-laden, and close to railroads—and, after a lot of strife, they got it. The land reserved for Indians tends to be arid and remote, with poor communications, which makes it hard to start and run a business—and causes many young Indians to head for distant cities where they struggle to compete with the workforce that is already there. Whether they live on reservations or not, just 1 percent of Indians own a business, while 11.4 percent of all Americans owned one in 2004 (data from Federal Reserve). Casinos—often permitted by tribal law in states where they are outlawed by state law—are the only businesses that seem to thrive and provide work on reservations.

There is, perhaps, a third reason why many Indians are uninterested in—I am tempted to say free from—the American dream: their sense of community, the thoroughly unAmerican idea that the tribe comes before the individual, that if the group is not safe and well fed, then no one can consider themselves successful or fulfilled. The Sicangu Lakota own the Rosebud Casino collectively. Perhaps then, Delaine Blue Thunder and his tribe do, indeed, know how to live in the present—without recourse to dreaming.

In my imagination I can see Delaine and the Horse Looking sisters, their strong features and quiet dignity. And I remember something Jack Kerouac wrote in *On the Road:*

> These people were unmistakably Indians... They had high cheekbones, and slanted eyes, and soft ways; they were not fools; they were not clowns; they were great, grave Indians and they were the source of mankind and the fathers of it... As essential as rocks in the desert, are they in the desert of "history." And they knew this when we passed, ostensibly self-important moneybag Americans on a lark in their land; they knew who was the father and who was the son of antique life on earth and made no comment.

NEBRASKAN PASTORAL

I AM WAITING FOR A live World Cup football game on TV, England against Algeria. Yesterday, Troy on reception said I could keep the room until the game is over.

I go to reception to check on this. The woman behind the desk says, "I know soccer's called football because they play the game with their feet. Right? I don't know why our football is called football, because they play it by throwing the ball, then someone else runs and catches it."

I raise my eyebrows, shrug, and say that their football is a little like our rugby.

"Yeah, I know," she says, "and your rugby guys don't wear all that shoulder padding and face protection." She is an Indian. She explains her knowledge of rugby by saying she has spent time in Maine.

Do they play rugby in Maine? I don't get a chance to ask; another guest grabs her attention.

England play badly again—a nil-nil draw.

WITHIN A MINUTE of leaving the Rosebud Casino and motel, I had crossed into Nebraska. It was a hot day. I let down the windows. Fifteen minutes later, I followed 83 into the middle of Valentine and parked between white lines at an angle to the pavement. Again 83 *is* Main Street: a posh Main Street with courthouse, library, town hall, bars and cafés, a well-stocked bookshop, and a small art gallery. In the bookshop, long-dead local author Willa Cather had a display to herself—with her classic *O Pioneers!* leading the way—and the aisles were jammed with women who in England might be dubbed "ladies who lunch."

Back on the pavement, I watched a truck trundle by trailing blue smoke; somehow this didn't disturb the gentility of downtown Valentine.

ON THE EDGES of towns and cities there are always plenty of car parks—usually outside fast-food restaurants, shops, or malls—but I often find it difficult to reach those car parks. By the time I have spotted a useful car park, I have usually driven past the entrance to the access road that leads to it (access roads are frequently parallel to the main drag with entrances at huge distances from the car parks I fancy). So I make a U-turn or drive around a block, only to be thwarted by a No Entry or One-Way sign. Then I just break the law quickly. Sometimes there is a jumble of access roads, car parks, shops, restaurants, and businesses, making it hard to know if a particular car park belongs to Kroll's Diner or Maple Park Dental or Triple A Muffler. But, if all you want to do is sit and eat an apple, what does that matter?

That afternoon, on the way out of Valentine, parking seemed almost too easy: I saw a group of parked cars way ahead, turned down the appropriate access road, drove up a ramp across a stretch of pavement, and parked between two of them. I got out my notebook and began to munch my apple. After a while I glanced at the pickup to my right; it was green and looked pretty beaten-up. To my left was a white minibus. It was very clean; so was the green pickup. I went back to my notebook. A little later a bald man in blue jeans looked at me as he walked past. He smiled with wide eyes and raised his hand in a kind of salute. I waved back. In front of me there was space for cars to drive past and then another row of cars, all with their backs toward me. The sun ricocheted off the trunk of a Toyota Corolla, and from the rear window of a Ford Taurus.

All the cars looked very clean. I looked again at the green pickup and saw that there was something stuck to its windshield. Numbers. I looked at the minibus. More numbers.

I reversed out of there, drove back to the main road and on around the corner where I found a long row of gleaming cars with dollar signs and numbers on their windows. Above them was a large notice: D and D Auto Sales. I had parked in the back row of a used-car lot.

THERE AREN'T THAT many towns in Nebraska, and there are very few on 83; on the map, only two between Valentine and North Platte, 130 miles to the south—and neither looked big enough for a motel. It was just after five o'clock. I drove out of town. The land was green, and there were ridges, valleys, and trees. I crossed a long, high bridge. Way below, though I couldn't see it, was the Niobrara River—a five-hundred-mile-long tributary of the Missouri that had been important both to the Santee Sioux who lived beside it to the west and to the smaller Ponca tribe to the east.

Across the bridge, 83 wound higher. Close to the crest of the valley, a small road ran off to the left; it was signed Cowboy Trail, so I took it and, after half a mile, found myself in an empty car park. (And this time it really was a car park.) The air was warm, and filled with black, floaty dragonflies darting and hovering. A track led north through long grass toward the river.

Alongside it pine and spruce stood isolated and in small clumps, and pale yellow foxgloves rose among the grass.

The path led to a footbridge, which once carried a single-track railroad. There were no rails now, just wooden planks to walk on and wooden rails to prevent walkers slipping over the side and down into the Niobrara far below. The river was wide and beautiful and brown, with evergreens along its banks and a green island to the east before a bend. I began to walk across and soon had to think myself out of an attack of vertigo. I was 150 feet above the river and, of course, it would be possible to go suddenly mad, hurdle the handrail, and drop through the Meccano-like metal underpinnings into the swirling water, or even worse, onto a circular concrete pier. I kept walking and grew calm, and stopped to look over and down and admire, rather than fear, the geometry of the towers of metal below me and their shadows, sharp and black on the water, like fishnet stockings trying to escape downstream.

I reached the other side and looked back. Upstream, to my right, the river seemed broader and lazier as it came toward me around a bend. Farther off, a modern bridge was supported on just three slender pillars—neat but dull. I watched as a truck drove across, like a toy in the distance. Of course. That was Highway 83; I'd driven over that bridge half an hour ago.

I returned to the car, walking more quickly, and saw a plaque that explained the Cowboy Trail: an old railroad that ran for 320 miles linking small towns in northern Nebraska is now rejuvenated as a trail for bikers, hikers, and horse riders.

IT WAS HALF-PAST six, still warm, the sky whitening a little at the edges. The road was two-lane and empty—and the dune-like landscape stirred memories of the TV Westerns I had watched with Uncle Godfrey. There were no crops or plowed earth, few trees, but everywhere grass, gray-green and, to my eye, natural and tempered with a thin gold where clumps had dried and died. These were the Nebraska Sand Hills. Human clutter was scant and what there was—occasional rows of fence posts, old and wooden and weathered—seemed to belong. I glimpsed a line of telegraph poles and stopped to look; their wood was silver-gray and they carried no crosspieces, just two cables, one beneath the other; they loped away across land that rose and fell—and eventually, smaller to me than a matchstick, disappeared.

There was a shape to this place that was exhilarating. Here the earth wasn't flat, like the unending prairie up in Canada and North Dakota where the immensity of the sky could make a human feel puny and frail, and where sometimes I'd felt marooned, forever at the center of a circle that shifted as I moved toward its edge. Here there were low humps and cones and ridges that broke the horizon—and long, sinewy vistas in between.

In South Dakota, I had seen landscape rounded like buttocks. In this part of Nebraska the land was like giant legs reclining, some bony, some fleshy and rounded, some with bent knees, some in creased trousers.

A metal windmill stood in a field in the lee of a low ridge. Again I stopped to look. It was like an elderly desktop fan, from a time before plastic, perched on a small pylon. It turned slowly and was, perhaps, drawing up water for cattle that had mooched off somewhere else—maybe many miles away, beyond the ridge; Stuart had said that the ranches here were "big." There was silence, but for the chirp of a bird and a rhythmic metallic clank.

I drew up by another windmill, closer to the road and in full sunlight, lifting water to a corrugated metal trough. It seemed fragile on its spindly, music-stand legs, yet it stood straight and permanent against a blue sky and a loose clump of trees that looked like oaks. There were no cows or steers to drink the water. Minutes later, though, I stopped again to admire a pastoral scene that would have raised the blood of Beethoven or Dvorak: a herd of black cattle—perhaps as many as one hundred head—grazed an open range that stretched south and west for two or three miles to an uneven line of hills; behind the cattle, a line of oaks and, halfway to the hills, a windmill. If only John Wayne or James Stewart had galloped into view... But I saw no cowboys that day.

I reached the little town of Thedford, an oasis in the Sand Hills. As I filled up with gas a long noisy freight train started to go by... and was still going by minutes later when, with siren blaring and lights flashing, the sheriff arrived in pursuit of another customer who had been quietly filling his tank: a little old man with a white beard who was accompanied by a little blond boy who called him "Grandpa." Several people came out of the garage, and there was much shouting and commotion. The sheriff wanted $168. By the time I left, he still hadn't got them.

SOUTH OF THEDFORD the landscape changed again, becoming more intense, prettier, terraced in places with little pointed hills matched by little pointed evergreens. I came to the haplessly named Dismal River and drove down from 83 to a small bridge that crossed it. It was past eight o'clock; a golden light lit the hills, the trees on the riverbank, and the seed heads of the long grasses.

The Sand Hills receded and darkness came on. I drove faster and came into North Platte sometime after nine. I took a slip road off 83, thinking it would lead into town—and found myself on a dark and crowded interstate heading west away from town. A sign announced that the next exit was in twelve miles, a town called Hershey. I put Van Morrison into the CD player, settled down in the slow lane, some way behind the taillights of a truck, and thought of Kerouac: "All alone in the night I had my own thoughts and held the car to the white line in the holy road. What was I doing? Where was I going? I'd soon find out."

In Hershey I came across Butch's Steakhouse, lit up, warm, and inviting. Six or seven people were at tables eating and drinking, and I was welcomed by a pair of friendly women. Yes. I could order off the menu, if I did so before ten o'clock. I chose "pork chops smothered," sat at the bar, and allowed myself a beer.

Those chops with their gravy and piles of vegetables reminded me of the rigatoni in Pierre; it was hard to know which of them was the best food I'd eaten since I arrived in North America.

There were no motels in Hershey, the women told me. "And don't go back to North Platte," one of them said. "Everything's full. This weekend they have an annual celebration." Instead, they suggested I drive west twenty miles to a town called Paxton.

HOLDING HANDS WITH VERNON

HIGHWAY 30 IS AN old road that meanders along a narrow stretch of plain between the Union Pacific Railroad and the South Platte River. Sometimes I can see the outlines of both without turning my head. The grass at the verges is shaggy and thick with dust, and the two lanes of tarmac are old and rutted and slope down from the broken yellow line in the middle. 30 is underused. There is almost no traffic. On this warm, sunny morning it is a treat to drive on and will take me from Paxton back to North Platte through a couple of small towns, Sutherland and Hershey. But, as well as the fun of driving on an empty country road, the wrong turn I took last night has led me into a heap of history.

In the teen years of the twentieth century Highway 30 was a major part of the Lincoln Highway, the United States' first transcontinental road, which ran from Times Square in New York to Lincoln Park in San Francisco through numerous towns including North Platte. The route was agreed on October 31, 1913, and people were soon traveling long distances along it, though it could take thirty days to drive all the way because much of it was unpaved and frequently blocked by rocks, landslides, and flooded rivers. Soon, though, its two lanes were carrying long lines of traffic, and it had been nicknamed Main Street, America.

170 In *Divided Highways,* his book about the building of the interstates, Tom Lewis writes: "In 1926, the Bureau of Public Roads designated this part of the Lincoln Highway as Route 30, making North Platte a stop on one of the nation's main transcontinental roads." In fact, most of the Lincoln Highway, from Philadelphia to Granger, Wyoming, became Route 30. Pleasingly, Lewis continues: "The bureau also designated a north–south highway that extends from Brownsville in the southern tip of Texas to Westhope, on the Canadian border of North Dakota, to be federal Route 83."

But, long before the Lincoln Highway was built, the Oregon Trail occupied this space. Blazed by fur trappers in the 1820s, it became, by the mid-1840s, the principal route for wagon trains heading west. In *Made in America* Bill Bryson explains that the Oregon Trail "wasn't a trail in the sense of a well-defined track. It was almost entirely a notional corridor, highly variable in width, across the grassy plains." Nor was the term wagon train "particularly apt. For much of the journey the wagons fanned out into an advancing line up to ten miles wide to avoid each other's dust and the ruts of earlier travelers..."

Homesteaders taking the Oregon Trail would often assemble with their wagons in Independence, Missouri, before moseying northwest to the Platte River, which led them to North Platte. There the river forks, and the trail followed the north fork, the North Platte River, into what is now Wyoming. However wide the Oregon Trail became, it seems that the shard of land between the North Platte and South Platte Rivers, where Highway 30 lies, was a part of it. Some four hundred thousand people are thought to have traveled this way in the years up to 1869, when the first transcontinental railroad reached California. As I head east along Route 30, a strip of grassy wasteland and a line of telegraph poles separate me from that same railroad.

I drive through sleepy Sutherland and soon reach Hershey where I find rows of tidy, painted-board houses, small and basic with wooden stoops and sofas out front. I stop for a minute and watch a gray-haired man in blue dungarees pull down the shutters on a red-brick commercial garage. LILE'S REPAIR SHOP is painted above the doors. The building looks old and the business reliable—perhaps the man is the second Mr. Lile, or the third.

A freight train, slow-moving, immensely long, pulled by two dirty yellow engines signed UNION PACIFIC, sounds a long siren-wail. The air is hot and the sky pure blue; it is already twelve thirty.

I enter the outskirts of North Platte—not the biggest city on Highway 83, but probably, with the exception of Laredo, way down south on the Mexican border, the most visited since it stands at the junctions of rivers, roads, and railroads. In 1867 the Union Pacific Railroad arrived here and built one of the largest rail yards in the U.S. Tom Lewis writes:

> Trunk line railroads from across the middle of the country sent their freight cars to North Platte, where trainmen joined them with others to create freight trains as long as a mile and a half. From North Platte the freights slowly snaked their way across the nation.

I'm expecting Route 30 to cross 83 somewhere in the middle of the city and, as I drive, I remember Kerouac again. He was here in July 1947 on his first trip west. He arrived on the flatbed of a truck late at night and wandered the streets in search of a pint of whiskey. "Tall, sullen men watched us go by from false-front buildings; the main street was lined with square box-houses. There were immense vistas of the plains beyond every sad street." Of course, the place is more built up now; as I near the center, the plains are out of sight.

I pass a sign—Jeffers Street Closed: 8 AM to 4 PM—and think nothing of it. Then I see another. And another. Soon there is a barrier and, behind it, people are riding past on horses. There is music and a crowd, and people sitting in the road on deck chairs. Some kind of parade is happening on Jeffers Street, and Jeffers Street *is* Highway 83. *My* road is closed!

I PARK IN a side street and walk, taking with me a plastic bottle of water that I keep refilled from taps in motel bathrooms. The sun is burning my scalp and I flip on my baseball cap.

People are sitting on folding chairs in front of the pumps on the forecourt of a closed gas station. Except for some babies in pushchairs, these are the only people in shade. I stand behind them, swallow some water, and wipe my forehead on my sleeve. Men in blue shirts and white cowboy hats ride slowly by, two by two. Then more men, with children on their saddles in front of them. People clap and wave and whistle. A truck, a kind of giant mobile home, crawls by; on its roof, a tiny girl rides a tiny pony and a small boy stirs a lasso into a downward spiral—both cute in outsize cowboy hats.

A man's voice, harsh and staccato, comes from a loudspeaker announcing items, acts, people, and sponsors—eliciting claps and cheers. Three men ride by; one, on a piebald pony, wears a feathered headdress. Next comes an immaculate stagecoach, pulled by four sleek black horses, and subtly lettered Wells Fargo and Company; pretty girls rest their elbows on its window frames and move their forearms up and down like Queen Elizabeth; and someone dressed as Snoopy sits beside the driver. Sweets are strewn from the back of a truck; coins are tossed into charity buckets; people drink pop and throw popcorn into their mouths.

I move forward a little, and a man in a chair looks up and says, "Howdy." He's sitting beside a woman and is wearing a straw cowboy hat, slim blue jeans, a blue shirt, and a belt with a big buckle.

They tell me their names: Phil and Chris Greeley. Chris says that I've arrived on the right day. The Buffalo Bill Rodeo, the event of the year in North Platte, is happening tonight. "You really should go!" Buffalo Bill came from this town, she says, and the rodeo is staged in the grounds of his ranch.

"I *will* go," I say. What a piece of luck!

Phil and Chris own a small ranch a few miles to the southwest, and Phil works on another ranch arranging hunting of pheasants and deer.

"So you're a bit like a cowboy?" I say as politely as I can.

"Yeah," He laughs loudly. "I guess that's what you'd call me!"

"Is that a compliment or not? If you're called a cowboy?"

"Oh yeah. It's a good thing to be. Pretty much my roots."

"OK!" I say with enthusiasm. "So your father and grandfather...?"

"Yeah, they were both cattlemen."

"He's got the broken bones to prove it, I can tell you!" Chris says.

Phil has a small, respectable kind of paunch—one of those that's confined and forward-pointing.

"My grandfather actually came to North Platte from Pennsylvania when he was twelve years old," Phil says. "He came on a horse, and in a covered wagon, with horse traders. And he went to work laying these cobblestone brick streets here in North Platte, and he made enough money to send back to Pennsylvania to bring the rest of his family out."

"OK! Yeah! *That's* interesting," I say feebly.

The three of us turn to watch a Scottish pipe-and-drum band march by.

Phil and Chris's son is in the parade, straight-backed and cowboy-hatted. He works on a ranch that sits beside 83 near Dismal River. Smiling soldiers in battle fatigues and forage caps ride past in an army truck and get a loud, prolonged cheer, as if the onlookers are demanding an encore. Then Miss Nebraska glides by, a cascade of golden floss perched and waving on the back of a gleaming sports car, shoulders and knees sparkling in the sun like polished chestnuts. The noise and excitement continue as, close behind, her blondness only a little more restrained, comes Miss Nebraska Outstanding Teen.

Phil and Chris leave and I talk to an older couple, the Rasbys: Joan and Duane. Till he retired, Duane worked in Bailey Yard where all those freight cars are still coupled together and sent off around the USA. "The biggest rail yard in the world!" Duane shakes his head at the thought of it, and both Rasbys glow with pride.

People are standing up, folding their chairs. I walk across the forecourt—and am accosted by a large man sitting behind the wheel of a nondescript saloon car.

Charles Cumston is a bore. Does my Englishness appeal to him? Or is it that, being English, I am too polite to cut into the stream of words and say that I have to go? I've been told that I'm a good listener, and now I rest my forearms on the passenger window of Charles's car, lean in, and excel.

Early in our acquaintance, he looks at me and says, "You're an old fart, like me."

I try to smile and look unruffled.

Then he says, "How old are you?"

"Sixty-one," I say.

"Oh! You're a youngster. I'm sixty-nine," he says, adjusting his belly under the steering wheel.

My self-image plummets—do I look *older* than sixty-one?—yet I go on standing there as he serves up glutinous slabs of his life history. Twenty years in the army: "Vietnam... Germany... Missiles, so no firefights." He smiles and scratches.

"Blimey," I say.

"Platoon sergeant."

"Great."

And twenty-one years as a railroad worker. Dates and promotions—but no emotions, or people, or fun.

At last I get away and walk toward my car—and think: How can that Charles Cumston see *me* as like himself? *His belly is all over the place! It barely fits under the steering wheel!* OK: I have a paunch—but it's a neat, little, forward-pointing one... like Phil Greeley's. And he must be only about forty-five, and he's got a pretty wife. And so have I! What's the matter with this Cumston guy?

ON JEFFERS STREET, south of the garages and DIY stores, there are some square, false-fronted buildings that would have been there when Kerouac passed through. One is a bookshop. Others sell antiques. They are shut. It's a hot Saturday afternoon.

Farther south I go into a Subway—and watch a huge unsmiling man order a sandwich. Under a series of rapid-fire questions from the sandwich maker, he chooses the size, the bread, and the ingredients. And the sandwich is made on the counter in front of him by *two* people wearing plastic gloves.

I want a sandwich, but I'm unsure about ordering. I pose—it isn't difficult—as an ignorant man from England and ask the huge unsmiling man about the different breads. He smiles and explains.

Then I watch an elderly man—called Vernon, according to a large metal sign on the back of his belt—and his dark-haired wife.

"Ain't that a sandwich!" Vernon holds it up for my benefit. And then he and his wife advise me: "Keep it simple."

So I do: six inches, rather than a foot; wheat bread, black forest ham, lettuce, tomato...

"Not too many relishes," Vernon's wife calls out. "They can take over."

"Just honey mustard, please."

I take the sandwich to a table a little way from the Vernons, stare out at the car park, and eat.

I can hear Vernon's deep voice and his chuckle. He reminds me of Uncle Godfrey; he has warmth, wrinkles, and twinkly blue eyes—but otherwise he is very different, a snazzy dresser: red baseball hat, patterned shirt, blue jeans, and that metal-covered belt.

I pass the Vernons' table as I leave and thank them for their help.

"Did you get it all down?" Vernon looks up and smiles. Then he takes my hand, squeezes it, and holds on, and says that he was in London in 1955 "working for Uncle Sam." "How's the economy?" he says.

I try to make the coalition government and their spending cuts sound interesting.

Vernon nods and beams—and I notice that he is wearing brown winklepicker boots with Cuban heels.

His wife interrupts, raising her eyebrows as she guesses at the cost of Prince William's wedding. "Billions, I bet." Then she says, "I'm sure Diana was assassinated."

"Could be," I say, hoping to sound as if I doubt it.

The old man laughs. And he keeps hold of my hand, which is strange but sweet. His grasp is loose; *I* seem to be holding *his* hand as much as he is holding mine. I'm not sure when to let go. Gradually I pull my fingers away.

A younger woman, whom I take to be their daughter, has joined them. I mention that I'm meeting my wife on Monday and want to get my hair cut.

Vernon's wife says, "If your wife loves you, she won't care if you got your hair cut."

Everything is shut, they say. It's 5 PM and a Saturday. And everything will be shut tomorrow as well.

"But," the Vernons' daughter says, "you can get it cut in Walmart."

SHE'S RIGHT. MY hair is cut by Kaylea, a sweet girl who wears a uniform pink T-shirt, blue jeans, and a ring through her upper lip to one side. The haircut is fine, and takes about ten minutes during which Kaylea chats in a loud voice about how she'd like to visit England, loves living in North Platte, doesn't know much about 83, but thinks Interstate 80 is a good thing because it goes coast to coast. She has never flown; she has no need to because her family lives thirty miles west of here and she goes there for vacations.

(*Note:* I shall soon be going off route and, like Steinbeck as he traveled with Charley, meeting up with my wife for a week. During his trip Steinbeck made a single rendezvous with Mrs. Steinbeck, in Chicago. Or so he said. Some academics now assert that he met her many more times, in many more places. I shall be meeting my wife once only. Thinking of that excursion reminds me of William Least Heat-Moon and his never-to-be-bettered American road book, *Blue Highways*. As he travels, he hopes to hear from his newly estranged wife, whom he calls the Cherokee. He does hear from her, but not in ways that are satisfactory. This takes up very little of the book and the reader is left to infer much. My Cherokee is, luckily for me, still mine—and she should be in Denver, two hundred miles west of McCook, Nebraska, on Monday.)

26

IN THE BLEACHERS

I DRIVE INTO A FIELD. Middle-aged men in matching blue shirts and off-white cowboy hats are riding about, self-importantly telling us drivers of cars where to go. I can't understand what my man is saying, and set off in the wrong direction. He canters after me, whoa-boys his horse, calls, and points. Chastened and under the eye of another bossy man on a horse, I manage to line Prius up beside an outsize black SUV which makes my little red hybrid planet-saver look dainty and gorgeous.

I buy a ticket for ten dollars and then stand in three successive queues. First, to obtain official acknowledgment that I am old enough to buy alcohol—there is no argument; the woman takes one look and hands me a silver wristband. Next to buy beer tickets. And finally to swap a ticket for a can of beer. The system makes a kind of sense; the beer is handed out by a crowd of efficient boys and girls who are clearly too young to buy or sell it.

I find my seat high up in the grandstand and gaze down at a patch, the size of a football pitch, of what looks like dry, friable mud. This grandstand is the only grandstand and it fills the west side of the arena, shading it from the evening sun. Facing me is a two-story pavilion, glassed in on the upper floor. The command center and hideout for VIPs, it has many words written on, below, and beside it. The biggest are NEBRASKAland DAYS WILD WEST ARENA and, between right- and left-facing buffalo silhouettes, BUFFALO BILL RODEO. From a flagpole on the roof flies what looks like, but can't be, the French flag. To the left, an electronic scoreboard and a digital stopwatch peep from beneath a pelmet of advertising.

Like everyone else in the grandstand, I am sitting in the bleachers with my back a couple of inches from the knees of the people in the row behind. To my left, a girl of about ten eyes me, sucks her popsicle, and somehow doesn't invite a greeting. To my right are three empty spaces which give me a clear view of more than half the stadium.

I tug at the ring pull on my Coors, sip the cold beer, wait—and remember Chris Greeley telling me that the word "rodeo" is Spanish for "roundup."

A rousing male voice comes from a loudspeaker behind me. It is thanking people and businesses who have helped make the rodeo happen. It stops speaking as a group of girls on horseback charge into the arena from the south. They are dressed in purple and black, with black cowboy hats, and carry purple flags. There are eight of them. Flags streaming behind them, they gallop full tilt in a complex dance of circles and figures of eight. Frequently they stop their horses dead, turn, and dash away in a new direction. The speed and coordination is exhilarating. They leave as they came in: suddenly and fast.

The empty seats are still there to my right. Another announcer, blue shirt, white cowboy hat, stands on the dirt at the far side of the arena, microphone in hand, and thanks more people and businesses. He speaks as if he knows everyone and everyone knows him. Maybe they do. But, to me, he is a little too pleased to let us know that he is familiar with the local plutocrats—and that he is himself one of them, naturally. Perhaps my reaction reflects a clash between an English love of modesty—often false, of course—and an American readiness to display pride, often noisily.

There is a disturbance to my left. Two middle-aged women followed by an enormous man squeeze past. The man plonks himself next to me, buttock to buttock. His stomach begins below his chin and balloons out and down to his groin; he has plastic tubes trained around his ears, across his cheek and into his nostrils, and is wearing a green check flannel shirt and braces.

An open wagon tours the arena, carrying five or six sailors in uniform and the wife and daughter of their commanding officer; it pulls up in front of the grandstand and all are introduced to the crowd, clapped, and cheered. Then soldiers, who returned from Iraq (rhymes with tie rack) two days ago after an eleven-month tour, are asked to stand up in the grandstand. They are scattered among us, thirty or so young men wearing baggy T-shirts and shorts or blue jeans; some hold small children or babies. There is raucous applause, catcalls, wolf whistles. Some raise an arm. All smile sheepishly. These men *are* modest. What comes into their minds at moments like this? What might they have experienced or witnessed?

The arena fills with perhaps a hundred people on horseback—most of them in groups of ten or so with matching shirts. Everyone wears blue jeans. Some carry flags. A choreographed routine is performed at walking pace; colored shirts interweave and form patterns. Among the riders are a few eccentrics who have no uniform: two children, one in white, the other in yellow; a young woman in a white singlet riding bareback and hatless. All of them come to a halt facing us in the grandstand. They remain still and, as it were, at attention. The announcer tells us that an eleven-year-old girl will sing "The Star-Spangled Banner." Everyone stands up and everyone who is wearing a hat, including the mountain beside me, takes it off and holds it over his or her heart. I stand hatless and small beside my neighbor. There are a few seconds of silence.

The girl has a hoarse, high voice which cracks, country style, now and then. There is no accompaniment, no other sound—save for the brief yell of a baby, and the snuffle of a horse. There are many verses. The sun seems to drop, the shadows lengthen, the air grows cooler, as the girl sings on. My eyes water and I catch my breath at the lone shrill voice, at the stillness that is broken only by the fluttering of flags and the nodding of horses, at the drawn-out concentration of sincerity.

Eventually it is over. We "put our hands together" to show our appreciation of the young singer. And the rodeo begins.

First, bull riding: a man comes through a gate riding on the back of a furious, prancing bull; he may hold on with one hand only; his free hand wheels, grabbing at air; he has to stay on the bull for eight seconds. Only five men are crazy enough to try this, and not all of them succeed—though no one gets hurt. Of those who do succeed, a winner is chosen by judges according to mysterious, time-honored criteria. Next comes bareback riding of bucking broncos: again a man—let's call him a cowboy—has to hold on with one hand for eight seconds; several fail. Then, steer wrestling: a cowboy on horseback chases around until he catches up with a steer (a young, castrated bull), leaps from his horse, and wrestles the steer to the ground by grabbing its horns and twisting.

The self-satisfied announcer has turned into an excited commentator. The crowd is screaming and whistling. I am on the edge of my bleacher. And the entertainment continues with tie-down roping: a herd of ten or so calves run around looking terrified while a cowboy chases them, lassos one around the neck, jumps off his horse, pushes the calf to the ground, and ties three of its legs together. Sometimes the cowboy fails at this in the time allowed and the calf gets away untied; when that happens I am thrilled, of course.

Daylight has faded, the stadium is lit by floodlights and there is darkness beyond. When we get to saddle bronc riding (like bareback bronc riding but with saddles!), I notice that one or two of the broncs are more docile than the rest which buck constantly. I speak to the large man beside me for the first time, asking if the riders have ridden the horses before. He smiles, leans down close, and gives me a thorough answer: they draw lots for horses, but they might draw one that they have ridden at another rodeo; there is no great advantage in that, though, he thinks. He and I get increasingly friendly. He asks what I'm doing in North Platte and about England—and then we watch together, making comments, like mates at a football match. We both laugh at a novelty act, a five-year-old girl pinballing around on a Shetland pony while a man riding a huge, docile bull fails to catch her. Surreptitiously I examine my friend's plastic pipes and see that they disappear under his shirt and connect to a tank, or bottle, strapped to his leg. I guess this contains oxygen but don't feel I can ask. Twelve cowgirls come on for a breakneck race around oil barrels; we both rate the same one—a tall girl on a sleek dark horse—and curse when she snarls up on a turn and comes in fifth.

We talk about Highway 83, and the large man says he has a newspaper that is all about 83. This seems strange and I must look surprised, but he assures me that it really exists.

As the evening ends, he writes his name and email address in my notebook and gives me directions to a church where I can meet him at ten the next morning. If I turn up, he will give me the newspaper.

AT AROUND MIDNIGHT I am sitting in a diner. I think about the rodeo and those daring young horsemen. Are *they* cowboys? They looked like cowboys, *real* cowboys: saddleworn and dusty, wearing chaps and with their hats hanging behind their heads by a string. I look at the rodeo program. Among the names listed are Cooper Link, Rooster Stewart, Cimarron Gerke, Dustin Schrunk, Troy Hubbard, Jesse James Kirby, Travis Sheets, Dooley Parsons, Chance Cole Frazier. They *must* be cowboys.

27

BUFFALO BILL AND A PASTOR

I THINK ABOUT BUFFALO BILL as I drive through North Platte toward the First Christian Church. This was his town. His image is everywhere. The Buffalo Bill Rodeo is held in the grounds of his ranch; the pavilion at the arena carries his portrait. Three different images of him, included in the logos of three municipal bodies, appear on my rodeo ticket. The cover of the rodeo program shows a painting of a man who died in 1997, dressed and coiffed with flowing hair and a twirly goatee to make him look like Buffalo Bill; the painting's caption begins, "Charlie Evans was the reincarnation of Buffalo Bill, and also the embodiment of the spirit of the Buffalo Bill Rodeo for almost thirty-five years." To me, Evans seems more handsome and trustworthy than the original—but less dashing than the comic-book character whose adventures I absorbed as a child.

When we were boys, Richard and I were enthralled by stories of Buffalo Bill dreamed up by writers and editors based in London. We emulated *that* Buffalo Bill, pretended to be him and saw him as a hero—even as a role model.

Why then am I not rushing off to look at his ranch and his house, which are said to be preserved as they were when he lived there between 1886 and 1913?

Because I no longer see him as a hero. Now I think of him primarily as someone who profited by taking something real and turning it into a circus. And thereby he helped to create a myth, in the original sense of the word: a purely fictitious narrative.

William F. "Buffalo Bill" Cody was an army scout and buffalo hunter; in his twenties he called himself an Indian fighter, and he fought and killed Indians on behalf of the U.S. Army. Later he became a friend of the Indians and stood up for them. Speaking to Canadian newspapermen in 1885, he said, "The defeat of Custer was not a massacre. The Indians were being pursued by skilled fighters with orders to kill. For centuries they had been hounded from the Atlantic to the Pacific and back again. They had their wives and little ones to protect and they were fighting for their existence."

From 1883 onward, he was an impresario, putting on Buffalo Bill's Wild West, a show that mixed wild animals, trick shooting, mock gunfights, and horsemanship with reenactments of recent events, such as Indian raids on settlers, who were saved at the last minute by Cody and a band of cowboys. Indians, principally Oglala and Hunkpapa Sioux, participated in his shows—perhaps because he paid them and there was little else left for them to do. They displayed their dancing, horsemanship, and skill with bows and arrows—and, of course, they played the Indians in the historical dramatizations. Ian Frazier describes this turnaround in *Great Plains:* "Only a few years after Little Bighorn, Buffalo Bill Cody... hired some of the same Indians who had fought Custer to reenact the battle in his traveling Wild West Shows. In arenas all over Europe and America, Custer died thousands of times more."

Sitting Bull saw Cody as a friend and toured with the Wild West Show in the U.S. and Canada in 1885, but, when invited to tour Europe in 1887, he declined, saying, "I am needed here.

There is more talk of taking our lands." In 1890, days before Sitting Bull was arrested and shot dead in the ruckus that followed, Cody traveled from Chicago to Standing Rock in a vain attempt to remove the Hunkpapa leader from danger.

I don't think Buffalo Bill was a bad man, but I do think it's a shame that a generation of children was misled by the producers of comics. The idea of strolling around Cody's house, which would have excited me when I was a kid, makes me feel uncomfortable now. I'm disturbed by the cruel paradox created by Cody, which is neatly summarized by Jenni Calder in *There Must Be a Lone Ranger: The Myth and Reality of the American Wild West:* "Indians in showy costumes performed in New York and London while others fought their last battles in the deserts and mountains, or starved on the reservations." And I agree with Carl Waldman, who writes in *Atlas of the North American Indian* that Buffalo Bill's Wild West Show "exploited and furthered the stereotyping of Natives."

While the Indian character became stereotyped as either bloodthirsty and warlike or plain simple, the appearance of Indians and their clothing became absurdly homogenized in live shows, movies, paintings, and comic-book drawings. Waldman writes: "Non-Natives once shaped the perceptions of how Native North Americans should appear—in Plains Indian warbonnets [feathered headdresses], for example, even if worn by individuals from other parts of the country besides the plains."

I PARKED BESIDE the First Christian Church, a modern building with gothic touches, walked around the corner, and saw Dillard, my neighbor in the bleachers, from some distance away. He was standing as close as he could get to the plate-glass door that led into the church. Perhaps he was hopping from one foot to the other—I'm not sure—but somehow this large man seemed to be exuding the excitement of a schoolboy.

He was clutching some papers, holding them high up, close to his chest, and he seemed excessively pleased to see me. Perhaps he had mentioned me to others in the congregation and a no-show would have been embarrassing. We were in a carpeted foyer. Ten or twelve elderly people stared when they thought I wasn't looking.

Dillard was wearing a dark checked shirt and had the tubes in his nose. He handed me two copies of a tabloid newspaper. The masthead read "Canada to Mexico via Highway 83"—curious, but I would examine it later. Then he held up a sheet of paper which he had typed himself. Pointing at it, he explained. Here were details of how to contact him—and, lower down, a list of places I might visit in and around North Platte. He told me about each of them: the railroad visitor center, an engine display in Cody Park, the Buffalo Bill Scouts ranch, the Lincoln County Museum, and an Indian earth lodge at Opal Springs, twenty miles to the south. There was a sense of urgency about him—the service must be about to start—as well as a determination to enthuse me. I responded by nodding as eagerly as he spoke.

Then he asked if I would like to stay for the service and for "a fellowship lunch" afterward. "You'd be very welcome and you'd meet some people."

I'd half-expected this—people in churches are often welcoming and press you to stay or call in again or donate some money—and I'd wondered how to respond. I am not religious. If I attended the service and met these people, would I be able to write honestly about it and them without causing offence? Would I be able to be frank with them about my lack of belief, or would I fall back on being evasive and insincere? I doubted that I would enjoy any of it; on the other hand it would be an opportunity to see what goes on inside an American church and meet some devotees.

I had to answer. I couldn't dither. I said that I had to get to McCook by noon. It was already half-past ten.

Before I left, the pastor walked by and Dillard introduced me. I think he was called Mike. He was wearing a deep-red shirt and a white tunic. A large white cross that looked like ivory, but probably wasn't, hung low on his chest. He was about forty and looked a little like Edward G. Robinson, an actor who often played gangsters. I guessed that he had charisma.

Dillard told him about my trip and said, "Can you think of anything off the top of your tongue along that road that might be interesting?"

Edward G. recommended a place called Adobe Walls between Spearman and somewhere he couldn't remember, "because it's where Quanah Parker, last, half-white, chief of the Comanches fought a battle with"—he paused—"well... a bunch of buffalo hunters." And then he suggested Tascosa near Amarillo (he pronounced it Ameriller), Texas, where there was a famous gunfight over a girl in Jenkins Saloon; several men—more than at the OK Corral—were shot dead.

A teenage boy, dressed in white, dark haired and olive skinned, perhaps of Asian Indian origin, approached and hovered. He whispered something to the pastor—about the ceremony—and floated off, followed by Edward G. Soon I was saying effusive good-byes to Dillard and promising to keep in touch.

PARADISE UNPAVED

SOUTH OF NORTH PLATTE, 83 is two-lane with little traffic, and rolls in a straight line for twenty miles over gentle green-brown ridges broken by lines and clumps of conifers. The sky is a gray horizontal wash and the air is cool. There are no towns, only an occasional farmhouse or barn, usually low down in a hollow. It's good to have left the city.

A sign advertises an eating place called Bearly-Nuff, Grub-n-Stuff. Five or six cars are parked uphill from a low L-shaped building. I go in and am greeted by a moderately large woman standing behind a Perspex display case.

Of course I can have a cup of coffee! "And would you like a piece of my pie?" She points to a row of six or seven pies, and names them: all different, all fruit, all homemade. A group of teddy bears sits on a shelf behind her.

"Blueberry, please." Several times as a child I met an elderly American cousin who ate blueberry pie every day—often twice; she lived well into her nineties. She also ate large piles of peas.

I am in a light, white-painted room, filled with small tables with white tablecloths. An elderly woman, neat, white-haired, handsome, is sitting beside one of the tables with a small baby asleep on her lap. There is no one else in the room—just groups of teddy bears watching from tables and window sills.

"Hello," the old lady says.

"Hi," I say.

I sit down at the next table and look at the baby. It has soft cheeks, delicate nostrils, and tiny hands; and it is very clean. In fact it is beautiful—and I say so.

She looks down and says, "Yes. Isn't he? I don't know him very well. My niece is his grandmother. He's four weeks old. I asked if I could hold him."

The baby's parents and grandparents are having lunch in another room, but she prefers to be here with the baby; it's quieter. She looks at the baby again. "They really are a miracle," she says. And then she says that she can't understand the people she has read about and seen on TV who harm babies and children.

I say that this puzzles me too—and that it happens in the U.K. as well.

She seems saddened to hear that. "There has to be some overall being beyond us," she says, "but I can't understand how he allows that." She sighs almost silently. "Perhaps he makes something perfect and says, 'Here it is. Here's your chance...'" She tails off.

The baby has been holding the old lady's little finger. I see him tighten his grip and squeeze, without moving in any other way or opening his eyes. Then he relaxes his hand without letting go; it's as if he's checking that she, someone, is still there.

My coffee arrives—with a dripping triangle of blueberry pie.

The old lady's name is Fran Greenwood. She is eighty-three years old. Her husband died two years ago. She used to be the local schoolteacher and she used to play the organ in church. In fact, she still plays the organ sometimes, but she makes mistakes because her fingers go numb. She has blue eyes and a strong face with high cheekbones. Only gray hair, lines, and a hint of weariness suggest her age. I can see her as a small-town schoolteacher: a Katharine Ross figure in a long skirt. And maybe her husband was as handsome as the Sundance Kid.

There are two farms in her family, she tells me: her grandfather's homestead and her husband's great-grandfather's homestead. Both are much larger than the original 160 acres, and both are worked by her son. "At first, he said he didn't want anything to do with farming, and he joined the air force. But, after that, he came and said he'd like to help with the farm." He keeps cattle and grows corn for feed. Fran hopes they'll keep both homesteads in the family, but isn't sure.

"Why can't you be sure?" I ask.

"Well, the machinery is getting old and I'm not sure we can afford the new stuff." And her son has too much to do. She helps a little. "I can go fetch stuff, oil or whatever, to save his time at least, but that doesn't help much. We did have hogs and that made money, but I think it was too much work. He actually had to live in the hog-farrowing building!" She doesn't smile at this. It clearly worries her.

My blueberry pie has cooled and I begin to eat it.

"I used to come up here as a young girl," Fran says. "At that time they had dances in the town hall. That was such fun. Now we have two or three ministers in the town, and they won't let them have any more dances in there because they put in a new floor. Well..." She looks across at me. "Why would you fix up a town hall and not use it?" She shakes her head. "We used to have a dance two times a month down there."

"Who stopped it? The ministers? Preachers, do you mean?"

"Yeah. He's new to this village. And he's gone on the town board—very strict."

"Is he Presbyterian or something?"

"I don't even know." She raises a hand and lets it drop onto the table. "If I saw him, I wouldn't know him. I just know that he's ornery."

The baby sleeps on. I eat my pie. And Fran tells me about the annual show, the annual horse race—and the proposal to pave Main Street.

"They've been putting paved roads in a lot of little places now—and some people said, 'Why don't they pave Main Street?' And the authorities, the county, were going to do just that. Well..." She looked up at me. "I've been married sixty-two years—lived here sixty-two years—and they've had a horse race every year in the fall. The young people bring their ponies. Most of them don't have saddles; they ride them bareback. And they start on the railroad track and they ride uphill on Main Street, past the town hall. They go so fast—the finishing line is right here—I worry that they won't be able to stop and they'll ride onto the highway." She waves toward the window overlooking 83. "Anyhow, it's fun. The kids love it. And, if they paved Main Street, that'd be the end of it."

Fran, excited now, goes on with the story. "There was a petition. Almost everyone signed it because of the horse race. The plan to pave Main Street was abandoned—and Wellfleet [pop 76] got into the newspaper with the headline, 'The town that wouldn't pave Main Street.'"

"Wonderful!" I say. "Fantastic! Hoo-ray!"

Fran smiles and shrugs. "I mean... it's not *that* bad. They keep it well graveled and well maintained and everything. It doesn't need to be *paved*."

The baby sleeps. He has squeezed Fran's finger once or twice, but otherwise he hasn't moved. In a few years he will—he *must*—race his pony up Main Street.

I pay my bill and begin to leave, and Fran tells me I must visit the town's lake: "It's beautiful." She gives me complicated directions, saying everything twice, and looks me hard in the eye, as if I'm a small schoolboy, to see if I've understood and will remember. Eventually, in her mind, I get there: "There are four or five little places where you can drive in and see the lake. Don't drive *in* the lake!" She giggles. "I'd hate anything to happen to you!"

I thank her for being such a good companion.

"Have a safe trip—or an interesting one," she says.

SOON I AM sitting on grass in a clearing beside the lake listening to the plunk of water lapping at a log, and the calls, whistles, and staccato chatter of birds. A cool breeze blows, quiet and then rushing, and then falls silent. No one. Just me lying back, closing my eyes, recalling a handsome old lady and a perfect baby.

MASSACRE CANYON

SOUTH OF WELLFLEET THE hills are covered with lush trees and grasses. Then, I drive up a hill, and at the top the earth is flat again—and a sign announces Frontier County. Now the road is lined with golden wheat fields and scattered, lonely trees. The grassy ranchland of Nebraska that I have grown used to has gone. Kansas and its wheat are not far ahead.

In McCook I turn west toward Denver on Route 34. (I will return to McCook in a week or so.) As I leave town I pass a trailer home with the owner's name written in large letters on a board outside; underneath, in the same large letters, is the word "VETERAN." In the U.S. many ex-service-people seem keen to advertise their past. That word appears on car license plates, clothing, hats, badges. Without my asking him, Charles Cumston told me about his war service as he sat behind his steering wheel in North Platte; veterans rode and marched in the parade in North Platte; and at the rodeo they appeared in the arena, and stood to be applauded in the grandstand. In Britain the exhibition of war service is rare. Retired servicemen don't publish their past. But this isn't just British reticence; the British, including the government, show less respect than the Americans, and give too little care to those who have fought in wars.

I stop in a wooded parking place where a tall, narrow stone, like a long finger, points upward among trees. A plaque explains that this is the Massacre Canyon Monument. Behind it is a visitor center, a low wooden building with a veranda, like a rustic cricket pavilion on an English village green—though a flagpole flying the Stars and Stripes banishes all thoughts of England. Inside I meet a kind-faced, gray-haired man, who seems as interested in me as I am in him and in this place. He gets me talking about my background, my parents, my children, my attitudes and beliefs. His name is Don Keller and he staffs this center voluntarily once a week; he is eighty years old and the great-grandson of a homesteader. He lives on the homestead, which has expanded to two thousand acres, and now his son looks after it with a little help from him. His mother is ninety-eight years old and lives nearby.

The monument and the center are tributes to Indians who died here on August 5, 1873, in the last battle between Indian tribes in the U.S.—when the Sioux fought the Pawnee over the right to hunt the buffalo that roamed here in large numbers. Sixty-nine Pawnee men, women, and children died, while the Sioux are thought to have lost only six.

Don says that he has Indian blood, Pennsylvania Indian, from eight generations back—and that fifty years ago people with Indian ancestry, such as his aunts, didn't mention it. They seemed to be embarrassed, he says—because the Indians were so badly treated.

I ask what changed all that.

He thinks for a while and says, "You know, I think maybe Martin Luther King did."

I'm surprised, but I have an idea of what he means. I've been thinking—not about Dr. King—but about the effect that

John Kennedy and the civil rights movement of the 1960s might have had on attitudes toward Indians. I tell Don that, in a few people I've met, I've sensed some racism toward black people, but not toward Indians.

He nods and says that there is still some prejudice against blacks. Then he says, "I grew up around here where there aren't any black people, or very few, but then I got to know them in the army. And, you know"—he smiles and raises a finger—"the military is the most color-blind organization there is. It doesn't matter in there."

Don served in Korea—he was an engineer and a Green Beret—so I ask him about veterans. He says that they are highly respected all over the U.S. As well as the government, many private organizations help them.

I wander around the visitor center; there are moccasins and jewelry made by Sioux Indians for sale. I buy a pair of earrings: jade, polished smooth, and shaped into arrowheads—and Don and I say our good-byes.

It's 6 PM and still warm. I sit at a picnic table and eat a sandwich. Don comes out and starts to lock up the center, and an old man wanders by with three dogs. "Do you think we're going to get somethin'?" he calls to Don.

I imagine they're going to discuss an upcoming baseball or football game. But Don says, "I haven't been paying attention to the weather. I've been in there all day. What do *you* think?"

"Looks funny. Somethin' I think," the old man says.

Overhead the sky is gray; down by the horizon, shining silver.

34 IS A two-lane highway, not unlike 83. Fields, dense with wheat, are carved out of a scrubby grass plain. These are the dry High Plains, west of the 100th meridian. The farmers are likely to be drawing water from the Ogallala Aquifer, a vast underground lake whose northern rim is in southern South

Dakota, nine hundred miles from its southern shore in Texas; the aquifer lies beneath western Nebraska and western Kansas, and seeps over into Wyoming and Colorado. Since the 1930s farmers and ranchers have pumped water from it to irrigate crops and pastures—and, until recently, they had no fear of it drying up. But now the water level has dropped in some places, owing to higher temperatures and less rainfall. More pipe has been added so that water can be drawn from deeper down, and farmers have been urged to use water more efficiently and to plant crops that need less moisture.

I stop beside a field that is half-harvested. The light has dimmed. The harvesters have gone home. A tractor waits where standing wheat meets cut wheat. Something—can it be a large rabbit or a prairie dog?—hops, bounces almost, across the road. I walk closer to it, and see a ball of tumbleweed blowing in the wind, skipping and rolling, just as they do in road movies.

A few miles on, the cloud grows heavy and there is an eerie gray light. The sun's rays pierce the vapor and move in the air like searchlights directed by some lighting designer in the sky. I stop again—on a straight and empty stretch of highway. Light falls on the land, far in front of me. The road is like an arrowhead, its tip at the place where sky meets earth: a point that glows silver and is, perhaps, five miles away.

I cross the Colorado border, and am almost ninety miles from 83, the limit of my self-imposed corridor. If this book were a play, now would come the interval and people would wander away and have a drink.

NIGHT DRIVE

STRANGE THINGS HAPPEN ON roads. On the night I left Denver—the earrings were a success, by the way—I drove along a dark, empty road at around half-past nine. The road was paved, two-lane, and straight, but rutted and bumpy. What I could see of the landscape was featureless; the light from Prius's headlights evaporated in the gloom, finding nothing to illuminate but road. I stopped to stretch and walk around, and turned the headlights off. There were plenty of stars, but no moon.

I drove on and, after a while, I began to have thoughts, ideas, that I wouldn't have in daylight: What would I do out here, where there are no houses, or lights, or other cars, if Prius breaks down? Then, some way ahead, I see red lights, taillights, disappearing and reappearing, and gradually over several minutes, without driving fast, I catch up with them. They belong to a pickup that's moving at about 55 mph. I don't want to overtake, so I drop my speed and follow a hundred yards or so behind.

A while later I see headlights in my mirror, a long way back, bouncing in and out of view on the uneven road. They come closer and closer and, after a few minutes, are a few feet behind me. Then the driver pulls out and overtakes. A small red car, it keeps up its speed and stays on the left side, the wrong side, of the road—preparing, I presume, to pass the pickup. But it doesn't pass it. It drives alongside it. Their taillights are next to each other, and they drive on like that, side by side, for three or four miles. Peculiar things happen: they move to the right together; they move to the left together; they sway apart and come close again. When the pickup brakes, the car brakes; the pickup is playing the lead, if there is one. But it's not a dance; the moves are random, prompted by the road, its camber and its ruts. Eventually the car drops behind the pickup, and the three of us proceed: the two of them close together; me about two hundred yards behind—and we seem to go slower, 50 mph and less.

I could overtake them both, but I don't want to. I don't know the road, though it's almost dead straight. I decide that they must be friends and that pickup must have asked car to follow him. But I'm just a little freaked. Are they driving slower in an attempt to entrap me? Car could pull out again, and they could stop and block the road.

I want to stop to peel the label off an apple. I am hungry and the tiny label on this Walmart apple seems to be glued on and impossible to remove with one hand in the dark. But I'm afraid that, if I stop, they will too—and they'll come for me, perhaps with guns, and steal the car and my laptop. The three of us are in a very remote part of the High Plains and it's ghostly dark. I keep driving and pick at the label of the apple with my left forefinger. But I can't lift it. In the end I stop the car. And they keep on driving, one behind the other, and draw ahead of me—well ahead. I deal with the label on the apple and, as I drive on munching it, their lights come and go in the distance, a mile or two ahead.

WHAT WAS HAPPENING out there in the night? Why did they drive beside each other? Why did the car, which had been traveling faster, settle back behind the pickup? Reflecting on this the next morning, I found it odd that I had assumed, in the dark of the night, that both drivers were men. Did the darkness evoke that assumption? Was that a primal response? Was I preparing for a fight, the worst kind of fight, to resist an attack by two male maniacs—crazy hillbillies like those I saw, years ago, in the film *Deliverance*? Somehow I knew that each vehicle carried just one person. But in daylight, I wondered whether one of them might have been a woman—the car driver, perhaps. Or maybe both of them were women. Would that have been better? Not necessarily. Women, too, can be homicidal killers.

Or maybe they were boyfriend and girlfriend on their way to a dance. Maybe in the High Plains people communicate by citizen's band radio, and friends know that they are just a few miles apart on the same road and meet up to chat while they drive.

NORRIS AVENUE, MCCOOK'S main street, is on a hill, wide, quiet, leafy, and paved with dull red bricks. Small shops seem to be snoozing through the hot afternoon and there is no one around. No film is advertised outside the 1930s picture palace, the Fox Cinema; instead, letters placed unevenly on the marquee announce HAPPY 40TH BIRTHDAY MICHELE BOYLE.

I'm hungry and luckily find Fuller's Family Restaurant—a low, newish building with a touch of the hacienda. Booths and tables for six or eight fill a large room with a low ceiling. At a table near the door six or seven older men are playing cards. One of them looks up, smiles, and stretches out his arm in a welcome-and-sit-wherever-you-like gesture. I sit in a booth, and a dark-haired waitress in her mid-thirties brings a menu and a glass of iced water. In front of me is a clump of condiments which includes ketchup, mustard, a sugar shaker, and toothpicks; every table has an identical clump; larger tables have two.

I order a BLT and stare into space. This place must be what Americans call a Mom and Pop restaurant, a rarity in a world of fast-food chains. There is no sign of Mom—she might, dare I imagine, be in the kitchen—but Pop is here, playing cards, smiling, and watching over us.

Close by, a man in his thirties sits opposite a woman with tight gray curls. They don't seem to have much to say to each other; I guess she's his mother. Is this a weekly ritual—it's Tuesday—or daily, monthly, annual, sporadic? Farther away two large, not at all slim men, sit with a large, not at all slim woman who is resting a bandaged leg on a chair; it seems likely that she is the men's mother. Soon they get up to leave; all three have difficulty walking.

I pull out the free Highway 83 newspaper that Dillard gave me. It's full of stories of a just-fancy-that variety that happened somewhere in the region of Highway 83 during the pioneer and Wild West era. Around the stories are advertisements for motels, cafés, antique stores, holiday homes, car showrooms, museums, funeral homes, and churches all along the road from North Dakota to Texas. In a matchbox-sized rectangle, Dillard's First Christian Church advertises Sunday School and Worship Service.

Belatedly I notice china animals sitting all around me, high on shelves on every wall—teddy bears, frogs, chickens, ducks, mice, cats, pigs, Disney characters—large effigies, twelve inches tall, or more. Looking more closely, I see not just animals, but houses, cars, buses, motorbikes, pixies, gnomes. I ask the waitress about them and she says they are cookie jars; there are twelve hundred of them in this room and the room next door. The proprietor—the arm-waving cardplayer—collects them.

And, she says, at Christmas time all twelve hundred are taken down and replaced with Christmas cookie jars.

As I leave, the waitress takes me into the other dining room to show me more cookie jars. I try to be appreciative. Then I ask how long she has worked here.

"I worked here—first job out of school," she says. "Then I traveled around thirty-three places for fifteen years and came back."

"So do you prefer McCook and this job to all those other places?"

"Well"—she hesitates—"it's best for me here. I got nine children, eight boys and a girl."

I feel like saying, "Good Lord!," but instead say that she doesn't look old enough—which is true.

PIONEER FAMILY

I DRIVE SOUTH OUT OF McCook into fields of waving wheat and soon pass a Welcome to Kansas sign. A couple of miles on I stop to talk to some horses in a field. They glance at me lazily and carry on grazing. Behind them the sun glints off the shiny green leaves of a field of maize.

In Oberlin, the first town in Kansas, it's mid-afternoon. The air is warm, the sun still high. I stroll down North Penn Avenue past detached houses with verandas and screen doors and lawns that merge, unfenced, with neighboring lawns and with the sidewalk. Shaded by trees, children are playing in a sandbox made from a tractor tire. This seems like the middle-class, suburban America that we British see in films—the place where, early in the morning, newspapers, thrown by paperboys riding bikes, thud onto porches; the place where James Stewart often seemed to live.

High on a plinth on an island in the middle of this comfortable small-town street stands a striking sculpture. A plaque on the plinth shows its title: *Pioneer Family*. Father, mother, daughter, and son stand back-to-back with joined hands, staring resolutely into the better future that will reward their tenacity and toil on the unbroken prairie. Oberlin was founded by pioneers in 1878. The sculpture was commissioned in the 1970s—perhaps by pioneers' descendants who now live on this street, grateful indeed for the better future they inherited.

A little farther downhill North Penn Avenue becomes South Penn Avenue, Oberlin's main street. The town library is on a corner. I go in, greet the librarian, sit on a comfortable sofa, and read *The Oberlin Herald*, a distinguished-looking broadsheet which announces proudly on its front that it is in its 132nd year. In other words it was founded in 1878, two years after Custer died at the Little Bighorn.

A piece by the editor, Steve Haynes, comments on the mind-boggling news that the Kansas legislature has voted to *raise* taxes. Haynes explains: "It wasn't the legislature that changed; the message coming back from the home front was that people agreed no further cuts were tolerable in social programs, public schools, roads, or higher education ... Anyone whose check depends ... on state and federal money was calling for an end to the cuts." The pressure of public opinion was such that even "our own Senator Ralph Ostmeyer voted for a one-cent tax increase to help save schools and other programs from more cuts ... And he is about as conservative, antispending, antitax as anyone in the chamber."

In current economic circumstances, and as a European-style socialist of the type that frightens Glenn Beck, I'm pleased for the people of Kansas but surprised that the editor of a Kansas newspaper is as pleased as I am. But then, I've learned that not everyone who lives on the Great Plains is a disciple of Mr. Beck or his mentor, Rush Limbaugh. Steve Haynes refers to a book that I happen to have read: "It was as if Kansas suddenly had awakened and realized that the author Thomas Frank in his book *What's the Matter with Kansas?* had been right, that people out there should be voting for their economic interests rather than their conservative beliefs."

Astonishing! The governments of these prairie states are dominated by conservatives who detest taxes and so-called big government, but it seems that the people can push them around—sometimes. Can this mean that democracy is, indeed, coming to the USA?

Farther down South Penn Avenue, high on the side of an old brick building, is a sign: Last Indian Raid Museum. The museum is closed but will be open tomorrow.

Later, in a café, I ask the waitress if she knows about this museum. She explains that the last Indian raid in Kansas was made on local farmers by Cheyenne Indians who were trying to get back to their homeland after escaping from the useless Indian Territory in Oklahoma, where they had been sent by the U.S. government. The waitress, a college student, home on vacation, frowns and says, "Maybe they were just trying to get things they needed, like food or horses."

IN THE EVENING I return to South Penn Avenue. The air is still warm. Pretty, flat-fronted shops are shaded by a concrete and steel impression of the sidewalks seen in Westerns. I walk the length of the street, to the grain elevator by the railroad tracks. I glance at the outsides of two or three bars, and go into one of them, the Re-Load. It's large, high ceilinged, and wood lined. Three young men are sitting at the bar: all jeans and cowboy hats. They turn and stare, expressionless and without speaking, long enough to make quite sure they don't know me; then they turn away and carry on with their conversation. There are no other customers. Two barwomen are wiping the bar and polishing glasses. One of them, a smiley, red-haired woman, pulls me a glass of Coors Light. I sit on a bar stool, sip the cold beer, and read the paper that Dillard gave me.

A man comes in: big-faced, unshaven, yellow baseball hat, jeans, and trainers. He stands beside me and orders a pizza to take away and a "red beer" to drink while it cooks. I ask him about his drink. He pushes the glass toward me, inviting me to taste it. It's Bud Light with about an inch of tomato juice in a half-pint glass; it tastes like tomato-flavored pop.

The man's name is Larry Ayres; I guess he's in his fifties. He tells me that his grandfather came from England as a small boy, accompanied only by his (the grandfather's) mother. His father and several brothers were supposed to travel on a separate ship and join them, but they never arrived.

"What happened to them?" I said.

Larry raised his eyebrows and shrugged. "Either they were on a ship that sank, or they just got lost. No one ever found out."

In the 1950s Larry's father bought the farm that Larry now owns, a 160-acre quarter section that was once a homestead. Until then his father had held land under a sharecropping agreement. There are still such agreements, and they suit some people because they reduce risk. If there's a bad harvest, a sharecropper pays little to the landowner, whereas a farmer paying rent or interest on a mortgage has to find the money somehow.

"I put the whole of my farm down to wheat," Larry says. The harvest is just beginning. Soon—today is June 29—the Oberlin grain elevator will be full of wheat. In October it will be full of corn.

Larry's pizza is sitting on the bar in a cardboard box. He has to go. He has a wife—he smiles—and she will be wondering where he is if he stays any longer.

We say good-bye and I pick up my newspaper. A minute later Larry taps me on the shoulder. He has come in from his car to suggest that I go to the grain elevator tomorrow and ask to be shown around.

When I look up to order another beer, I find that, as well as the two women, there's a man behind the bar. He's wearing an off-white cowboy hat, blue jeans, and a belt with a big buckle—a fairly fit, good-looking man with a gray drooping mustache, perhaps in his late forties. He puts my beer down in front of me and leans both hands on the bar. A clean, white shirt, unbuttoned over a blue T-shirt, trails over his jeans; there's a hole in the T-shirt that reveals a patch of pink skin. "It's too darn hot!" he says, and wipes his forehead with the back of his hand. He walks to the double doors to the street and wedges them open. Insects yo-yo and flutter in the glow of a streetlight and, beyond, the sky is dark.

We talk—for some reason about farming. "Wheat planted before the winter gets a few inches high and overwinters," he says. "It's protected from frost by snow. Then it goes on growing till harvest, which is around now. Corn is sown in March or April, and harvested in October and November. After the wheat harvest, another crop, like soybeans, can be planted."

Then he says with a shrug, "But I'm not a farmer."

"Are you the landlord?" I ask.

"I own this place."

"Well... in England, we'd call you the landlord."

"Well... here,"—he grins—"they call me an asshole."

I chuckle and wheeze, but manage to say, "In England, we'd call you an *arse*hole."

He smacks the bar and bends at the waist laughing.

We calm down and I ask his name.

"Mick... Mick Barth... Barth with an arr."

He says that in the past he has earned a living by driving truckloads of cattle. "But I'm not a truck driver. It's"—he pauses—"boring... I like meeting people—like this, now. My wife doesn't understand that..." He laughs.

The doors are still open to the street and from time to time, as we talk, he catches a June bug in his hands. I ask about them and he shows me one, a brown, hard-cased insect. He squashes it with thumb and forefinger and puts it in the trash with the others.

Then he tells me that he's a cowboy. He says it not in a showing-off way, but as a simple matter of fact. "That's more a way of life, an attitude, how you're raised, than a job," he says.

He tells me that he has ridden in rodeos. "Some bucking broncos, but more roping steers—and in a team where one guy ropes the neck and the other gets the legs."

"That's really difficult, isn't it?"

He looks at me, pauses, shakes his head, and says, "No."

Rodeo riders can make a lot of money, he says, but they have a lot of costs. "They have to pay for all the horses, except the bucking ones." He still does a little rodeo. "Anything for a bit of adrenalin."

As I'm leaving, Mick is jumping about trying to catch a flying insect. Black and bigger than a June bug, it has been dive-bombing the barmaids. Eventually he swats it with a rolled newspaper, picks it up, looks at it, and says he's never seen such a thing before.

Nor have I.

CHEYENNE RAIDERS

In south penn avenue, not far from the Last Indian Raid Museum, three men in head scarves are standing by their Harley Davidsons. Two of the head scarves are red—one patterned, one plain; the other is dark blue with silver-gray, lozenge-shaped motifs. The men are in their seventies, I guess. They are lean, and wear jeans and tight-fitting T-shirts; two wear denim jackets with the arms cut off. Two are chatting, one shading his eyes from the sun. The third has scuffed black boots and a scrawny ponytail that pokes out below his scarf; he drinks water from a bottle and stows it in his pannier.

I watch them from the car and remember that, a few days ago, I met two young men in a bar. Dustin had a wispy blond beard, and a shiny, many-colored head scarf tied around his head; plenty of hair escaped from under it in all directions. He looked like a 1960s hippie. His friend Jared, on the other hand, looked like a French intellectual from that same time: gray sports jacket and floppy dark hair, brushed and falling from a side parting to his shoulders. From their appearances I took them to be rebels of some kind, as hippies and long-haired Frenchmen once were.

When I heard Dustin's name, I asked the obvious question. "Are your parents fans of Dustin Hoffman?"

But Dustin seemed to be barely aware of the great actor. *The Graduate, Midnight Cowboy, Tootsie,* and *Rain Man* meant nothing. "It was *someone* off a movie credit list," he said. "They were watching a movie, I know that, and the name came up in the credits and they said, 'Hey! That's a neat name.' But it could have been Dustin, the key grip." (Oddly, this mirrors the naming of Dustin Hoffman, whose parents expected him to be a girl; having to come up with a boy's name in a hurry, they found a mention of Dustin Farnum, a silent-screen actor, in a magazine.)

Dustin's friend Jared knew that Dustin Hoffman is a movie star but, when we got to talking about politics and who supported whom in the Obama election, Jared shrugged and said his dad was a Republican, as if his dad was usually right and that was all that needed to be said.

Dustin thought about it and said, "I would probably have voted for Obama because there's a need for something new."

Neither of them voted in that election, and it seemed clear that, despite appearances, neither is a hippie or an intellectual or a rebel.

On another day, on 83, I drove behind a low-slung, beaten-up, black saloon car for several miles before we both pulled into the same gas station. A fierce-looking, very hairy man—beard, hair, tattoos—got out of the black saloon, walked over to me, and asked politely what part of Minnesota I came from (Prius has Minnesota plates). I explained that I was from London, which led him to call over his friend, a muscle-bound man in a cowboy hat and a loose, armless T-shirt. The three of us talked about England, trucks and truck drivers, and the road in America. Both told me that they always keep to the speed limit. Yet, to me, they looked like don't-anyone-tell-*me*-what-to-do rebels.

So: new theory. What shrieked rebellion in the 1960s—when I was in my teens and wanting to change the world—doesn't now. Not in America, anyway. And often not in Britain either (consider Mick Jagger). Obvious, I suppose.

And these men with head scarves and Harley Davidsons are probably just that, nothing more.

THE LAST INDIAN Raid Museum contains: fossils, quilts, radiograms, muskets, plowshares, and reconstructions of a homesteader's sod house and of rooms in timber houses built by early settlers. Glass cases display Indian memorabilia: clothes, headdresses, moccasins, jewelry, bows, arrows, arrowheads, fishhooks. Outside, on the cut grass, are several old buildings, preserved and pristine: the town jail, a Lutheran church, a 1930s gas station, a grocer's shop, a 1920s one-room schoolhouse, and many more. All of this drips with pioneer grit, craftsmanship, thrift, and tradition, especially Indian tradition. For local people the museum must be of enormous value: a route to their origins and ancestors.

However, I've become blasé—*already*. I've seen similar stuff—buildings and bedrooms and iron beds, bows and arrows, moccasins and wampums—in museums, old houses, and interpretive centers along the road. I know that, in their own time, these things were important to people. But, viewed a century or more later, and in quantity, they take on a generic quality—provoking an oh-there's-another-very-small-bed-beside-a-rack-of-children's-washed-and-ironed-nightshirts reaction—rather than touching me because they are specific or personal. But then maybe my imagination is faulty, and my need to keep moving on constrains it.

But this museum has something special: the last Indian raid in Kansas. And because of it, I am invited by a friendly blond woman to sit in a creaky, revolving, leather-upholstered chair of the type that newspaper editors sat in a hundred years ago, and to watch a film on an old television set.

Photographs of settlers and landscape materialize and dissolve, and a voice-over tells the story. And, as I listened, and as photographs of handsome, unsmiling Cheyenne chiefs came onto the screen, I realized that I knew this story. It's a famous story—a desperate, tragic story. I had read it in *Bury My Heart at Wounded Knee,* where Dee Brown gives a whole chapter to it. And I knew that, in the 1950s, Mari Sandoz wrote an entire book, *Cheyenne Autumn,* about it. The book became a best seller, and John Ford made it into a movie starring Richard Widmark, Carroll Baker, James Stewart, Edward G. Robinson, Karl Malden, Sal Mineo, and Dolores del Rio. They played the white people. The Cheyenne chiefs, Dull Knife and Little Wolf, were played by Mexican-American actors Gilbert Roland and Ricardo Montalban, and the lesser Cheyenne roles by Navajo Indians who spoke in their own language and are reported to have delivered nonsense lines of great amusement to those who speak Navajo.

In 1876 the Northern Cheyenne fought beside the Sioux at the battle of Little Bighorn and helped to defeat Custer. In 1877 they surrendered to the U.S. Army, along with the Oglala Sioux and their leader Crazy Horse. The Cheyenne expected to be able to live close to the Oglala and to their own homeland in the Black Hills. But instead, they were forced to trek hundreds of miles south to a reservation in Indian Territory in Oklahoma—on the promise that, if they didn't like it there, they could return north.

For a year the Northern Cheyenne stayed on the reservation in Oklahoma. It was a dry, barren place with no buffalo for them to hunt; they were miserable, short of food, and stricken by diseases that were new to them and against which they had no immunity. American promises to provide food and medicine were broken, as was the promise that they could return home if they wished. Many died of measles, malaria, and starvation. Dull Knife and Little Wolf pleaded for their remaining people to be allowed to return home. And, when permission was repeatedly denied—usually by bureaucrats in Washington—a large group, led by the two chiefs, decided that they would rather die in battle than on hot, alien land so far from home. So, during the night of September 9, 1878, 297 men, women, and children left their tepees and moved quietly and swiftly north.

There followed an epic display of courage, cunning, and endurance as the Cheyenne were chased across the plains of Kansas and Nebraska by a force which grew to ten thousand soldiers, sent out of five forts, aided by three thousand civilians.

The Cheyenne had fewer horses than people, so they took turns to ride and run, while the U.S. Army used three east-west railways and thousands of horses in its efforts to keep up with them. It is an exciting and heartbreaking story that continues over many months. There are moments of uplift and some Cheyenne survivors. Back in the 1950s, one of the reviewers of *Cheyenne Autumn*, Maxwell Struthers Burt, was moved to write: "In all American history there is nothing finer than the loping march of the Cheyenne up from the Indian Territory and their subsequent incredible frozen flight. The march of Xenophon and his ten thousand was as nothing compared with it."

The last Indian raid in Kansas is part of that story. It happened over two days, September 30 and October 1, 1878, three weeks after the Cheyenne had fled the reservation—three weeks during which they were chased by the U.S. Army, fought them off, and lost lives. Nineteen settlers, who lived along a ten-mile stretch of Sappa Creek, close to what was then the hamlet of Oberlin, were killed in a series of raids by small bands of Cheyenne warriors. Mari Sandoz says that Chief Little

Wolf allowed the raids only because his people had to have more horses to give them any chance of escape. He wanted no bloodshed, as the settlers were not soldiers, but accepted with reluctance that it was certain to happen because his young braves were angry—and perhaps because twenty-seven Cheyenne, including women and children, had been slaughtered by a force of hunters and soldiers by the same creek three years earlier.

The film I was watching showed the settlers to be hard-working farmers and homesteaders—some single men, but mostly families with children—who had arrived in the area during the previous three years. Those murdered were men and teenage boys. All were named, some with photographs—as were the widows and fatherless children. All were innocents. None of them threatened the Cheyenne. Despite this, and despite the museum's setting in a white American community, the film presented the predicament of the Cheyenne with sympathy, and seemed to blame the settlers' deaths as much on the U.S. Army and government, with their cruel mismanagement of the Cheyenne and their numerous broken promises, as on the Cheyenne themselves.

The screen went blank. The film had lasted little more than ten minutes. I felt flat. Nineteen people had been killed as they tended crops, cattle, horses, and even their children at home. More than 130 years later, I was alone in a large, wood-floored room filled with glass cases. The floor creaked as I walked around, head down. Arrowheads from arrows shot during the raid were laid in neat rows behind glass. A bullet that killed a Cheyenne warrior lay on its side, dull and rusting. Sheets of paper, wrinkled with age, held hand- and type-written accounts by eyewitnesses.

I decided to visit the graveyard where the nineteen are buried.

I PUSHED OPEN a door, expecting to find myself in the museum shop. And got a surprise. A tall man wearing a cowboy hat was sitting in a low chair right beside me, by the door.

"Hello," I said.

He didn't answer.

I looked at him.

He didn't move. And I saw that he was a dummy, a shop-window mannequin decked out in period cowboy clothes—white shirt, red neckerchief, buckskin jacket.

The blond woman, who had sat me in front of the television, was standing some way off talking to another woman. I walked toward her.

"How did you like our museum?" she said.

"It's great! That guy sitting there gave me a fright . . . "

"Oh, he scares us all the time." She laughed, a hooting kind of laugh. And her friend laughed too, a little higher pitched, more of a chirp.

"I came through and there he was, right in my face."

"I have a little story about that man"—blond woman pointed at him—"that I love to tell people. This lady came through. She was . . . oh—maybe mid-sixties, mid-seventies—and she had her granddaughter with her, or great-granddaughter maybe; she was about fourteen. And, when the lady came through that door, she was talking to him. She was just carrying on a conversation and her granddaughter was behind her. And she said, 'Grandma, do you know he's a dummy?'

"And the lady said, 'Well, isn't most men?'

"And then she said, 'No, I mean grandma, he's a mannequin.'

"'A mannequin? A mannequin? A ma . . . A *mannequin!*'"

At this the three of us hooted and chirped like chickens disturbed by an air-raid siren.

When we became quiet again, blond woman looked back at the cowboy. "That's the kind of fella I want."

"Well, that's just like women," I said, trying to keep pace with the prevailing stereotypes. "They talk and the man's just meant to . . . shut up."

"Well, he's the silent type. He's the *strong,* silent type."

More hoots and cackles and chirrups—and then I managed to say good-bye.

IT WAS 1 PM and hot outside in South Penn Street, burning and broiling. Cars were parked on a slant, noses to the pavement, many with their windows down. I walked to the end of the street where the railway tracks come across. Sleepers were bedded down in the dirt and dust, and there was no platform because there would be no passengers, just grain tumbling from elevators into goods wagons. A line of wagons, painted brown, stood beside an elevator, a newish one, an assembly of white-painted tubes like giant cigarettes; on one of the tubes a stalk of wheat was painted like a tobacco company's logo, below the word "CO OP." There were shadows beneath the wagons, but none on the ground—just sunlight, and splashes of sun-dazzle bouncing from the shine of the rails.

Across the tracks from the co-op were older elevators, gray against the sky like battleships. The sun lit the silver sloping roof of a rectangular elevator: the traditional design—like the pair I'd come across late at night in Melita, Manitoba.

I went into a low building with air conditioning and carpet tiles, and startled a woman called Brenda. She said she would ask if I could be shown round. I stood in a corridor with a primitive painting of cornfields until she returned, apologetic: the manager wouldn't allow it just then; it would be dangerous, and they were busy getting ready for harvest. But, with encouraging smiles and hand gestures, Brenda explained the rudiments: the grain is delivered by truck to the foot of the elevator, weighed, cleaned, and hoisted to the top on a kind of vertical conveyor belt fitted with "buckets"; there it drops into tall storage bins according to its type or grade; when the time is right, it is allowed to fall to the bottom again and is elevated once more, this time to a bin from which it drops through a chute into goods wagons.

I nodded and said "OK" several times—and showered Brenda with thanks as she let me out into the steamy heat of Kansas.

EVERYONE KNOWS THAT there is more space in America than in Europe. It is one of the reasons why, once Columbus had found it, the place filled up with people; and is probably why everything is larger: houses, trucks, steaks, people—some of them, anyway—and cemeteries. High up on the edge of town, Oberlin Cemetery covers acres of mown grass—and the dead have room to stretch; there is none of the shoulder-to-shoulder intimacy with strangers that the dead have to live with in Europe. And the graves are tidy and well kept; there is respect here—perhaps even a little ancestor worship.

Outside the cemetery, against the fence that faces the road, a large weatherproof notice—erected by the Kansas State Historical Society and the Kansas Department of Transportation—tells the story of the flight of the Cheyenne in three succinct paragraphs printed in clear white lettering on a brown background. It does not criticize the Cheyenne. Rather it states that they were "angry and embittered by their plight" and describes their escape as "a remarkable feat." The deaths of innocent locals are mentioned near the end, introduced by the only word that conveys an opinion about the killings: "*Sadly,* it [the escape] resulted in the death of forty Kansas settlers and herders. Nineteen of them were killed here in Decatur County, and their graves formed the beginning of the cemetery located east of this marker."

To describe the deaths of forty people as sad and to make no criticism of their killers seems to acknowledge that the Cheyenne—and, perhaps, all the Indian nations—were unfairly and cruelly treated, and are not altogether to be blamed for raids and murders. Or, to put it another way: *sadly,* their retaliation was a reasonable response. That seems to be the opinion of the Kansas Historical Society and of the Department of Transportation, and I guess—the notice seems to have been here for some time and has not been defaced—of many Americans.

But something puzzles me. If European Americans can recognize that the Indians were so badly treated that their killing of white people was reasonable, and can, in effect, forgive them, why do so many white Americans bear a grudge against black people? Their ancestors were ill-treated too—and were, on the whole, unable to retaliate. Why do they not get the same degree of compassion?

Inside the cemetery, a smooth four-sided stone needle, perhaps thirty feet tall, commemorates the murdered settlers and lists their names. To one side, against a low wrought-iron fence, five tombstones, small, almost square, with rounded corners, are arranged in a row like gappy teeth, and set in concrete. An inscription reads: Markers made by E.F. Bliss, 1878. The words on the stones themselves are worn, but large and clear. Four of them commemorate members of a family called Laing, a father and his three sons; E.F. Bliss carved their names in elegant curved capitals and wrote below each name: KILLED BY INDIANS SEPT 30 1878. The words on the fifth stone are a little different—E.F. Bliss was instructed by a different family—and read simply: "J.C. Hutson Born Dec 25 1840 Died Sept 30 1878."

Behind the monument, and in line with it, are more tombstones: newer, matching, and precisely aligned in rows, with space between for burial, as in a military graveyard. These stones appear to date from 1911, when the monument was built. The four Laings and "John C. Hudson [*sic*]" are here with the others.

33

SELF-OBSESSION AT MONUMENT ROCKS

SOUTH OF OBERLIN, 83 rises and falls over low hills as it travels in a straight line for some twenty miles. It is two-lane with tarmac shoulders and the surface is smooth, enabling relaxed, finger-and-thumb driving—until I see a combine harvester ahead, spread across both lanes, moving slowly south, wide and wobbling like a fat man on a tightrope with a balancing pole. A black SUV is following it, and I trundle along behind at about 15 mph. When we reach the crest of a hill, I see that this mighty green-painted machine is at the rear of a convoy of three—and I remember Stuart saying that a combine harvester costs at least three hundred thousand dollars and that smaller farmers employ professional harvesters who bring their own combines.

More cars line up behind me and, when there are eight or ten of us patiently grinding along, the combine slows and moves to the right, onto the shoulder so that much of the header (the wide part at the front that does the cutting) overhangs the grass verge. I follow the SUV and squeeze past on the left with two wheels on the farther shoulder. We reach the next combine and it too moves across to the near shoulder. It lurches and wobbles. The driver doesn't seem to have it under control. It rocks sideways. The end of the header hits the ground and scuds along the grass, and the combine comes to a halt. This fat man has fallen off his wire—and now he resembles a crashed airplane resting on one wing.

The SUV driver slows to look, and drives on. The combine driver, a tall man in blue overalls, is climbing down from his cab. The combine in front has stopped safely, and the driver is already jogging back to help his mate.

The black SUV is now moving at the regulation 65 mph. I cruise along behind and realize that while I was driving slowly I turned the radio on, but somehow, with the drama unfolding in front of me, I haven't been listening. Now I find that, once again, I am alone with the ranting Glenn Beck! I listen to some extraordinary nonsense: a gross distortion of what liberals or "progressives" think. Beck speaks very slowly, loudly, and indignantly, as if he's talking to someone very stupid (as, of course, on the whole, he is) with whom he's having an argument—his tone that of a schoolboy on the edge of losing his temper as he protests and pretends that he has been falsely accused of some minor misdemeanor. This rubbish is sponsored by Goldline for thirty minutes, and then, if anyone can stand it (and I fear they can—I think of my friend Dallas, who bought me two large bourbons in New Evarts), by Carbonite for another thirty minutes. Whoever they are, I must try to make sure I don't buy anything from either of them.

Eventually I slide in a CD, *Concierto* with Jim Hall, Paul Desmond, Chet Baker, and others; Desmond's sax and Baker's trumpet on "You'd Be So Nice to Come Home To" are balm for the ears.

I REACH THE city of Oakley (pop 2,045), take a quick look at Main Street and its scattering of antique and junk shops, and drive on down 83 in search of Monument Rocks—marked on my

Michelin Road Atlas as a national landmark. I am encouraged to make the detour—the rocks are a few miles off the highway—by Jamie Jensen who describes them as "surreal" in his book *Road Trip USA: Cross-Country Adventures on America's Two-Lane Highways*. (Jensen's book is a guide, with photographs and maps, to eleven road trips across the USA, and runs to more than nine hundred pages. I have with me a copy of one chapter; ominously titled "The Road to Nowhere." It's devoted to Highway 83—and is good on many things including history, even prehistory.)

It's a warm evening and I drive thirty miles over flat, barren-seeming country; the sky is blue and filled with sun-tinged clouds that would have delighted Botticelli. Then I drive eight miles or so on dirt roads—the type that are rutted and kick up dust and intersect at right angles because they once marked the boundaries of homesteads. The land is dry, a place of cattle grids and thistles and little else. Small rusting signs point to Monument Rocks; there are miles between them, but whenever I begin to think I might be lost, another one appears. And then I see them, perhaps a mile away, sharp and white in the evening sunlight—and they *are* surreal. In this immense featureless flatness, they look like a wedding cake tossed aside and broken in a field. Jensen says they are seventy feet high and eighty million years old; they were left standing after the erosion of an ancient seabed.

I get up close, park, and walk about. There is no one here. The land and the air are warm, the evening somehow blissful. The rocks stand in a group, spread across a space the size, perhaps, of eight football fields. They are irregularly shaped and horizontally layered in off-white, beige, brown. I walk away and turn back and they seem like chalk cliffs rising from the sea—islands in the plain, a hot, barren archipelago.

A herd of black cattle is grazing close by, ignoring the rocks and me. I sit on the ground, lean against a cliff, and absorb heat and silence and the scent of herbs.

A car comes bumping along the track and a man, a woman, and three teenage boys are soon clambering around. Happily they ignore me, and I try to ignore them. A boy, small against the sky, calls from high on a rock, and his brothers appear beside him, calling too.

The man walks over to say hello, and learns that I'm from London. His wife is Filipino, he says—and then talks about himself: his vacation, of which this excursion is part; his time in the military; his job. He has relations in Liverpool and tells me precisely where they live. The street name means nothing to me; I've been to Liverpool once—years ago. He's the first American I've met in these weeks who knows that I'm from England and doesn't ask why I'm here. Well... why should he?

34

BISCUIT TROUBLE

THE ASIAN INDIAN MAN who runs the Annie Oakley Motel in Oakley is very friendly this morning. He tells me that he came to the U.S. from India. An Asian Indian woman, pushing a cart carrying soap, coffee bags, toilet paper, and a mop, passes us on the pavement outside the rooms. She is his aunt. She moved from Uganda to live in Wembley in north London. She is here on a two-month visit during which she will clean the rooms.

The television news is full of the death of Senator Byrd, someone I have not heard of until today—but if I were American, I surely would have. Mr. Byrd entered Congress in 1952 and became the longest-serving congressman in the history of the United States, dying in office at the age of ninety-two. A southern Democrat, Mr. Byrd was a member of the Ku Klux Klan in the 1940s, and in 1964 voted against Lyndon Johnson's Civil Rights Act, which became law despite him. Over the years he gradually became more reasonable, gained in importance, and ended up an important member of the party that supports the first black president.

On TV, Senator Byrd's death prompts talk of the founding fathers. In the late 1770s, when they—Washington, Jefferson,

Benjamin Franklin, and friends—were able to plan the future of their new nation, to write the Declaration of Independence and the United States Constitution, freedom played a big part in their thinking—hardly surprising given that they had just fought for and won freedom from the Kingdom of Great Britain, and that many citizens of the new country had fled from tyrannies, religious as much as political, in Europe. Yet, despite all that, they ignored the rights of American Indians and black people. Eighty years later, three years before he became president, Abraham Lincoln began to fix part of that omission by declaring:

> There is no reason in the world why the negro is not entitled to all the natural rights enumerated in the Declaration of Independence, the right to life, liberty, and the pursuit of happiness. I hold that he is as much entitled to these as the white man.

We British might regret that we don't have a written constitution—merely a bundle of laws created over hundreds of years by parliament and by judges—and that what we have has not been thought through, and is more the product of expediency than of ideology: Henry VIII extricated us from the Catholic church because he wanted to get shot of Catherine of Aragon and marry—conceive an heir with—the more glamorous Anne Boleyn; Robert Walpole became the first prime minister because the new king, George I, being German, couldn't speak English. I think about this as I sit over coffee and a blueberry muffin in a gas station on the edge of Oakley. And I wonder whether their written, easily quoted, constitution might, directly or indirectly, make some Americans more defensive of their "liberty" than is good for them.

I am thinking of those Americans who are resistant to the idea of anyone, including themselves, getting support from the state—even though huge numbers of people are unemployed and live in poverty. Is this because somehow they have come to see state help as the government threatening their freedom: both their freedom to make money without paying taxes that might be used to assist the less fortunate; and their freedom to be poor, sick, and miserable in private without interference from government?

In Britain most of us don't see it like that. The setup is thoroughly imperfect, but we are happy, to varying degrees, to go along with the idea that the state will use some of our taxes to help those in need. We value individual freedom, but we also think—many of us—that the fortunate should help the less fortunate.

Perhaps Americans—as the descendants of people who escaped from tyranny—take freedom a little too seriously?

Is it possible to take freedom too seriously?

Yes—but only once you've got it.

As I sip coffee and ponder, a man comes into the gas station and asks if he may bring his cat into the restroom and wash it. "The cat shat all over the box," he says.

The two women cashiers look at each other and shrug. "Sure," one of them says, "I guess." She smiles, and the man hurries out.

I remember reading something by Amartya Sen, the Nobel Prize-winning philosopher and economist. He defined freedom in a memorable way, making more of it than simply freedom from the interference of other people or the state. He wrote about the freedom of people to lead the kind of lives they value and "have reason to value." Governments like that of the U.S., rather than threatening freedom, can perhaps help people toward Sen's type of freedom—principally by bringing about freedom from ignorance and poverty.

THERE ARE SEVERAL combine harvesters on the road south from Oakley. Cars and trucks wait their turn to straggle past. An ad comes on the radio: "Let us harvest your wheat. We have four combines and are in your area now." Clouds of golden dust move slowly across the landscape where harvesters are at work. Sometimes, there is gold on one side of the road and deep green on the other where lush young maize swollen with irrigation stands a foot or so high. Long-legged, spidery contraptions, perhaps one hundred yards long, stalk the fields dispensing water pumped from the Oglalla Aquifer.

It's hot and nearly midday. I turn right and drive a mile or two to Lake Scott State Park, pay for entry, and receive a brochure and a map. I drive down a lane with trees to my right and a steep ridge to my left and come to a small, stone-built house. A sign says Steele Home. I can't resist a quick look. Coming in out of the sunlight, I find it hard to see but soon make out a table and someone sitting at it, an elderly woman playing patience. She smiles and says hello. She speaks quietly, like a nun, and asks if I know about the Steeles. I don't, so she tells me.

Herbert Steele homesteaded the land in 1888. He married Eliza five years later, and they had three children, two girls and a boy. None of the children lived to adulthood—the nun whispers this. Years later the Steeles decided to leave their land, their 640-acre homestead, to the state to be used as a park for all to enjoy. It took time, but eventually the Kansas Forestry, Fish, and Game Commission accepted their offer. Herbert had died, but Eliza was there to make a speech at the opening of the park in 1928.

The Steeles' house has changed little in more than a hundred years, the elderly woman says. The basement was the Steeles' first home, a one-room house dug out of the mud, high above the stream at the back. Later, using local stone, they built three rooms on top, a living room and two bedrooms, one for them and one for the children. I look at their chairs, their table, their piano—all of beautiful polished wood—their beds, their faded patchwork quilts, their photographs, a doll that belonged to one of the girls. The place is beautiful, empty, and sad. But the elderly woman is cheerful, uplifting. She reveres the Steeles for their pioneering energy and for what they gave to the people of Kansas; she and a group of friends volunteer so that the house can be open as often as possible and so that the Steeles will be remembered.

As I leave, a young Canadian couple in snazzy cycling gear walk in. The elderly woman puts down her cards, and welcomes them.

I walk up the road and begin to see why Herbert Steele settled here. Set in the middle of the flat, parched plains, the homestead was a wooded valley, with a river running through it. How smart was the good Mr. Steele! But what a task to take on alone in 1888. No wonder the elderly woman admires him.

On the hill, way above me, is something man-made, a tiny, thumb-sized protrusion against the sky. The map shows it: a monument to both brave Steeles. A faint, chalky path winds up toward it. I fetch my baseball cap and water bottle, and start climbing.

Soon the path peters out. I clamber between bushes and spiny cactus, tracking around the hill when the direct route is too steep, hauling myself up with my hands when there are no footholds. Small birds hear me coming and fly, tweeting, from bush to bush—and sometimes I slip on small stones, disturbing stripy lizards that slide away like quicksilver.

At the top I stand for a moment like stout Cortés and all his men—silent, but short of breath, upon a peak in Kansas. Instead of the Pacific (which Cortés didn't see either; Keats got that wrong), I see a large pink rock inset with a brass plaque commemorating the Steeles. I am puffed and hot. I sit down, lean against the rock, and drink.

Back at the bottom of the hill, a path leads to the ruins of an Indian pueblo, a stone building that Herbert Steele discovered on his land in the 1890s. Archeologists came and decided that from the 1660s it was home to Taos Indians who had fled north from the Spanish, and that they shared it with the local Apaches who were also not keen on the Spanish. It had no doors or windows which made it easier to defend; the Taos and the Apaches entered through holes in the roof and climbed down ladders. The holes made by the ladders are still there.

In the 1930s the river was dammed at the northern end of the Steeles' land. The Steeles had liked the plan to build a dam, realizing that it would make their homestead more of a park, a place for people to take a break from their exertions on the hot, unrelenting plain, have fun, fish, and swim,. As I drive toward the dam, I pass a group of adults and children swimming off a small beach—and then the Canadian couple, their bikes parked under a tree by the water. I climb steps to the rim of the dam. Vast concrete slabs, set in a curve, slope down to the lake; stiff grass and reeds grow in the cracks, and a warm wind blows gray-green water into ripples which lap against the artificial shore.

I drive down the east side of the lake, see no one, stop among trees beside the water, and sit at a wooden picnic table where I eat apricots and gaze at the movement of the water on the lake. A dead tree lies in the shallows, sprawling and twisted, stripped of bark and bleached almost white by the sun. The wind makes a rushing in the cottonwoods, and above me a bird sings shrill and staccato. Otherwise nothing and silence. My head droops and my eyelids close.

I RETURN TOWARD 83 and to the seemingly infinite flatness of the plain.

I'm hungry. 83 passes through Scott City, where I find a small supermarket. I fancy eating cheese and biscuits or, better still, cheese and oatcakes. I pick up a packet of sliced cheese and walk the aisles in search of oatcakes. Of course, they may not be called oatcakes in the U.S., but I can't see anything that looks like oatcakes. I ask a gray-haired man who is squatting near the floor, packing a shelf with cans. Oatcakes mean nothing to him, so I say that they are a type of biscuit. He leads me around the shop and, as we walk, I remember that what we call biscuits, they call cookies. And, stupidly, I apologize and tell him that I meant cookies. We change direction, and then I realize that I have got it wrong: oatcakes are savory; they will not be with the cookies. I tell the man this and, with no change of expression, he turns around and we head for the biscuits again. I am still unsure; I don't know what American biscuits are like. I say, "I'm sorry. I'm from England. We don't call biscuits biscuits."

He stops and looks at me. "What *do* you call them?"

"I'm not sure... Not cookies. We don't have cookies." I suddenly remember the word "crackers" and blurt it out, "Crackers! Oatcakes are a little like crackers."

He looks at me, still polite and apparently keen to be helpful, though there is sweat on his forehead which wasn't there before. He says, with only a hint of exasperation, "Crackers?" And we shoot off down another aisle. He points at a set of shelves. No oatcakes, but cheese biscuits, savory biscuits, crackers. I thank him repeatedly, and leave with a box, the contents of which are sugar-free, flavored with herbs, and turn out to taste fine with cheese.

I drive on toward Garden City. A man, a bigot, called Mike Huckabee—somehow the name seems familiar—comes on the radio and lies about what happens in British schools. Everyone gets a prize, he says. Oh yeah?

Later I rediscovered something that I had forgotten, probably because it turned out to be useless information: in 2008 Mike Huckabee put himself forward as a potential Republican

candidate for the presidency of the USA. Simon Schama
described him in his entertaining book *The American Future:
A History from the Founding Fathers to Barack Obama:* "Baptist
230 preacher, ex-governor of Arkansas... a victorious veteran of
a hundred-pound battle with girth, a perfect emblem of the
Republican commitment to shrinking government."

BEEF AND RACISM IN GARDEN CITY

GARDEN CITY IS LARGE—LARGER than North Platte, much larger than Pierre—the largest city I have visited since Bismarck. I drive around and turn off into a park, stop under some trees, and, with the windows down, hear screaming, shouting. I have parked close to one of Garden City's proudest possessions, the world's largest concrete outdoor swimming pool. I can see the water through a chain-link fence, a massive, rectangular melee of swimmers and splashers, mostly kids and teenagers. For a moment I think about joining them. Would the authorities lend me a pair of swimming shorts?

In a city this big there should be a bar where I can watch World Cup football—the tournament has reached quarter-final stage without England; we have been knocked out, as so often and ignominiously, by Germany—but there don't seem to be many bars of any kind in Garden City. Online, I find the Time Out sports bar and drive there—Garden City is big; I have to drive. On the way I stop at Herbs Hamburgers. My buffalo burger is brought by Bernice, who is black; she came to Garden City with a group of friends from Chicago because there are jobs here. All but one of the five staff working tonight are black, and I remember how few black people I have seen on this trip: just two, a man on the street in Mobridge and the bouncer at

the Longbranch Bar in Pierre.

There are black bouncers outside the Time Out sports bar; they wave me in. The place is dark, spacious, high ceilinged, filled with deafening music and almost empty of people. A wall-sized screen—so big that the picture lacks definition—is showing baseball. Six or seven young men sit at a marble-topped bar staring at their drinks with their backs to the screen. Two talk quietly, heads together; the rest are alone with their beer. I climb onto an empty stool at one end. The youth on the next stool tips his bottle into his mouth, swallows, unhooks the bottle from his teeth, and puts it back on the bar. He is chinless and morose—uninterested in the likes of me. Anyway, the music—AC/DC's "Highway to Hell"—casts a blight on the likelihood of conversation.

The barmaid redeems my evening. She pushes a beer across, leans on the marble, shouts into my ear, and asks where I am from. She is young, olive skinned, a little plump, with short, asymmetrical black hair, low-cut singlet, tattoos, and several drawerfuls of earrings; they are lined up like bikes in a crowded rack right around the rim of each ear, with one in each tragus (those little triangular promontories that separate cheeks from ears). She is made up with kohl around her eyes, a beauty spot high on her left cheek, and glossy red lips. She wants to know why I am in Garden City and, when she hears that I'm on my way to Texas—now less than seventy miles away—says she has never been there. This may be because she hasn't been in Kansas long. She has lived, perhaps was born, in Portland, Oregon. Her father is half-Iranian and her mother is from Missouri. Her name is Sarah, "with an 'h,'" she says. Without my asking, she tells me that she designs her own tattoos. So I look more closely and they are quite something: red, green, purple, and blue stars and butterflies swarm over her arms, shoulders, and chest.

There is another barmaid, but this is Sarah's bar; she gives the place some pizzazz and it's a shame that someone so radiant has to serve drinks to a bunch of tongue-tied, fluffy-cheeked adolescents and a middle-aged Englishman. But that changes. Two tall young men, who might be Asian Indian or perhaps half-Iranian, come in and stand beside me. Both wear T-shirts so white that they light up the gloom. Sarah knows them and brings them drinks. One of these languid fellows has "Jesus" tattooed in tasteful copperplate lettering on the side of his neck and a beard plaited like coarse string. They take seats farther down the bar. Sarah moves away and chats to them.

There is no football here. I finish my beer and put dollars on the bar. Sarah brings change and shouts good-bye then she leans a little closer and almost whispers that the best bar in town is at the Clarion Hotel. "That's where upper- and middle-class people go," she says, and throws me a red-and-white smile.

Of course, I knew it was a myth that America is a classless society. The impossibility of the Kennedys, or even the Bushes, the Pitts, the Streisands, the Beyoncé Knowleses, pushing a trolley around Walmart proves that.

Back at the motel I watch TV. The fearful antisocialist, anti-progressive, antiliberal faction may monopolize the radio stations that I can receive in the car. But, mercifully, the other side, the side that says let's take a few risks—some of them may fail but, if we're lucky, some of them won't—to try to make the world a better place, has the wonderfully funny Jon Stewart on *The Daily Show,* followed by *The Colbert Report*.

NEXT MORNING I drive to the old part of town and walk around red-brick-paved streets that are quiet and green with trees. Large, white-painted wooden houses with balconies, verandas, and gables stand stolidly apart from their neighbors.

On Main Street: clothes shops, travel agents, a bank, an abandoned cinema, and a beautiful four-story building that was once a hotel. It's hot and, as I walk up and down, I can hear music: specifically Paul McCartney's "Hey Jude." I've encountered this before, in Minot and Oberlin—not "Hey Jude," but music playing quietly in the street from several speakers so that you lose the song as you walk and pick it up again, say, five strides later. I'm unfamiliar with this—it doesn't happen in England—and several questions come to mind. Does anyone ever object? In many parts of England, some curmudgeon probably would. And who chooses the songs? Is there a committee? If so, is it democratically elected? Or is there a dictator? And, a more philosophical point, which edges into a conservation-of-energy issue: Does the music stop when no one is listening?

I come to an imposing stone building which takes up a whole block and is surrounded by grass and trees. It has a restrained art deco look. The U.S. flag dangles from a flagpole and the words "FINNEY COUNTY" are written in fine brass capitals, up high, below the roof. I recognize the name: it is associated in my mind with four infamous murders that are described in agonizing detail in Truman Capote's classic *In Cold Blood*. This is the courthouse where Perry Smith and Richard Hickock were tried and found guilty of killing a farmer named Herb Clutter, his wife, and two teenage children in their home on the edge of Holcomb, a small town five miles west of Garden City.

I buy a takeaway coffee, and ask the barista whether the city has a library. It does. It's ten minutes' walk away, on Walnut Street. The friendly barista gives me elaborate directions.

I soon get lost—and see two men planting daylilies, which I happen to know are also called *Hemerocallis,* on the corner of Spruce Street. I ask them the way to Walnut.

Neither of them knows, though one has lived in Garden City for fifty years, and the other for thirty-two years; in fact, he *is* thirty-two. Thirty-two gets out an iPhone and looks at a map. Walnut is two blocks north.

Expecting that they know about plants, I ask if they are planting *Hemerocallis*.

"No," says the older man. "They're daylilies. You may know the Latin name, but to me they're daylilies."

Mark Twain is sitting on a bench outside the library; he and the bench have been cast in bronze. I sit down beside him. He has smart shoes, incredible hair, eyebrows, and mustache, and is holding a book with no title. I think about putting my arm round him and waiting for someone to come by who will take our photograph. No one comes.

Karen in the library gives me two maps, shows me the local history books, and talks about Prince Charles because, she says, she is the same age as him (curiously, or perhaps not curiously, she looks a little like Camilla Parker-Bowles, with rather less makeup). Karen was born in Kansas, went to live on the east coast as an adult, and returned recently. She says it's like the 1950s and '60s here, while in the east it is at least 2012. "This town is very conservative, so there's nothing to do except go to Walmart." She smiles, and confirms what I discovered last night: "There are very few bars."

"Go to the zoo," she says. "It's a social activity." She laughs. "All those monkeys."

She returns to her work. I scan the shelves, flick through a few books, and sit down at a table with *Cultural Pluralism and Social Capital in Garden City, Kansas* by Molly DesBaillets. Originally an MA thesis published in 2008 by the University of Kansas, it reveals something rather astonishing: in the last thirty years Garden City has successfully integrated some ten thousand immigrants from Central America and Southeast

Asia into a population that was only eighteen thousand in 1980. The city has managed this despite being in Kansas, a conservative Republican state so far to the right that, from time to time in recent years, the teaching of evolution has been banned in schools. The achievement has been so startling that journalists and filmmakers, as well as social scientists, have traveled from all over to report and analyze.

The background to this is beef. In 1980 "the world's largest beef-processing plant" was opened within a few miles of the city, and another huge one arrived in 1983. A labor force prepared to work for low wages was required, and large numbers of immigrants were recruited from Mexico and El Salvador and from countries farther away, in particular Somalia, India, Vietnam, and Laos. By 2000, 73 percent of the children and teens enrolled in schools were from "minorities." This makes Garden City what Molly DesBaillets and other pundits call "a major-minority community," the first in Kansas.

The path to assimilation of so many immigrants was smoothed by the presence of a long-established Mexican population, whose ancestors were enticed to the city in the 1900s to work in the then-thriving sugar-beet industry. Otherwise successful integration seems to have come from hard work, good sense, human kindness, and the profit motive. In the 1980s, such bodies as the city's government, the Chamber of Commerce, church groups, and a specially formed nonreligious group called Emmaus House set about providing "a food pantry," housing, health care, multilingual teaching in new schools, and much more. A group of social scientists arrived, studied the city for two years, and made many recommendations that were acted upon, ranging from a soccer program to the suggestion that the ultimate beneficiaries of the immigrants' labor, the meat-packing plants, provide more money for the new community. All this enabled the building of "social capital," defined by Molly DesBaillets as "networks that enable access to resources"—and perhaps too loosely by me as projects and bodies that bring people together.

Karen appears and I tell her about Molly's thesis. She nods with enthusiasm. She is proud of the city and of how well people get on. The Chamber of Commerce makes sure, she says, that enclaves and ghettoes don't develop, that people of different nationalities are scattered, that there's a German restaurant beside a Somalian one beside a Vietnamese one.

But there are two facets of the city that she doesn't like. One is an area to the south of town called the South Wind Country Club. "South Wind *is* a ghetto," she says, "because only lawyers and doctors can afford the three-million-dollar houses down there."

Her other beef is with the meat industry. The way the cattle are treated, especially in feedlots, has made her "almost a vegetarian." Cattle are kept "standing close together in their own shit, so that sometimes their hooves rot. Every inch is used for something. Blood for dog food—red pellets. Hides for leather. Bones for gelatin. Hoof for buttons—yes, buttons! And their shit is returned to the land as fertilizer."

She says that there are three types of truck—and I should look out for them. "Trucks with holes, to let the air in, bring cattle from the range. Refrigerated trucks carry the meat. And soft-top, covered trucks take the hide and bones. Covered,"—she gives me a look—"so people don't see legs sticking out."

"Oh my god!"

"And there are a lot of trucks. At Tyson they slaughter six thousand head of cattle a day."

"Blimey!" I mutter.

UNTIL THE 1960S most American cities had their own slaughterhouses, meat-packing plants, and specialist producers of meaty items like bacon, sausages, and "patties," the raw meat for hamburgers. A few places, Kansas City, Omaha, and Chicago—especially Chicago—dealt with meat on a larger scale, packing it and sending it to outlets around the United States and exporting it to Europe. In 1960, Currier J. Holman and A.D. Anderson started Iowa Beef Packers (IBP). Their big idea was to dispense with expensive, skilled, unionized slaughterhouse workers and butchers, and instead create what Eric Schlosser in *Fast Food Nation* calls "a disassembly line." For eight hours at a time, workers stood in line holding knives, and, as the cattle rolled endlessly by, each worker made his or her own unique cut, over and over, thousands of times. As A.D. Anderson proudly said, "We've tried to take the skill out of every step." At the end of the line came another breakthrough: instead of sides of beef, neat packages emerged—steaks, joints, ribs, and the rest—all ready for sale in supermarkets at a price all (some would say most) Americans could afford.

In the half century since then, the hundred-year-old meatpacking district of Chicago has turned into a ghost town and IBP has grown into the largest beef packer and second-largest pork packer in the U.S. It was sold to Tyson Foods in 2001 for $3.2 billion.

Eighty percent of the U.S. meat business is now controlled by four big companies—including IBP, renamed Tyson Fresh Meat—and almost all of it has moved from big cities to remote towns like Garden City. By operating way out on the plains and closer to the cattle, the meat packers save on rent, the costs of shipping cattle to big cities, and, most importantly for them, labor. Out on the plains, unions are weak—and workers, most of them immigrants, accept lower pay and more readily tolerate long hours, hardship, indignity, and injury.

In 2004, in his book *What's the Matter with Kansas?* Thomas Frank noted that Garden City, with its neighbors Dodge City and Liberal, packed 20 percent of the nation's beef and had the facilities to slaughter twenty-four thousand cattle each day. The three towns made Kansas "the biggest beef-packing state in the country through most of the last decade."

And how has this affected the cattle? In a piece titled "Power Steer," published in *The New York Times Magazine* in 2002, Michael Pollan tells how he bought an eight-month-old calf from ranchers in South Dakota so that he could follow it through the rest of its life and eventually eat it. Pollan's calf, a black Angus steer known as No 534, had lived pleasantly for six months munching grass on the range with his mother. Then he was weaned and given, by his unusually kind breeders, two months of "backgrounding" in a pen where he learned to eat a "new, unnatural diet of grain" from a trough, as he would have to do for the rest of his life. After that he moved five hundred miles south to a feedlot in Kansas called Poky's—in Scott City (the town where I had biscuit trouble).

I didn't visit Poky's, as Pollan did, but I saw feedlots close to Garden City. There is no grass, just what looks like mud and is, in fact, manure, spread over endless acres, enough to accommodate many thousand steers—Poky's has space for seventy-four thousand; others are even larger. Typically cattle are placed in pens that hold about two hundred. Every feedlot has at least one feed mill, a sprawling collection of circular and rectangular metal tanks, linked by pipes and gantries. There the feed—usually a mix of corn, alfalfa hay, growth hormones, antibiotics, and protein supplements—is measured, often by computer, ground up, and sent to the troughs. The smell around a feedlot is appalling, owing to open drains and the animals' waste being stored in vast pools known as "lagoons." Referring to feedlots in Colorado, Eric Schlosser writes: "The two Monfort feedlots outside Greeley produce more excrement than the cities of Denver, Boston, Atlanta, and St. Louis—combined."

No 534 lived for six months in Poky's feedlot, growing ever fatter and more sturdy. From there he was taken, with thirty-five of his pals, one hundred miles down 83, past Garden City, to the National Beef plant in Liberal for slaughter. He was fourteen months old, a common age now for steers to be turned into beef. In the 1950s, beef cattle were slaughtered when they were two or three years old. In the 1920s, they lived for four or five years, generally outdoors and eating the food they like: grass.

Humans suffer too in the modern meat business. Safety standards are low, and statistics show meatpacking to be the most dangerous of all factory work in the U.S. Workers losing a finger or an arm is not uncommon, and many unspeakable deaths have occurred. Eric Schlosser describes several, among them a man mangled in the cogs of a conveyor belt, and a man drowned, along with two others who tried to rescue him, in a vast vat of blood that it was his job to clean.

And we who benefit from cheap meat are also at risk. The meat-packing giants have taken trouble lately to improve food safety, but the potential for epidemics of food poisoning and even death from the likes of E. coli 0157:H7 has increased along with the scale of meat-packing methods. In an interview with PBS, former U.S. Secretary for Agriculture—and Kansas congressman—Dan Glickman, said: "The risks to the public are greater than they've ever been before because disease, or a pathogen, can affect millions of people, as opposed to just a few. So even though I think the systems are better today, the risks are probably greater as well."

I LEFT THE library wondering whether I would ever be able to face eating beef again.

Around the corner from the courthouse, I found a café called Traditions. Revolving circular stools, chrome and red leatherette, stand in front of a bar topped with cream Formica; the floor is tiled, black and white; booths to one side display more Formica and red leatherette; everything is shiny clean. I sit on a red leatherette stool. Behind the counter a young dark-haired woman and a lean gray-haired man in a loose white T-shirt are busy serving customers. The man is an alert, talkative character and a great salesman. Despite everything I've just heard and already knew about beef, he persuades me to buy a beef sandwich.

It turns out that the man—his name is Mike Wade—owns the place. Until a year ago he had a career in "autobody work"; he abandoned it to buy a half share in this delightful sandwich bar and soda fountain which has been here, virtually unchanged, since 1943. "I saw that, if I didn't take the opportunity, I would be in autobody work until I retired. So..."—he throws his hands in the air—"I *had* to do it."

On the long wall behind the bar is the 1940s menu with 1940s prices and larger-than-life paintings of banana splits (2 dips, 29 cents), ice cream (cones, 5 cents; dish 10 cents), ice cream soda (19 cents), milkshake (19 cents), sundaes (3 dips, 24 cents), fresh limeade (10 cents), lime freeze (19 cents).

As Mike and I talk, the dark-haired waitress makes a cappuccino for an elderly man in shorts—all skinny legs and gray ponytail. A few weeks ago, Mike bought the other half of the business. He wants to make it commercially successful while preserving the 1940s décor and trappings. There is a hint that others have struggled to make it pay. Traditions is just off Main Street, in the old town center—still a district where people shop, work, and live—but the beef-and-potatoes, jeans-and-T-shirt, computer-and-dishwasher shopping is now on the northeast edge of town where the concrete hangars of the likes of Walmart, Sears, and J.C. Penney have been plonked. Molly DesBaillets writes, sadly, that one "is now more likely to see community members greeting acquaintances in the aisles of Walmart than on the sidewalks of Main Street."

Mike pulls out a camera and takes my photo, I take one of him with my camera, and he takes one of me with my camera: a digital sign of friendship, a modern-day exchange of beads and furs. He'll make a print of me and stick it on the wall, he says, pointing to a space beside a framed picture of Elvis.

AS I LEAVE Traditions, I glance at the shop next door, at a window crammed with old stuff: lamps, toys, jewelry, clothes, teapots, tables, pictures, comics, books—anything that is old or secondhand, attractive, or quirky. The door is open. Inside, I can see a small framed painting of a woman in a yellow dress sitting on a chair. She has dark hair and wears it in a kind of crimped bob; she might be from the 1930s. I go in—I want to look at her more closely—and am greeted by a big man who is standing behind a glass counter in the middle of the shop. Below the counter shelves brim with jewelry, ornaments, knickknacks. There is a lot to look at—and a strong smell of aftershave to contend with.

Big man and I talk sporadically as I move around and he learns about my interest in Highway 83. "It was a buffalo trail, from Texas up to Canada. They migrated to follow water and grass. There was a river crossing here at Garden City, the Arkansas River." As he speaks, he is putting handwritten price stickers on tiny plastic bags of what looks like brown cotton wool. "And the Indians gathered where the buffalo gathered," he says.

He sees me looking at the plastic bags and the stickers, which say "50c." "Buffalo hair," he says. "I collect it sometimes from the bison refuge, from the fences down there."

A woman comes in with her young daughter; they are clean and neat and wearing dresses as if they are going to a party, which they probably are. They are looking for a present. There are a lot of paintings for sale, some old, some new. Some of the new ones are by the big man, pastoral scenes—horses, cattle, wagons, rivers, farms, the open range—with plenty of trees, sky, and water. They are skillful, accurate, brightly colored. Some are painted on metal disks from which wires bent at right angles stick out all round. I recognize the shape—part of some agricultural tool. Big man is watching me. "The tines of old harrows. I like painting on those. They're appropriate to my subjects."

The well-dressed mother and daughter buy something and leave. Big man is full of generosity and time. He gives me things—three bags of buffalo fur, some Indian arrowheads that he picked up from the plain himself, old postcards that he pulls from a shoebox and thrusts at me: "the Sugar Factory, Garden City," a beautiful red-brick building photographed in the 1950s; a surreal 1930s photograph of a man aiming a rifle at a giant grasshopper; an old picture of the Garden City Swimming Pool, packed with people at the height of summer, photographed from above somehow, as if from the top of a tree. I turn it over and read the caption: "Nation's largest, free, municipal, concrete swimming pool 220 by 330 feet, holding nearly three million gallons of water."

Big man is saying something. "You'll find all the immigrants down there. Well… I guess you know, you've got the Pakistanis."

I'm not sure what he's getting at.

Then he says, "You won't find any Caucasians down there—not with their slime."

It came as a shock, unexpected from the big, friendly man who liked old things and to paint pretty, perhaps idealized, landscapes. But it would have been a shock if it had come from anyone.

I should have argued. But I said nothing. I wanted to get out. I went toward the door and looked again at the dark-haired woman in the yellow dress. I lifted the picture to have a closer look.

"You can have that for ten dollars. It's marked at thirty-five." I looked at the back. A sticker read "$75," and a printed card, attached with crumbling Scotch Tape, gave the artist's name, Juanita Craig, and her address—and beside that, in handwriting: "Girl in a Gold Dress painted about 1940."

I said I'd take it.

He took my ten-dollar bill and pointed out faults in the painting. "Her left arm isn't right."

I didn't care. I liked it. Perhaps he was insulted that, with so many of his paintings on view, I preferred one by someone else—one by a woman who, judging by her name, may well have been Mexican, married to a Scot.

He wrapped it and, as a final gift, gave me a printed cartoon-style map of the city that he had designed and illustrated in 1997. He made much of writing "For David Reynolds" in the bottom corner and signing it.

I thanked him with no enthusiasm and walked to the car, angry at my meekness and at the composure that had allowed me to buy a painting I liked, cheap, from a racist. I should have stated my opinion, quoted Abraham Lincoln, and *then* bought the painting. I wondered: Had Karen, the librarian, and Molly DesBaillets got it wrong? Were the different races in the city not as well integrated as they thought? Or was big man an exception: a lone nutter?

Had he *really* said "slime"? Yes, he had.

There is racism in the U.S. There is racism in England too. Nowadays it is usually hidden, not flaunted. Does that make it any better than big man's racism? Hiding it suggests that a racist knows that his view is not widely shared or popular. The shock I suffered just now came from big man assuming that I share his view. Or, worse, not caring whether I share it or not.

Did I let him know that I don't agree with him? Perhaps. By my silence. By making no comment. By buying a painting as if nothing had been said. But I should have made myself clear. I should have shouted.

36

TRUMAN CAPOTE AND THE CLUTTERS

I DROVE TO HOLCOMB ON a narrow side road which ran beside a railroad track. For five miles the road was straight, the country flat and featureless, in tune with the first line of Truman Capote's *In Cold Blood:* "The village of Holcomb stands on the high wheat plains of western Kansas, a lonesome area that other Kansans call 'out there.'"

The road entered Holcomb at its southeastern corner, a place of small, worn bungalows. I turned west at a junction and drove past playing fields, a low, spread-out school, and a strip mall—and stopped beside an area of grass, bordered in the distance by trees. A large brown notice with white lettering announced Holcomb Community Park, Dedicated to the Herb & Bonnie Clutter Family.

Herb Clutter was a forty-eight-year-old farmer—successful, well liked, and an employer, depending on the season and the weight of the harvest, of up to eighteen men. He had energy, a social conscience, and a concern for farmers and farming, all of which involved him in many activities and committees, local, statewide, and national. He was respected not just in Holcomb and Garden City—where he taught an adult Sunday School class—but in Topeka, the capital of Kansas, and in Washington. His wife, Bonnie, trained as a nurse before raising four children; she was popular and much involved with the local

community.

In the early hours of November 15, 1959, two ex-convicts on parole from Kansas State Penitentiary entered the Clutters' home while they slept. They had been falsely informed that Herb kept a large sum of money in a safe. There was nothing for them to steal. Instead, Dick Hickock and Perry Smith murdered Herb, Bonnie, sixteen-year-old Nancy (the Clutters' youngest daughter), and their only son, Kenyon, who was fifteen. Two older daughters were living away from home.

After reading a brief account of the murders in *The New York Times*, Truman Capote, already a well-known novelist and playwright and the author of *Breakfast at Tiffany's,* traveled to Holcomb with his childhood friend Harper Lee (who would later write *To Kill a Mockingbird*). Together and separately, they interviewed everyone involved in the sad, ghastly, pointless crime: surviving members of the Clutter family, their friends and neighbors, the police who caught up with the culprits six weeks later, the sheriff in whose tiny jail the two accused lived for many weeks, the sheriff's wife, the lawyers, and the murderers themselves. Capote befriended many of these people, including the guilty pair, and spent six years writing *In Cold Blood*. It was published in 1966, the year after Hickock and Smith were hanged. Holcomb, unremarkable and with a population then of about eight hundred, was made famous by the murders of the Clutters—a fame that became worldwide and enduring after publication of Capote's book.

It was beginning to grow dark. I left the car, walked around the edge of the park, and came to a broad, clean, almost white, stone path that led across grass for some thirty yards to a circle of stone on which sits the Clutter Memorial, a block of polished granite supporting a sheet of brass on which are inscribed five paragraphs that pay tribute to the Clutters, detailing their lives and achievements. Their deaths are mentioned in one short sentence only. Instead of evoking greed, madness, and murder, as much of Capote's book does, these words describe lives well lived. The memorial was constructed only recently: in 2009, in time for the fiftieth anniversary of the Clutters' deaths. The idea was proposed by Bob Rupp, a local man, who in 1959 was a seventeen-year-old high-school basketball hero and a friend of the Clutters; he was dating Nancy Clutter, and was the last person to see any of them alive. Speaking of the memorial to the *Garden City Telegram* in October 2009, Rupp said, "The focus is where it should be, on a family that greatly touched not only the Holcomb community, but also Garden City, Finney County, and the state."

Locally there is some resentment of Capote and his book: both of the fame and money he gained from a tragedy that belonged to them; and of his supposed fictionalization of aspects of the story. (Capote himself called *In Cold Blood* "a nonfiction novel," a concept that was dubbed a "new literary art form" by *New York Times* critic George Plimpton.) Of course, as a good writer must, Capote gave one consistent view—his own—of the place and the people. And a problem may be that, gripping and beautifully written as the book is, Capote's standpoint is that of a sophisticated, literary New Yorker—a man from a milieu that many who live here on the plains see as alien. Would, I wonder, the people of Holcomb have felt comfortable at the "Black and White Ball" that Capote threw at New York's Plaza Hotel in 1966 to celebrate the publication of *In Cold Blood?* Capote called it "my great big all-time spectacular present to myself," and asked his 540 guests—who included Marlene Dietrich, Frank Sinatra, Greta Garbo, Jacqueline Kennedy, John Steinbeck, and Andy Warhol—to wear masks.

Many nights ago in New Evarts, South Dakota, Daryl, the designer of grain elevators, told me, "We're different from the people on the coasts. This is the *real* America." And, while I didn't agree with Daryl's view of the world, I felt some sympathy. Now, staring down at the Clutter Family Memorial, which makes no mention of Truman Capote or his book, let alone the many films that followed from it, I feel more than sympathy. After all, the four Clutters who died that night had *lived their whole lives before* Capote showed up to write about their deaths. They deserve this short citation written by friends and displayed not far from their home.

KAREN AT THE library wanted me to visit her sister Sonnie who runs a sweet shop which I understood was called "You".

In a smart strip mall, back in Garden City, I found not You, but Ewe—and a thin, tallish woman with a lined, intelligent face standing in the middle of a large island of plastic bins filled with sweets: like the old Woolworth's Pick 'n' Mix counter but on a far greater scale.

Sonnie talked affectionately about Karen, her *younger* sister, and how she'd lived in the east where she'd picked up a lot of strange ideas. It seemed that Sonnie saw a logic in that, a connection between geography and how people think. It was as if she were saying, "The east is another country. They vote Democrat there." And that she, too, would have those ideas if she'd happened to have moved east. But she hadn't, so she was a Republican—but, I guessed, liberal with it.

We talked about Holcomb and the Clutters and films: *Capote,* the 2005 film with Philip Seymour Hoffman; and the black-and-white *In Cold Blood,* made in the 1960s. "That movie is how I knew what happened," Sonnie said. "We didn't live here then. Besides, I was a child."

A largish man came in and began to choose large quantities of sweets. While Sonnie served him, I picked up a business card from the counter. "Ewe Specialties LLC & Perfect Occasions: Wedding Rental, Party Supplies, Bulk Nuts, and Candy." Maybe the largish man was having a party.

The three of us discuss Dodge City, whether I should go there—and I'm reminded that it was the setting for one of the longest-running television Western series, *Gunsmoke*. In the real world, it was a railroad hub of the cattle trade between Texas, Chicago, and the east of the United States in the late 1870s and early 1880s, which meant that a constant stream of cowboys arrived, newly paid and desperate for fun and female company after weeks on horseback droving cattle. A tumult of bars, gambling joints, and whorehouses grew up around Dodge's Front Street and, it is said, there were frequent gunfights.

Sonnie thinks I might be disappointed by Dodge because the town has been turned into "a playground for tourists." But the man who is choosing sweets thinks I should see Front Street: "It's just down the road and it's part of history."

As I drive away, my head full of images of cowboys in bars, I remember one of the antics my friend Quentin got up to in our school dining hall; he would suck in his cheeks, narrow his eyes, slide two glasses along a long table, and rasp: "Set 'em up, bartender."

SINCE THE CLARION Inn was where "upper- and middle-class people go," I put on my black cotton jacket before walking there to get a drink and perhaps dinner.

I sat at the bar, facing a screen showing baseball. I was the only person in the room wearing a jacket. Beside me were two men—clean shirts, blue jeans, early middle-age, not fat, probably middle-class.

"Excuse me. I'm from England. Do you know what hush puppies are? They're here on the menu with the catfish."

"Ah... I'm not sure." One man looked at the other.

The other was resting his hands on the bar. He shrugged his thumbs. "I think it's... ah, almost like a dumpling—fried."

That didn't sound too good. I negotiated with the barman and he offered asparagus instead of hush puppies.

The first man was saying, "I can insure against hail. No problem whatever. It's drought that I can do nothing about."

He was a farmer who owned two farms, one close to Garden City, the other near McCook in southern Nebraska. His friend, who was sitting next to me, was an agronomist, employed to advise him how to get the best from his land. They were amused that I was driving *slowly* from Canada to the border with Mexico. The farmer drives two hundred thousand miles a year between and around his farms. He grows wheat and corn and keeps cattle, and seemed very content with life.

The place filled up and the music, strong on bass, got louder. The three of us ordered more beers. The farmer gestured to the barman. My beer was to go on his bill. I thanked him.

Then the catfish came. And it interested them. They had never eaten catfish. "I'm from Nebraska, so I usually eat steak," the farmer said—and shrugged his thumbs. The three of us stared at the catfish. It was on a square white plate with about eight asparagus shoots lying parallel to it. At first we couldn't see it properly because it was coated with some kind of pastry that formed a hard shell. I managed to crack this by lunging at it with the knife provided. Inside it was hot and white and steaming—and it tasted fine, like fish.

The bar filled with people, a DJ opened up in a corner and lights flashed on the dance floor behind me. I finished the fish and bought a round of drinks; my companions were drinking Scotch and I had one too. The bar was shaped like a horseshoe, and now there were three barmen ricocheting around like pinballs, upending bottles, jerking the tops off bottles, throwing bottles into a bin with a crash, snatching credit cards and cash, jabbing at symbols on foolproof tills. A fourth man worked more calmly, coming and going with crates of beer, armloads of spirits, plastic bins of empties. A big man stood on my right, ordered a bottled Coors, paid two fifty, drank it in a few seconds, and ordered another. A flabby young man bought numerous complex cocktails for a group of flabby girls and boys behind me. Twenty minutes later he ordered them all again.

On the screen above the bar, a baseball pitcher—a large man in a white outfit and a blue hat—lifted his knee almost to his chin, drew back his arm, lunged forward, and threw the ball. The striker—an even larger man—waved his bat at it—and missed.

Next to me, the agronomist was looking at the screen too.

"Why do they do that—the pitchers—that thing with their leg?"

"It's to do with ... ah ... balance and ... ah ... thrust—putting power into the throw. With that leg movement, the guy rocks back on his standing leg and gains power and thrust from it when he throws." He picked up his glass, tipped it toward him, and contemplated the spoonful of whiskey at the bottom. "He doesn't just throw with his arm. The leg, the standing leg, pushing forward, is a big part of it."

A young woman wearing a ball gown that displayed her shoulders and arms came in alone and sat down next to my farmer friend. He took no notice. I watched the man on her other side, a young man in a baseball cap, glance at her, glance away, and carry on talking to a fresh-faced, bald man who was standing behind him. The young woman was perhaps twenty-eight or thirty. She stood out in the room, not just because she was alone, but because she was better dressed, better looking, wearing less makeup, and taller than the other women—and she was slim without being skinny. She sipped at a long bright green drink. I imagined she was waiting for someone.

Farmer, agronomist, and I ordered more Scotches—and discussed Indians. I told them about my evening in the Rosebud Casino. Agronomist laughed and said, "You go on that Indian reservation up in South Dakota in your car and they'll—heh!, heh!—have all the wheels off and goodness knows what all. Anything they can trade for drink or drugs."

I said that I thought he was exaggerating, and he conceded he was—"but only a little." He grinned and raised his eyebrows at his drink.

I think that his vision of Indians as thieves and drug addicts is a myth. Thieving will happen on reservations occasionally, as it will in any dark city street. In the 1980s I visited New York City once or twice a year. People—locals from Midtown, Greenwich Village, Queens—said, "Don't drive through Harlem. When you stop at the traffic lights, they'll—heh!, heh!—have all the wheels off and goodness knows what all. Anything they can trade for drink or drugs." I drove through Harlem more than once with an English friend, at night. The first time, we locked the doors. And we stopped, terrified, at traffic lights—and nothing happened. We left the doors unlocked after that—and still nothing happened.

Flabby man bought eight more assorted cocktails. Woman with shoulders and ball gown was talking to baseball cap and fresh-faced bald man. I excused myself to go to the gents. It was cooler in there and the music was more melodious than the bass-and-drum machine in the bar, but of course I couldn't linger. When I returned, another Scotch was waiting. And soon my companions asked for their bills. It was late; they had an early start; they would take their drinks up to their rooms. A small barman with big sideburns riffled through a pack of credit cards as if he were looking for the ace of spades.

When my friends had gone I sipped Scotch and watched baseball. People were sitting on both sides of me, busy, talking to friends. Shoulders and ball gown had gone. A man was sitting in her seat. The place, the people, got louder, crazier: dancing, yelling, fists pumping, bottoms out. I paid my bill, climbed off my stool, and pushed through the crowd toward the door.

37

WHERE THE DEAD GUYS AREN'T

THE ROAD SOUTH FROM Garden City is like the road that comes in from the north: a straight two-lane run across immeasurable acres of wheat stubble with, here and there, a patch of glossy green corn or soya beans or milo, a type of sorghum. I'm still wondering whether to visit Dodge City. Sonnie called it "commercial," and Jamie Jensen says "it can be something of a disappointment."

Yet I have an urge to go. It's a famous place in the history of the Wild West, a place where history will, no doubt, be thoroughly, frustratingly entangled with myth. It began with one three-room house, built beside the Santa Fe Trail in 1871 by a rancher named Henry Sitler. In 1872 the Santa Fe Railroad arrived, linking the future Dodge City to Kansas City and Chicago. A town rapidly grew around Sitler's house and became a center for trading and shipping buffalo hides. The inhabitants wanted to call their town Buffalo City but that name had already been taken, so they named it Dodge City after nearby Fort Dodge. After six years, during which 1.5 million buffalo hides passed through, there were no buffalo left in the region; all of them had been slaughtered. By then, the cattle business had taken over and, for ten years beginning in 1875, Texas longhorns were driven up the Great Western Trail from southern Texas for shipping from Dodge. The town's lawlessness and hell raising, which began when it filled with buffalo hunters, continued. And the place was policed by drifters and gamblers like Wyatt Earp and Bat Masterson, who were both employed as lawmen, and by the gunfighter who was also a dentist, "Doc" Holliday.

I turn east toward Dodge on an innocuous highway numbered 144.

This road too is straight, but there is something about the emptiness of the landscape—the scrubby, brown-green range—and the spacing of the telegraph poles, their shape and simplicity—one crosspiece close to the top—that takes me closer to my boyhood hero, Dan Matthews of *Highway Patrol*. It's a warm day; the window is already down—so I rest my elbow on the sill and cruise, sixties-road-cop-style, with one hand on the wheel. There's no traffic and, unlike Matthews, I have no job to do. I am here, fully awake inside one of my childhood dreams, where life is easy on an American road.

I put on a CD that I bought in Garden City: JJ Cale's *Roll On*. It's what I hoped for, slow and shuffling. I turn from 144 on to 56 and head northeast on another almost empty road with telegraph poles. Less than an hour after leaving 83, I mosey through the scruffy industrial outskirts of Dodge City which now has a population of twenty-seven thousand, more than five thousand of whom work for two meat-packing companies, both of which have amusing names: Cargill Meat Solutions and National Beef. Soon I pass Gunsmoke Street and Wyatt Earp Avenue, and sidle into a car park in front of a sidewalk that, at a glance, looks like Main Street in *High Noon*...

Only, at a second glance, it doesn't. There's no saloon, no livery stable, no sheriff's office, just the Golden House Chinese

Food Carry Out, Windmill Food, and a nail bar. A sign points to Tourist Information. Unsure how far it is, I drive; it's two blocks away in a new building in front of a car park.

Inside I meet a charming and helpful man. He is tanned and squat with a bristly white mustache, and is sitting behind glass as if we were in a bank. I ask for his suggestions as to what I should see during the rest of the day.

He suggests that I go to the Boot Hill Museum; the entrance is at the Great Western Hotel. He tells me that at six o'clock I can eat dinner, at seven o'clock watch a gunfight, and at half-past seven attend "a variety show with Miss Kitty and her cancan girls." He smiles and says, "That will keep you occupied until about nine tonight."

"I don't expect to be here that late," I say.

"Well," he shrugs. "The gunfight is included in your ten-dollar admission fee."

I walk out into hot sunlight, and drive Prius a few yards to the Great Western Hotel car park. I walk up some steps, push open a door, and find myself in a large shop full of tat: cheap cowboy hats, replica guns, sheriff's badges, thimbles, bottle openers, mugs, scented candles. I wait to buy a ticket from a bored-looking, fattish girl, who is chewing gum while a fat woman leans all over the counter, with her souvenirs spread all around, trying to find a few extra knickknacks in the racks by the till, before she finally hands in her credit card. She pays no attention to me or to a sour-looking man in a white T-shirt who is queuing behind me. I remember Sonnie standing among bins of sweets saying that I might be disappointed by this town—and try hard to relax while I wait and observe the fat woman struggling to decide whether or not to buy three more gimcrack key rings with Colt 45s dangling from them.

The fattish girl behind the till chews and blows a pink bubble. And I wish I was anywhere but here.

Eventually fat woman pays, gathers her fat—and leaves the world to gum girl and to me.

Clutching my ticket, I emerge through a door at the back of the shop onto a swathe of parched grass, and find that I am facing a long facade that is labeled Front Street. Yet it can't be the Front Street that was there in the 1870s, the city's boom time. It's too new, too freshly painted in subtle pastel colors, too perfect. And what about the other side of the street? There is nothing here, only the grass I am standing on.

A fat young woman dressed up to look like Old Mother Hubbard is standing on the sidewalk. And I find that I'm thinking about fatness: that, perhaps, in the USA there are four categories of fat: fattish; fat; very fat with tight skin, or balloon-like; and very fat and wobbly. The terms "mountainous" and "immensely unslim" might apply to the two very fat categories.

Young Mother Hubbard wanders into a fake old-time grocer's store which looks like another shopping opportunity—offering, perhaps, Mrs. Earp's blueberry pie and Bat Masterson's onion pickle.

I peer into the next window and see a bar where a man dressed in a frock coat is talking to a room full of jean-clad customers sitting at tables. I go in, and sit as unobtrusively as I can on the nearest chair to the door. Frock coat is an actor playing a quack doctor hawking a spurious cure-all medicine. A young man dressed in period rags limps in. He has numerous ailments, including blindness and deafness. An amusing rigmarole ensues at the end of which the poor boy hands over twenty dollars and receives a bottle of medicine. He drinks the medicine and collapses on the floor. Children are giggling. Adults, including me, are smiling.

I move on, into another room, and see guns arranged on walls. And then—there they are: black-and-white photographs of Earp, Masterson, the "Doc," and several of their pals, mustaches drooping in unison in homage to their hardness. Later, after they'd moved on from Dodge City, those three became ever more famous. Until eventually they ascended into myth as they featured in more and more books and movies. Wyatt Earp, for example, has been played by the following actors (and by many more, less famous): Randolph Scott (1939), Henry Fonda (1946), Joel McCrea (1955), Burt Lancaster (1957), James Stewart (1964), James Garner (1967), Kurt Russell (1993), Kevin Costner (1994), Val Kilmer (2012).

I find that I can move between the different shops on Front Street without going outdoors; they all connect. Surely the real Dodge City wasn't so well planned. I look at a saloon, a newspaper office, a bank, a drugstore, a barber's shop—all of them reproductions. Eventually I come out on the sidewalk. Farther along is a functioning café, designed as a period replica, but with modern accoutrements such as an espresso machine and a credit card reader; four smiling waitresses are dressed in white shirts, long skirts, and green aprons. I remember that I haven't had lunch. It's about 5 PM. As I eat a juicy, beef brisket sandwich, a fat man with a bushy beard and his wife who wears pink sit across the room eating ice cream; they seem like fun, twinkly people. In a corner some loud oafish teens flick salt at one another. A pair of adults look in to check on them and, understandably, abandon them again.

Later I come across the teens, three boys and a girl, as I look round a genuine 1880s house whose "interior reflects the middle-class lifestyle of Victorian Kansas." One of the boys seems almost angry with boredom. As they leave, he whines at his friends, "Where's the place where the dead guys are buried?"—as if sight of it might rescue his day.

The Boot Hill Museum is indeed boring for the most part, and disappointing, especially the place where the dead guys are supposed to be: a small fenced patch of grass at the top of a slight slope—presumably Boot Hill itself. Here a few gray planks with crosspieces nailed to them stick out of the earth at odd angles. Some carry crudely carved inscriptions: "Five Buffalo Hunters," "Unknown Cowboy," "Alice May Coombes, died 5 May 1878." That no bodies are buried here is made clear in the single-sheet guide to the museum that came with my ticket: "The Boot Hill Cemetery... was closed in 1879 and the remains of those buried there were moved to the northeast of town... No one famous was ever buried here." I think of angry teenage boy and hope, for his parents' sake, that he doesn't read this. It is obvious that the planks are just decoration, pushed into the ground not long ago to give visitors something to look at. A printed notice gives details, drawn from contemporary newspapers, of the deaths of about twenty people who were buried here, including those whose names appear on the planks. Twelve of the deaths appear to have been violent, for instance: "Barney Cullen, January 1873: railroad employee who was killed during a shooting spree in a saloon."

One man, perhaps a cousin of one of my ancestors, has a notice to himself: "Jack Reynolds, a notoriously mean and contemptible desperado, got into a quarrel at Dodge City with one of the track-layers and without any ifs or ands, he put six balls in rapid succession into Jack's body. The desperado fell and expired instantly." September 8, 1872—*Kansas City Commonwealth.*

So, at that time in the American West, there *really were* mean men who, perhaps, sucked in their cheeks, narrowed their eyes, and thought, or pretended, that they were "hard"—and these mean desperadoes were considered contemptible at the time. Why then, ninety years later, had my friend Quentin and I, fourteen-year-old schoolboys in England, sought to emulate them? Were we trying to show that we were rebels, outlaws, desperate for freedom from the constraints of school? Was the drabness of postwar England (something we didn't notice, and only became aware of retrospectively by comparison with what happened later) a factor?

I go into a low building next to the graveyard. Inside are darkened rooms and dimly lit cabinets: an exhibition titled People of the Plains. The teenagers are there, breathing through their mouths and gawping at old photos of Indians. Are they bored by the Wild West because they have more recent sources of myth to absorb them: perhaps World War II or Vietnam? Or are they bored because they recognize that most of the Boot Hill Museum is hokum? Or is it just the dust of a museum, any museum that contains no computers or games—or dead guys?

There is an idea that myths help humans to make sense of the world and their place in it. The anthropologist Claude Lévi-Strauss demonstrated that the myths and stories that turn up in different cultures all over the world are surprisingly similar; he suggested that they are evidence of the existence of a universal law of human thought and that they play a role in resolving conflict.

In *The Raw and the Cooked,* Lévi-Strauss examines 187 myths drawn from Native American tribes throughout North and South America, in almost all of which either a raven or a coyote plays a mediating role. He suggests that these myths tend to underlie "illusions of liberty." I like to think that his theory applies to more modern myths, and that—as long as children and cultures embrace appropriate myths and stories, ones that bear on resolution of conflict and notions of freedom—it doesn't matter where the myths come from. The stories of cowboys and Indians and the mythical conflict between them in the second half of the nineteenth century that I and millions of boys and girls, and indeed adults, all over the world enjoyed in the twentieth century might seem, in that light, to have had a civilizing influence on our lives. Both cowboys and Indians, the myth says, strove and fought for freedom—of the individual for the former, of the tribe for the latter—and someone, a good cowboy or Indian or soldier or lawman, featured as a mediator. And might it be significant that the U.S. Army, the real oppressor of the Indians, played a minor role in our childhood stories and reenactments?

The People of the Plains exhibition displayed photographs of cowboys, Indians, pioneers, buffalo hunters, and soldiers, alongside their clothes, their homes, and the stuff they used every day. It was the best part of the Boot Hill Museum because it showed reality. Short typed essays had been fixed to the walls with nails. One was about cowboys, and from it I learned that not all cowboys were white or of northern European origin:

> African Americans made up one-quarter of the cowboy population. Many Mexican vaqueros also worked on the trail drives. Referred to as "buckaroos," the Hispanic cattlemen taught the early American ranchers how to ride horses and to herd cattle.

How many black cowboys have been seen in Western TV series, movies, or comics? How often has a Mexican been shown teaching an American how to ride a horse?

I left the Boot Hill Museum and took the same road out of Dodge City back toward 83. The sun was low, and the clouds were low too and lit from above. There was no traffic, and distance seemed to be measured by the mesmeric flicking by of telegraph poles.

The flicking by became a lullaby. To keep myself awake, I put The Hot Club of Cowtown's *Continental Stomp* into the CD player: fast, loud, acoustic music with violin and guitar and a great female voice.

GUNS AND FREEDOM

IT WAS AFTER NINE and dark when I reached Liberal, the last town in Kansas. I checked into the large, square, two-story Liberal Inn Hotel and went to its restaurant, where a waitress greeted me.

"I'm on my own. I'll sit at the bar," I said, and took the nearest seat, cornerwise to a middle-aged man with dark, slicked-back hair.

The room was large but there weren't many people in it—two old men farther along, three couples eating at tables, and the waitress, slim in jeans with fluffy blond hair. For some reason—perhaps because there were so many empty seats—I apologized for crowding my neighbor.

At first he didn't understand, so I repeated what I'd said.

He waved his hand. "No problem. Come on. No problem."

I noticed his shirt, silver-and-black herringbone, closely woven. It looked expensive and I put him down as a businessman, and wondered what we would talk about. I was pretty sure we'd talk; I'd found that people sitting beside each other at bars in the U.S. usually do.

I asked for a beer, studied the menu, and listened with mild embarrassment to smart shirt attempting to flirt with the waitress.

"Can I tell you a joke?" he said.

She looked at him and sighed. "Yes." She was, I guessed, in her late thirties—and well used to this sort of thing.

"Hold my hand."

She took his hand, and feigned a smile while rolling her eyes. The smile made her look a little like Dolly Parton—but taller and without the alarming bosoms.

"Are you married?"

"No."

"Have you got a boyfriend?"

"No."

"Will you come out with me?"

"No."

"Why are you holding my hand then?"

She pulled her hand away. "It's no good, Jimmy. You've done that before."

"Well." He grinned. "I gotta keep trying, haven't I?" He swallowed some beer.

She didn't answer and turned to me. "What can I get you?"

She wrote down my order, disappeared, and returned with a full plate—steak, chips, carrots, beans, mushrooms, onions, gravy. She put it down in front of Jimmy. "Where you going, Jimmy?" she said.

"Denver. Gotta move out early," he said. "Gotta be there at two."

Jimmy isn't a businessman. He's a truck driver, who, it seems, after a day's driving, showers, changes his clothes, combs his hair, drinks a few beers, and tries it on with waitresses.

I get his attention by making a feeble remark about how he and his colleagues are always overtaking me. I tell him my theory that, when the speed limit is 65, as it frequently is on 83, the truckers drive at 68. He tells me I'm wrong—at least with reference to him. "If the limit is 65, I drive 65. If the limit is 70, I drive 70. If the limit is 75 . . ." and so on.

He's freelance, paid by the hour. He rents the truck, has many costs, and needs to drive a lot to make a living. Right now, he has a 377-mile job moving meat from Liberal to Denver, and it isn't enough miles, barely worthwhile, he says. He lives in southern California, one hundred miles east of San Diego. He has driven on every interstate in the country, and in every mainland state except Maine.

I guess that he's in his mid-fifties, and from his surname and his looks—a little overweight, but handsome with cheekbones and a jaw—Irish American. He's been divorced twice—and tells me, eyes bulging a little, that he'd like to kill his first wife.

As the evening moves on, he gets more friendly. We buy each other beers—and later decide that that's silly; we might as well pay for our own. I must have mentioned Indians because he said that he was almost 50 percent Native American—and proud of it. "I'm fifty-seven varieties," he says with a laugh.

The barmaid smiles and says, "Most of us are, I guess."

"So you must have sympathy for the Native Americans and the blacks," I say.

"I have a lot of sympathy for the Native Americans. Not so much for the blacks." He looks away and scratches his neck. "You know, the slaves were enslaved by their own people, who sold them to the whites who transported them."

"I didn't know that," I say—in a tone intended to convey skepticism rather than surprise.

As we drink, Jimmy becomes ever more talkative. Probably because he knows I am English, he tells me that Princess Diana was murdered. Then he comes up with something I've not heard before: "The Japanese were *allowed* to invade Pearl Harbor. The Jap ambassador was waiting to deliver a declaration of war, but they wouldn't let him in because they wanted the invasion so as to get the American public onside for entering World War II."

I mumble something, while wondering if that idea is widespread in America. It might be, because, though the event was much longer ago, it's similar to Jimmy's next theory which I heard in another bar a week or so ago: "Al-Qaeda were *allowed* to fly into the twin towers, so as to get the people onside for the invasion of Iraq." He backs this up with details of what he says is the strange way that the towers collapsed.

We order more beers. And Jimmy moves on to Obama, who "changed his name to Barack Hussein Obama, when he went to Africa and found his father there living in a dictatorship. He is a *Muslim*. Isn't that a *Muslim* name? Barack *Hussein* Obama!!" Jimmy is getting mildly agitated—perhaps because I don't seem convinced.

We order more beer, and I ask him about guns.

For a moment his eyes sparkle with what I take to be irritation. "They are part of the Constitution, the right to carry guns, the right to freedom."

"Sure," I say.

He says nothing else about guns. Their equivalence to freedom is clearly all that needs to be said. And soon he climbs down from his stool, says, "Good night. Nice meeting you," waves at the waitress, and leaves.

BACK IN MY room I turn on the television. *The Larry King Show* is on CNN; King's guest is Bill Maher (rhymes with bar), comedian and host of *Real Time with Bill Maher*. They discuss Larry King's imminent retirement after twenty-five years of hosting his show. And then they move on to the state of their nation.

Maher says that a recent *Vanity Fair* poll has revealed that 24 percent of Americans believe that Obama wasn't born in the USA. His next statistic is even more remarkable: the same percentage believe that Jesus Christ will return to Earth during their lifetime. Maher points out how "egotistical" this is: "He's gonna want to come back while *I'm* around. Just for *me*."

And then: again that same figure, 24 percent, think that Obama *might*—Maher stresses the *might*—be the Antichrist. "So," Maher says, "I think one out of four Americans is just a total nutcase, Larry."

King's lips sag at the corners. He lifts his forearms from his desk in a gesture of hopelessness.

Then, in an eerie echo of a conversational gambit I tried on Jimmy, Larry King raises the subject of guns.

Maher deplores a new liberalization of gun laws in Chicago. And, almost incidentally, mentions Arizona, where the authorities are clamping down on immigration from Mexico: "Arizona, my favorite state, should rename itself Whiteyville."

They get back to guns. The Republicans, Maher says, keep finding more and more places where people should be allowed to have guns, such as churches and bars.

"Why do we love guns?" King asks.

"Having said that," Maher continues, "*I* have a gun. I am not going to give up my gun,"—he pauses, as if for a moment unsure of his own motive—"because there's too many other nuts out there with guns, Larry. We are such a gun culture. It's a case of not going back—and you don't want to be in your home and somebody breaks in and *they* have guns."

Maher chuckles and grins through all this, while King nods wearily—and I, doing both, feel my spirits rise.

TWO PANHANDLES AND THE CHEROKEE

THE FIRST SETTLER IN the area that was to become Liberal was a man called S.S. Rogers. He had water on his land and regularly gave it away to thirsty travelers. The travelers—or at least one of them—thanked him by saying, "That's very liberal of you." And the word became the name of the fledgling town.

The receptionist at the Liberal Inn Hotel, a chatty brown-haired woman, told me this. It happened in 1872, and S.S. Rogers wasn't trying to sell ice cream or drugs. I want it to be true because it displays the word's true meaning: generous. And it seems likely to be true. In 1885 S.S. Rogers built a general store including a U.S. Post Office which was called Liberal. In 1888 the railroad arrived and the town was officially incorporated. Within a year the population was eight hundred. Nowadays, Liberal is one of the three big beef-processing cities of southwest Kansas, along with Garden and Dodge. Guyman, nearby in the Oklahoma Panhandle, is a center for processing hogs.

Today is July 4, Independence Day. The receptionist says that nothing much will happen in Liberal. If people want to celebrate they go to big cities where there are fireworks, or they stay at home, have a few friends over, and let off their own fireworks.

ACROSS THE ROAD from the Liberal Inn Hotel, life-size cutouts of the characters from *The Wizard of Oz* stand in a raised flowerbed in front of some small trees. Behind them is a museum that contains Dorothy's (Judy Garland's) house and the Yellowbrick Road. Dorothy is a fictional character who comes from Kansas. Where in Kansas is not specified by her creator, L. Frank Baum. So some smarty-pants has to be congratulated for building her house in Liberal.

I ignore Dorothy and drive south out of town. After three miles I come to a sign, pitted by a few bullets, that says Welcome to Oklahoma: Native America, reflecting Oklahoma's history as Indian Territory and the many tribes that still hold land in the state. I'm entering the Oklahoma Panhandle, which measures 166 miles east to west and just thirty-five miles, via 83, north to south. The Panhandle was once part of the short-lived independent Republic of Texas but was surrendered when Texas entered the Union as a slave state in 1845, because slavery was prohibited to the north of the line that became its southern boundary. For years after that it was known as No Man's Land—and, in a way, that's how it still seems.

FROM 1834 UNTIL 1889 the land that is now Oklahoma—the rest of which is east and southeast of here—was known as Indian Territory. It was the place to which the U.S. government dispatched scores of Indian tribes when they got in the way of white expansion—or in the way of what journalist John L. O'Sullivan in 1845 described as "our manifest destiny to overspread the continent allotted by Providence for the free development of our yearly multiplying millions." The idea of manifest destiny, held long before O'Sullivan gave it a name, was that white Americans had a right to create across America an agrarian utopia that would serve as an example to the rest of the world. And, of course, the demands of God, or Providence, and the need to spread Christianity were part of the general idea.

Yet God didn't spare the Indians. And surely no god worth worshipping would have blessed the enforced removal of Indian peoples from their ancestral lands to any place, let alone to this so-called Indian Territory, much of which was dry, flat, treeless, and covered in grass that appealed only to buffalo. Every removal of Native Americans to Indian Territory brought about tragedy and, frequently, death. The story of the flight of the Northern Cheyenne, who found that life on that land was literally killing them, is one example.

Another story, even more shocking, is that of the Cherokee, one of a group of tribes known then by Anglo-Americans as "the five civilized tribes"—the others were the Choctaw, Creek, Chickasaw, and Seminole. The five tribes lived in the southeastern United States—the Cherokee in the mountains that now span the border between Georgia, the Carolinas, and Tennessee. All five tribes had a tradition of living in towns and practicing agriculture as well as hunting. Faced with white men from Europe, the Cherokee tried to accommodate them and learn from them. Churches and roads were built; missionaries were invited to open schools; and European methods of farming were adopted. They grew cotton, they spun and wove, they kept slaves. A Cherokee named Sequoyah worked hard to devise a Cherokee alphabet, based on the eighty-six syllables that they used, so their language could be written down. Missionaries who were teaching the children in English were skeptical, but when, after twelve years, Sequoyah succeeded, all his tribesmen wanted to learn and thousands did.

The Cherokee then produced a bilingual newspaper, the *Cherokee Phoenix;* the Creek put out a Bible; and laws were written down. By the 1820s and '30s, they had set up law courts, magistrates, police, a militia, and the first public school system in the South—and they had put in place a system of government based on that of the United States.

Christopher Davis, author of *North American Indian,* writes, "In fact they were too successful." Six thousand people, a quarter of the tribe, broke away and migrated beyond the Mississippi because they wanted to retain their Indian identity.

Meanwhile, in 1828, the Americans had elected Andrew Jackson as their seventh president, a man who believed in manifest destiny—though the expression was yet to be coined—and who wanted to move all Indians west of the Mississippi. Jackson was a soldier, a popular general both in the 1812 war against Britain, when his men nicknamed him "Old Hickory," and in wars against the Creek and Seminole who called him "Sharp Knife." In 1830 Jackson introduced the Indian Removal Act in Congress which, in effect, stated that the five civilized tribes must move from their homelands to lands beyond the Mississippi. The act was passed in the House of Representatives by just five votes. But many spoke against it, including Davy Crockett, the representative for Tennessee. Some cited the guarantees, given by Washington, Adams, and Jefferson, the first three presidents, of federal protection for all Indians.

Edward Everett, a Massachusetts congressman who later became president of Harvard, said:

> The evil was enormous, the inevitable suffering incalculable... Nations of dependent Indians, under color of law, are driven from their homes into the wilderness. You cannot explain it, you cannot reason it away... Our friends will view this measure with sorrow and our enemies alone with joy. And we ourselves,

> Sir, when the interests and passions of the day are past, shall look back upon it, I fear, with self-reproach and a regret as bitter as it is unavailing.

Simon Schama describes the passing of the Removal Act as "one of the most morally repugnant moments in American history," and Jackson as "the ethnic cleanser of the first democratic age."

The Cherokee, under their chief John Ross, who was one-eighth Cherokee and seven-eighths Scot, appealed to the Supreme Court where the Chief Justice, John Marshall, upheld their case, ruling that they were a nation, that treaties had been made with them, and that therefore the state of Georgia might *not* hold a lottery to sell off their land.

But Jackson ignored the Supreme Court and calmly rescinded the relevant treaties. The lottery went ahead. And when John Ross returned from arguing the case in Washington, he found his house occupied by a lottery winner and had to move his family into a log cabin.

Jackson wanted the Cherokee to leave their land voluntarily, but Ross refused to go and persuaded his fellows to resist. In 1838, by which time Martin Van Buren was president, the deadline for voluntary removal expired. The Cherokee, including women, children, and the elderly, were rounded up by seven thousand troops, led by a general, and herded into corrals. There many died. The rest were loaded onto leaky, overcrowded boats. The survivors of the boat trip were pushed onto railroad boxcars, from which the dead and dying were thrown as the train progressed. Then came an eight-hundred-mile walk, in a long line. A passerby described a line of two thousand Cherokee three miles long: "A great many ride on horseback and multitudes go on foot—even aged females apparently nearly ready to drop into the grave were traveling with heavy burdens attached to the back—on the sometimes frozen ground and sometimes muddy streets with no covering for the feet except what nature had given them."

Eventually Ross was allowed to take command of the transportation. Even so, a quarter of the sixteen thousand who left Georgia died. The journey they were forced to make became known as "The Trail of Tears."

The other four civilized nations had already been removed to Indian Territory. A few Cherokee escaped to the mountains of western North Carolina where their descendants still live, and three hundred to five hundred Seminole—their tribal lands were in Florida—fought U.S. soldiers in the Everglades, killed fifteen hundred of them, and never surrendered; their descendants call themselves the "Unconquered People."

It might be thought that now, getting on for two hundred years later, there is no opportunity for redress of the misery suffered by the five nations. But there *is* something, suggested by Simon Schama: Andrew Jackson's face, complete with what Schama calls "his imperious quiff," could be removed from the twenty-dollar bill where it has been since 1928. And it might be replaced (my idea, not Schama's) by the face of a woman—Sacagawea perhaps, or Rosa Parks. There are no women on U.S. banknotes.

THE HARVEST IS over and the land looks worn out, flat and dismal with few trees and fewer houses—just sweeps of dusty stubble, plowed earth, and scrubby grassland. The air is warm, almost hot, and the sky is blue above rolling clouds. 83 is two-lane, gray, rough, cracked here and there. There are no telegraph poles, save for an occasional line looping east or west and away out of sight.

Once in a while a pickup overtakes, or zips by going north. The map shows two or three small towns or villages, but they amount to almost nothing. And soon I reach the Texas State

Line, white letters on green; and Drive Friendly the Texas Way, the same colors around a painted Texas flag, white-and-red horizontal bands against a vertical blue one with a single white star.

I'm in the Texas Panhandle, in the Lone Star State—and immediately everything changes. There is plenty to look at: hills, valleys, gulches, a small canyon, rocky outcrops, long graceful curving bends in the road—the first real change in the landscape since I left Swan River. 83 is different too. Although this is famously a rich state, the road is a little narrower, with gentle bumps and sways; at the same time it is homier, cozier, worn reddish-brown over black.

As I drive into Perryton, the first town in Texas, I pass a small sign in washed-out black capitals, CLUB 83, and in smaller letters underneath, DANCING. Club 83 is housed in a brand-new, shiny silver, corrugated-iron, windowless Nissen, or Quonset, hut. Electric cables leading to the unobtrusive sign suggest that at night CLUB 83 DANCING will be lit up, pulsating to the beat, and visible for miles in every direction. Sadly, it's too early for me to stop.

South of Perryton, on a bend at the bottom of a hill, I come to a stopping place and a notice: Texas Vietnam Veterans Memorial Highway. In the shade of a lush patch of cottonwoods, I lean on Prius and read: "In gratitude to the thousands of men and women who served our country during the Vietnam War, the people of Texas dedicate this highway which runs across our state from the southernmost tip to the northernmost point. It is our hope that all those who travel U.S. 83 will pause to remember those who gave up their lives or their youth or their hopes in that long and bitter conflict. We vow not to forget those who did not return to us and we pledge to remember the sacrifices of those who did come home."

In fact, the whole length of 83 in the U.S. is designated Veterans of Foreign Wars Memorial Highway. All of the six states supported this individually and it is marked on some road signs in North Dakota and Nebraska, but this is the first time I've seen a dedication or anything to read.

A few miles on I cross the wide and almost dry Canadian River. Fifty yards to my right is the outline of an old bridge, the predecessor of the concrete one that is carrying me and 83. I drive over to its southern end where a plaque describes it as a wagon bridge, built in 1916 and restored in 2000. More specifically it is a Parker truss bridge, made up of twenty-one steel hoops, or trusses, resting on concrete piles, held together with steel struts, and painted rust brown. It is 3,255 feet long, and in 1916 was the largest steel structure west of the Mississippi.

It is late afternoon and warm. I walk halfway across on a surface of sun-bleached boards. The air is scented with herbs. Birds dart and sing in the long grass of the dry riverbed and in the trees. Suddenly, loud squawking—and a flock of pigeons flaps unaccountably skyward from beneath the new concrete bridge.

It's hot in the town of Canadian. I walk up the brick-paved slope of Main Street and I buy a cold lemonade in the foyer of the Palace, a beautiful old movie theatre. I am served by a man called Shane Spencer who owns the place and restored it. He says that Canadian celebrated July 4 on July 3: yesterday—because it was Saturday. There was a parade, fireworks, dancing, free movies, and numerous attractions. But there's a rodeo tonight starting at seven. It's now a quarter-past six. Shane recommends a motel that is between Main Street and the Rodeo Arena. I drive there, check in, splash my face with cold water, flip the television on and off, and walk back, north along 83, half a mile to the arena.

The grandstand is smaller than at North Platte and the entrance fee is five dollars instead of ten, but the evening is more fun because it is less slick. At least some of the cowboys come from local ranches, and not all of them are lean young men—in fact, some are middle-aged and quite fat. The twanging guitar of the great Duane Eddy is piped at us, and two clowns sweep the arena with besoms. The announcer is full of wit, but there are no in-jokes and no sycophancy directed at his good pals, the local panjandrums. In the rows in front of me are numerous cowboy hats, mostly stiff, pleated-at-the-crown, cream or white Stetsons; serious ranchers often have these custom-made at a cost of around five hundred dollars.

As in North Platte, I am sympathetic to the poor steers that feature in many of the events; there is a group of them and they are constantly being chased, lassoed, thrown on the ground, and tied up. The completion of Stray Gathering, for example, occurs when one, often fat, man sits on a steer with his knees on his neck while another ties the animal's feet. In other events they have their ears and tails pulled (that didn't happen in the swanky Buffalo Bill Rodeo in North Platte). And these steers are *very* small. Two of them are brown while the rest are black. One of the brown ones has white splodges on his face. I feel especially sorry when he gets a rope around his heel and is jerked to the ground. And I am overjoyed when the cowboys throw their lassos and miss, and the steer skitters away. I can see them curse as they have to loop up the lasso and try again.

Near the end, there's an event that I don't at first understand. Several Texas longhorns—adults, rather than steers, with beautiful long, pointed horns—are released into the arena. Teams of three chase after them. The longhorns don't like this. Men and beasts struggle. Eventually, one man grabs an animal around the neck, another hugs its midriff, while the third seems to fiddle about underneath. Soon the third man runs across the arena holding a small bottle and empties it in front of the judges.

There is a large, Hispanic-looking man sitting next to me. I ask him what is happening.

"They're milking them."

"Oh!" I say. "So they're female?"

He gives me a look. "Yep." And turns away toward his wife and son.

When the rodeo ends I walk through the small car park. A horse, saddled and bridled, stands patiently in a parking space, alone among cars and pickups.

AT HALF-PAST TEN, outside Pizza Hut, it is still warm and everyone except me is wearing flip-flops. Many of those waiting are Hispanic, young couples and young families, and I remember that I am now in Texas; after the Indians, the Spanish were here first—and Mexico isn't so far away. Doors and windows are open to the street, and some of the men seem to have forgotten to put on their trousers. One handsome young dude, with a tall and striking young woman, has chosen an expensive-looking orange-colored shirt to hang over his stripy boxers and chunky brown legs.

40

COTTON AND SLAVERY

SOUTH OF CANADIAN, THE land is green, open, rising, and falling: idyllic, Western country. John Wayne and Gary Cooper could easily be out there, were it not for a rash of small circular storage tanks that intrude on a timeless pastoral scene like turds on a well-kept lawn. They are often in groups of three and many are painted black. Some of them sprout pipes and valves. This is Texas, so, of course, they contain oil.

A few miles on, the tanks disappear and the landscape seduces unhindered. This is the range—for me the realization of a vision that comes from *The Waltons,* the Ponderosa ranch in *Bonanza, Oklahoma!* and the song "The Surrey with the Fringe on Top," and, indeed, "Home on the Range." Once again the sky is blue, the clouds are puffy, and the air is warm. All is so suddenly well that, when I reach a town called Wheeler, I turn the car round and drive back three miles to take photographs in case the landscape changes again farther south.

83 goes straight through Wheeler. I see a grand building, a block away to the right, turn off, and park in front of it. It is roughly the shape and style of Buckingham Palace, though somewhat smaller and faced in part with deep-red brick,

with four columns topped by Ionic capitals and a stone pediment. Written across the top in plain, widely spaced letters is WHEELER—COUNTY—COURT—HOUSE. I've seen several courthouses in towns along 83. They are always old and imposing. It seems that those early settlers, as soon as they had established even a small community, would set up the basic tools of law and order: a sheriff with deputies and a ramshackle office, a tiny jail, and, perhaps, a wooden courthouse. Then they relaxed, took time, and collected money for the raising of imposing, well-proportioned buildings of brick and stone, with a touch of the castle about them to reassure the law abiding and frighten the criminals.

HALF AN HOUR on I reach Shamrock, where 83 meets the old Route 66—now, unhappily, replaced by Interstate 40 which bypasses the town. Again 83 runs north–south through the town and doubles as Main Street. It's a hard-boiled, run-down, dusty place with a handful of well-preserved showpiece buildings. At the junction of 83 and the old 66 is a huge and, in some ways, beautiful art deco building that once housed a filling station and a café called the U Drop Inn. This is the place that, back in Swan River, Wilbert Schoenrath, a friend of Stuart's, told me I must see. It's now a Visitors' Bureau, though 1950s gas pumps, of the type immortalized by Edward Hopper, stand pristine under a portico outside. In a back street, a cream-painted wooden bench swings from chains over a wide veranda that fronts a Spanish-style, red-brick building with rounded arches. This is now a museum but was, according to a plaque attached to its front, "The Reynolds Hotel, built by attorney Marion Reynolds" between 1925 and 1928; it "was open for about fifty years and housed many a weary traveler." Close by is another pristine art deco filling station, complete with pumps that once dispensed Magnolia gasoline. These are handsome buildings, perfectly preserved, but they are closed, no one is around, and there is a deadness about the town, brought about, I'm sure, by regular traffic no longer passing through en route from Chicago to L.A.

WILBERT SCHOENRATH ALSO told me to look out for the "Bonnie and Clyde bridge," an old metal bridge south of Shamrock where the gangster couple had a spectacular crash.

I find it parallel to a concrete bridge that carries 83. It's closed for repair but, when open, takes 83's northbound traffic. It's a steel-framed truss bridge, similar to the one north of Canadian but a lot shorter, just three trusses instead of twenty-one. I have seen these bridges in films; they used to be out there on country roads, all girders and geometry. To me they evoke both kids fishing in bright sunlight, and bootleggers on dark nights in the Prohibition era; I can imagine the roar and rumble as black whiskey eights driven by the likes of James Cagney and George Raft thunder across.

I look down, and see the Salt Fork of the Red River swirling, orange brown, not far below. On June 10, 1933, Clyde Barrow, driving fast, as he usually did, missed a sign warning that this bridge was being repaired—just as it is today—and shot down the bank into the water. A couple called Pritchard, who lived nearby, saw the accident, rescued him and Bonnie, whose leg was badly burned, and Clyde's brother Buck—but didn't recognize them. They took them to their home and called for help. A sheriff and a marshal arrived and were instantly disarmed by Bonnie. Buck Barrow shot the Pritchards' daughter in the hand while shooting at their car to disable it to prevent pursuit. The trio then drove the two lawmen into Oklahoma, handcuffed them together, and tied them to a tree with barbed wire.

Hollywood made Bonnie and Clyde into heroes or, at least, attractive villains. I saw the film in the late 1960s and was thrilled by a pair of gorgeous, beautifully dressed gangsters (Faye Dunaway and Warren Beatty) rebelling against society and the police—and, at a stretch, against the failures of capitalism—during the Great Depression. But, like most Westerns, the film perpetuated—in this case, perhaps, created—a myth. Glamorizing psychotic thieves and murderers can't be good—and the argument that one person's glamor is another's brutal realism doesn't wash with *Bonnie and Clyde* because the film blatantly eschews the reality.

I STOP TO look at three fine chestnut horses. They line up and stare at me amiably from the farther side of a ditch filled with rushes. I walk up a grassy track beside their field. They follow slowly, showing mild interest as if my arrival is better than nothing happening at all.

Across the track, to the north, a field is planted with line upon line of plants that stretch up and over a low slope. They are about three feet high with green spiky leaves and red stalks. I can see a few white, pink, and puce flowers, dotted around the field. Cotton! Unobtrusive, tolerably pretty, and probably the most important crop plant in U.S. history, it caused slavery to continue for years longer than it might have otherwise—and was at the root of the American Civil War, in which seven hundred thousand Americans died. Not long after that war Frederick A.P. Barnard, an eminent scientist, chancellor of the University of Mississippi (1856–61), and president of Columbia College, New York (1864–89), wrote:

> But for the increased and constantly increasing importance of cotton to the industry of the world, those of the American states which were fitted by soil and climate to the production of this plant would not have become rooted in the belief that compulsory labor was essential to their prosperity. And had it not been

> for this belief, and for the discordance of views which grew out of it between the cotton-producing states and the other members of the American Union upon matters, both political and moral, of vital importance, the terrible convulsion which has shaken the Union to its center could never have occurred.

Yet to its credit, cotton bolstered the fledgling U.S. economy around the turn of the nineteenth century—at a time when it needed to be bolstered—by responding to a surge in demand from Europe, especially from Britain where the Industrial Revolution was under way. When I learned about that revolution at school, it seemed as if it was caused by Kay's flying shuttle, Arkwright's water frame, Hargreaves's spinning jenny, Crompton's spinning mule, and Cartwright's power loom—all inventions that, along with the power provided by Watt's steam engine, brought the spinning of cotton and the weaving of cloth out of the cottages of English peasants and into factories—which were called cotton mills because, before the steam engine, they were powered, erratically, by mill wheels.

In 1787, the year when delegates from the first thirteen American states met in Philadelphia for the convention at which the U.S. Constitution was to be agreed and written, Britain imported no cotton from the U.S., getting it instead from other sources including its own colonies. Twenty years later, in 1807, it imported 60 percent of its cotton from the U.S. The factories, many of them in Lancashire, close to the port of Liverpool, didn't just want more cotton; they wanted better quality. Cotton from India, for example, produced 20 percent less yarn than American cotton, and was more difficult to spin. By 1800 America was able to supply what Britain wanted—in part owing to a man called Eli Whitney.

In 1792 Whitney graduated with a mediocre degree from Yale at the age of twenty-eight, the oldest in his class. Unable to get a job in his native Connecticut, he went south to work as a tutor on a cotton plantation in Georgia—and there he watched as slaves spent whole days using only their hands to separate one pound of cotton lint from its seed. Whitney, who liked to tinker with machinery, had soon invented the cotton gin, a simple gadget with which one slave could "clean" fifty pounds of cotton in a day, just by turning a handle. In 1794 he obtained a patent and began to manufacture gins in a factory in New Hampshire. Despite his patent, others copied his machine and some of them improved on it. In the end Whitney made little money, but his invention revolutionized cotton and changed history.

But cotton growing and picking remained extremely labor intensive; the plants needed frequent weeding throughout their six months of growth and every cotton boll had to be picked by hand. There were few white laborers in the U.S. in 1800—most white men outside the cities were proud to be independent farmers, some of them with very small farms. But there were plenty of slaves. In fact, some people thought there were too many. George Washington had four hundred, many of them inherited. Only one-third of them could work in his fields. In *Cotton and Race in the Making of America* Gene Dattel writes, "Like other slaveholders, Washington was trapped in an economic system. He wanted to dispose of his slaves but abhorred the act of selling them. He and other slaveholders could not find replacements for their slave labor, hence they did nothing."

The first slaves in what would become the U.S. were brought from Africa to Virginia in 1619. By 1780, 287,000 had been brought across the Atlantic—many of them by British slave traders. The children of slaves were born into slavery, so by 1790 there were seven hundred thousand slaves in the U.S. (out of a total population of 3.9 million)—who, had it not been for the sudden demand for cotton, might well have been freed in the early years of the nineteenth century. In most of the thirteen states that formed the fledgling U.S., slaves worked as house servants and on farms. Only in Virginia and Maryland did vast numbers labor on tobacco plantations, and in South Carolina on rice and indigo plantations.

In 1787 it was conceivable that the U.S. Constitution would mention slavery—and perhaps put in place a plan for its abolition. Several of the delegates in Philadelphia were in favor of abolition, even though many of them, such as the future presidents Washington, Jefferson, and Madison, owned slaves. At that time slavery entailed a moral conflict for many wealthy Americans. On the one hand, they owned slaves. On the other, they disapproved of slavery. Madison called slavery "a deep-rooted abuse," yet he inherited 108 slaves from his father and owned 130 at his death. Jefferson called slavery "an execrable commerce . . . this assemblage of horrors" and while drafting the Declaration of Independence in 1776 wrote the immortal words "All men are created equal," yet he inherited slaves from his father and father-in-law, and over his lifetime owned 650.

The founding fathers' hesitation seems to have had several sources. One was a fear of what would happen if slaves were suddenly freed. Jefferson feared a race war and believed that emancipation should happen slowly: that first, the conditions in which slaves lived and worked should be improved, and the transatlantic trade abolished. And he thought that freedom, when it came, should be combined with deportation, to Africa or the West Indies.

Another difficulty arose with the large slave owners, often called "the planter elite" and defined as those who owned more than twenty slaves—and used them to work their plantations. The abolitionists accepted that emancipation would happen only with their agreement—and that it wouldn't be forthcoming.

Third, the point of the convention in Philadelphia was to create a constitution that would unite the thirteen states of the new country and protect the freedoms gained by the War of Independence. That meant an effective government, legitimized by regular elections (many feared anarchy if the existing system, of one vote per state with unanimity required to make decisions, continued), a strong economy, and a federal tax system which would fund investment and an army. Those aims were more important than abolishing slavery. And they knew that some of the delegates from the southern states would walk away from the convention if abolition was on the agenda. And some from the north would walk too; Newport, Rhode Island—home to large numbers of Quakers, many of whom profited from the slave trade—was the principal port of entry for slaves from Africa.

So slavery was not mentioned in the U.S. Constitution. And abolitionists comforted themselves by reasoning that more and more Americans now saw it as an unhelpful embarrassment, that tobacco farming—the biggest user of slave labor—was in decline, and that therefore slavery would soon die a death.

Had it not been for the sudden boom in cotton, they might well have been right. Indeed, slavery was banned in the northern states by 1804, and an act banning the import of slaves was passed in 1807. But, of course, that didn't end the trade in slaves who were already there, or as yet unborn. In fact, the trade intensified as slaves from the north were sold to cotton planters in the south and in the new, cotton-planting territories—Alabama, Mississippi, Louisiana, Arkansas, and Texas—to which settlers rushed to set up new plantations. Only two of the original thirteen states—Georgia and South Carolina—had the weather for cotton.

The north-to-south trade increased the slaves' misery: husbands were separated from wives, children from parents and siblings, as many, not all, slave owners took the highest prices they could get while disregarding basic principles of humanity and morality.

After abolition, in 1865, many freed slaves—by then there were four and a half million—continued to work in the cotton fields as sharecroppers; there was little else for them to do. They were still poorly rewarded and treated badly, but not as badly as before, unless they happened to be assaulted or murdered by the Ku Klux Klan, which was founded on Christmas Eve 1865. And they were, in effect, subject to segregation—a system that became law in the southern states in 1896. Not until 1947, when cotton picking at last became widely mechanized, did their lives substantially change. Then, in the wake of World War II, during which Americans had grown used to migration, millions left the land and headed for the cities.

I looked at the cotton in front of me, and imagined it being harvested in a couple of months' time by a man—probably a white man—listening to music through headphones while driving something large and painted green.

41

HOT AND WILD

THE AIR IS HOT and sticky as I leave the Panhandle and enter the broad sweep of Texas that lies south of the bulk of Oklahoma and of the Red River which marks the border. Soon I reach Childress and find the old, red-brick downtown dying, turning into a place of broken glass and crumbling curbstones, where a torn sign in a darkened shop window whispers in vain: CLOSED Please Call Again. Yet, one block to the north—where 83 crosses 287, the east-west route linking Wichita Falls to Amarillo—an avenue of gaudy illuminated logos, set high on concrete sticks, lines a seething mile of filling stations, fast-food cafés, and motels.

I pull into a Shell station which has a Subway attached. I know now how to behave in a Subway; I know not to try anything new. I eat at a tiny table by the window with a view of cars and gas pumps, and watch people queue for sandwiches. A prime, wobbly fat, immensely unslim person, *almost* the largest man I've ever seen, is standing there, with a small, fattish blond woman; he is shaped like a bowling pin—tall with a little head, little legs, and a body that swells out and out and out, and down and in again in three dimensions.

I finish my sub, return to Prius, and sit behind the wheel studying the map. Bowling pin and wife emerge carrying a pile of sandwiches and soft drinks. They go to a large, black SUV and hand food and drink through the windows to a pair of children—and somehow bowling pin squeezes into the front seat behind the steering wheel. I notice that there is something dribbling onto the asphalt from the SUV's engine. Should I go over and tell bowling pin? Yes.

Do I? No.

Why not? I'm not sure. I've overcome much of my natural reserve and have spoken to quite a few large people. Perhaps it's some kind of inertia brought on by the environment.

I drive off toward the junction with 83, and find that I am craving a postprandial cup of coffee. Why didn't I buy one in Subway? I drive up the strip, make a U-turn, and drive back. I settle on a gas station that includes a café called Allsup's. Inside, I have to help myself to coffee, which isn't easy. First, I use the wrong kind of cardboard cup—one that is intended for cold drinks—and am told off by a passing jobsworth. Then I find that there is no milk that is not sweetened. If I want a white coffee, I have to choose from three flavors of Coffee-mate: hazelnut, vanilla caramel, and pumpkin spice. The jobsworth tells me that that's it; they don't have actual milk or unsweetened milk powder. I wonder whether to drink my coffee black—but then remember that I like to take risks now and again, so I go for vanilla caramel. I queue to pay and after a few minutes am confronted by a tall, fat man wearing a skin-tight, black top made from a material that looks like plastic.

"Hi," I say, and offer him a five-dollar bill.

He doesn't reply. Instead he points to a small printed notice: Credit Cards Only. If I want to pay cash, I have to queue at the other till.

I get out my credit card and he tells me to swipe it in a particular way—but I fail to understand.

"You do it. I'm too stupid." I hand him the card.

He swipes successfully, and I'm free to drive out of Childress slurping something that tastes like warm fudge ice cream.

SOUTH OF CHILDRESS is beautiful tree-filled countryside, a place of red earth and rivers. Jack Kerouac was here in 1950. Perhaps not curiously, he took a different view: "At Childress in the hot sun we turned directly south on a lesser road [83] and highballed across abysmal wastes to Paducah, Guthrie, and Abilene."

Unlike Kerouac I drive slowly, sniffing the air and stopping twice to photograph abandoned homes which stand alone, their timbers sprung, listing like shipwrecks beside empty seas. I haven't seen such picturesque dereliction since Manitoba.

In Paducah I come to an imperious building with the words "COTTLE COUNTY COURTHOUSE" etched tastefully below its roof. The architects and self-important locals who put up this affirmation of civilization were even more adventurous than their fellows up the road in Wheeler. It has many wings and an art deco symmetry and angularity, while also appearing Spanish—or, more precisely, Moorish. Central archways contain patterned openwork, intended to admit cooling air, of a type seen in Spain and in grand old mosques in cities like Rabat and Cairo; the long history of the Spanish in Texas must explain this.

I walk right round and find that front and back are identical; I can't tell which is which. Both Moorish arches are crowned with a pair of handsome figures carved in stone in a style that somehow, like the building, links ancient Egypt to the 1920s. Between these figures inscriptions are carved—different inscriptions. Walking round again, I notice something insignificant—when set against this splendid architecture—that marks what must be the front: a glass-housed, all-weather elevator for hoisting wheelchair users up the courthouse steps. It is the front, then, that carries these reassuring words: "TO NO ONE WILL WE DENY SELL OR DELAY JUSTICE." While at the back is a more sanitary message: "HE WHO COMES HERE MUST COME WITH CLEAN HANDS."

The courthouse fills the center of a square where I see no humans, save for two or three in passing cars. Around the sides of the square are shops, most of them derelict. A long three-story building is identifiable only by its name, COTTLE HOTEL, carved in stone between rows of broken windows; the boards that secure its ground floor have soaked up so much weather that their grain stands out in black and white, like giants' fingerprints. Across the street, stiff clumps of grass grow behind a chain-link fence in the forecourt of a defunct New and Used car lot. I seem to be looking at the remains of a small-town America that thrived fifty years ago—and was displayed to the world in movies. Somewhere on the edge of this once-attractive town will be predictable mega-outlets supplying predictable stuff more cheaply than these shops ever could. The only viable defense against the chains, for the time being anyway, seems to be the one played by the Husteads in Wall, South Dakota: take over the town yourself; or—to put it another way—if you can't beat 'em, join 'em.

I DRIVE ON slowly. A cooling breeze brings a scent of herbs through the open windows. Low-growing shrubs and yellow daisies line the road and, in a parking place, small lizards dart into cracks in the concrete and wait motionless and watchful.

Guthrie is small and, like Kerouac, I pass through it quickly. Then, for half an hour, there are no towns or villages, nor even a cow or a bull, just a few farm or ranch houses, in a long vista that flows between woods and copses and lone trees.

The road drops into a shallow, wooded valley. At the bottom a low, flat bridge crosses a river. A sign proclaims the Salt

Fork (another one) of the Brazos River. It looks wild, deserted, intriguing. I park at the top of the farther slope and walk back.

It's six o'clock and the day is still hot. As I walk, one or two cars pass. Then a white four-door pickup slows, and a man leans out and says, "Do you need a ride?"

I explain that I'm walking down to the bridge to take photos.

He smiles and says, "Oh, I understand." He makes a U-turn and drives back up the hill.

Only then do I realize that he has driven past me, turned, and come back to check whether I need help—and that, if I had, he might well have driven me in the direction I was walking, which was not the way he was going. I remember Shane in Canadian saying that Texans see themselves as different from other Americans; that they prize their individuality yet are proud to be friendly.

I stroll on down to the river. It's wide—perhaps two hundred yards across—and the water is swirling, roiling, a reddish-brown, somewhere between chocolate and chestnut, a blend of the colors of the surrounding earth. Narrow islands are covered in small trees, and low cliffs—layers of gray cracked rock that sprout with green—form the northern bank.

I walk back uphill. Trees, shrubs, prickly pear, scrubby grass are all around. It's a place for wild animals rather than cattle. And, back in Prius, a mile or two on, I come upon a coyote, trotting toward me at the side of the road.

BENEATH A BRIDGE over another fork of the Brazos River, the Double-Mountain Fork, the water is calm and approachable; a holiday village squats, shaded by tall trees, close to the grassy bank. A plaque, placed by the Texas Historical Commission, gives the history of a long-lost town called Rath City, and says much about the swift fate of the buffalo and of the Plains Indians, who depended on those herds that had been so huge:

In 1876 during an international demand for buffalo hides, Charles Rath (1836–1902) founded this town... He sold supplies and bought hides from the buffalo hunters. On one occasion in 1877 there were 1,100,000 hides at his trading post. The town... boasted a corral, hide yard, saloon, and restaurant. Skins stretched across poles sheltered the hunters. A tower beside the corral was used as a lookout to ward off Indian attacks. By 1879, the buffalo disappeared and the town vanished.

42

FEAR AND A HANDFUL OF PLUMS

I DROVE ON IN THE still, warm evening, passing through small, sleepy places such as the curiously named Radium, which seemed to be one house and a power station. In front of a wooden house with peeling white paint, not far from Abilene, a sign announced FARWOOD FOR SALE. On the edge of the city, 83—now four lanes, with a fat ribbon of grass in its middle—crossed Interstate 20, a major east-west route; motels and fast-food outlets were strung along it both ways, and I was reminded of Jamie Jensen's advice to travelers on 83: "You'll notice that most of the roadside services are found along the east-west crossroads, especially the major old transnational highways..., or today's interstate superslabs. North-south travelers have always been a rare species."

I turned into the forecourt of America's Best Value Inn. I had stayed at a good motel of that name in Garden City and assumed this would be similar.

The proprietor, an Indian from the subcontinent, was busy looking at the video he'd made the previous day of his small son's birthday party; he seemed very excited and proud of his film. He was a very hairy man, short, and with a manic look. He called his wife from the back and told her to check me in.

She leaned her head on her fist as she watched me fill in the usual form.

"Happy birthday for yesterday," I said to the little boy.

He squirmed, shrugged, locked his hands together, and smiled sideways at me.

His mother gave me the key to room 117, and I drove Prius fifty yards to park outside the door. I dumped my bag on the bed and looked quickly around. It seemed OK. The coffee jug wasn't very clean, but few motel rooms are perfect.

THE DAY DARKENS as I drive a couple of miles downtown in search of food and, maybe, a beer. In the "Historic Downtown" I cruise up and down parallel, dimly lit streets named Hickory, Cedar, Cypress, Pine, and Walnut. Everywhere is shut except a hotel, which seems dark and uninviting, and a coffee bar on Cypress Street called Monks.

From behind the counter in Monks, a young man says they have no food except muffins. He is apologetic, almost distressed, by this and says that my only option is a place called Sonic. He tells me where it is and says, "The food may not be that great, but it's kind of fun."

Sonic turns out to be a drive-in where colored lights flash while you sit in your car and are brought food and soft drinks by young women on roller skates. One of them glides over, and makes me aware that the menu is on the wall beside me; then she waits attentively while I read it and ask questions. There are numerous types of hamburger, some of which—like the *Super*SONIC Bacon Double Cheeseburger—I might enjoy, but somehow I don't fancy eating alone in the car; the other customers all seem to be young couples having fun. I thank the waitress, reverse out of my parking bay, and head back to Monks; a muffin or two will do.

The young man seems pleased to see me again. He apologizes about Sonic, and brings a warmed blueberry muffin and a peach smoothie to my table. Monks is a sweet place, dimly lit and scruffy, with mismatched furniture that looks as if someone picked up whatever was available at a Salvation Army shop on the day they happened to call in. Haunting, edgy, country music echoes softly as if the band were a long way away, at the back of a cave. There are about six other customers, all young. At the next table three young men—one black, one white, one, at a guess, Hispanic—discuss TV comedy. One doesn't like *Seinfeld*. Another likes *The Simpsons:* "They are *still* relevant." All three like *Futurama*.

I look at the walls, at small drawings, larger paintings, and photographs for sale, and at handbills advertising exhibitions, concerts, plays, events. Belatedly, it occurs to me that Monks is aimed primarily at students.

The young man appears at my side. "I know what it's like traveling and not being able to get stuff to eat," he says. He holds out an apple and a plastic bag filled with plums. These are his personal fruits, and he is asking if I would like them.

Naturally, I am deeply touched. There is something almost biblical about this—which is ironic because later I discover that this man, like so many good people, is an atheist. I tell him that I have an apple in the car (which I do), but I would love to eat some of his plums if he can spare them.

He has plenty more at home, he says. He puts the bag on the table and returns, carrying the apple, to his counter where I see him cleaning and washing up.

I read yet another story in Dillard's newspaper and eat plums—and gradually the other customers leave. I offer to leave too, but the young man is in no hurry. He seems to want to talk, to know where I'm from, what I'm doing.

"Wow! Brownsville! That's still a long way," he says.

Is it? It doesn't feel that far to me—now that I'm almost halfway down Texas.

He tells me a horror story. A friend of his was dragged out of his car and mugged in Brownsville. I must be careful. There is a war going on down there—between drug cartels.

I tell him I like the music. He smiles. He likes it too. "It's a band called Cotton Jones. Well... actually, not a band, two people—mostly."

He has wavy dark hair and a wide face. His name is Grant Perkins. He comes from Lubbock, a city about 150 miles to the northwest, and he's here because he's taking a master's degree in English literature. Abilene has three universities, he says, even though it's a small city. He likes its smallness. He apologizes for its being boring, for everything being shut. "It's famous for being boring. There are T-shirts that celebrate that." He smiles. "And it's very conservative; it has more churches than any other city in Texas." He smiles again and shrugs. "But not that many people go to them." And that's when he tells me he's an atheist.

The music has stopped. He goes away to put on another CD, comes back, and says, "You'll like this. It's..." I don't catch the name and ask him to spell it.

And he does, before saying it again, "Micah P. Hinson."

He says that Texas gets more liberal as you go south, and this is partly the influence of Hispanics, who grow in number the farther south you go and who tend to depend more on the state—though he doesn't think people's politics always match their liberal, or conservative, attitudes. "Liberal can mean culturally liberal," he says. "And then people don't necessarily vote the way they think, because the individual doesn't fit their idea of someone who can represent them."

By now Grant has sat down at the end of the table.

I ask him that question about Indians and blacks that came to me in the graveyard at Oberlin: If white people are sympathetic to the descendants of the Indians whom they once oppressed, why are they—many of them—not sympathetic to black people or, for that matter, Hispanics?

Grant replies quickly, almost without thinking. “Because there are so few Indians. They are no threat. On the other hand, blacks and Hispanics are competition for whites.”

“Yes,” I say. “Of course.”

He picks up one of his own plums, bites into it and swallows. “Racism is a big thing in the United States, still”—he takes another bite—“though people, politicians, don’t tend to talk about it.”

He finishes his plum, wraps the stone in a paper napkin, and walks away holding it. In the silence I hear the music of Micah P. Hinson, and I think about what Grant Perkins said about Indians and blacks, and how obvious it is now that he’s said it.

Soon afterward we shake hands and, as I leave, he calls out, “Good luck in Brownsville.”

BACK IN MY room at America’s Best Value Inn, I find that the TV remote doesn’t work, so I sit in a chair six inches from the screen, squinting and pressing buttons. Then I hear the constant plish of running water and realize that the loo, flushed a few minutes before, will replenish itself forever, unless I do something. I remove toilet rolls from the top of the cistern (there is no roll holder), take off the cistern’s lid, fiddle with the rusty rods and ball inside, and manage to fix it. Then I notice that the phone, which is in a corner on top of the microwave, is dirty and dusty. I pick it up; there is no tone. I check that it’s plugged in, which involves moving a heavy fridge. There is still no tone. It is now 1 AM. Shall I ask for the phone to be fixed? My wife just might want to ring me in the morning; I emailed earlier to tell her where I was.

I find the hairy proprietor in reception, tell him about the phone, and mention the TV remote and the unclean coffee jug.

He says that thunder and lightning last week upset his telephones, and then his insurance company was slow to take action because of July 4. "I offer you two solutions. One: You can make international calls on my phone free. Two: I give you another room where the phone works."

Solution two suits me better and, after much thought, he gives me the key to room 119—and says that, although it has a bigger bed, he won't charge me extra.

After checking that the phone works, I move into my new room. And then I notice that, despite being a more expensive room, it has no fridge, unlike 117 where I was cooling my water, orange juice, and an apple. Nor does 119 have any clothes hanging facilities, not even a rail. The desk chair is an old office chair with a filthy, stained nylon cover. Later I find that the loo has the same unceasing flush problem. Again I remove the cistern lid—this time I somehow drop a new loo roll into the loo (no loo-roll holder again)—and fix it, almost.

I'm a little irritated. It's nearly 2 AM. Stupidly, I put this hotel into Google on my laptop, wondering idly if I can complain to the parent of this franchise. There are fourteen reviews. Three are strangely positive—a wonderful hotel, just what we wanted, great value. Eleven vary from disgruntled to furious. One guest had three people entering his room early in the morning—even though he'd double-locked it. Another had bites and feared bedbugs. Another was unable to have a shower until the proprietor had tightened the tap with a screwdriver. And another didn't eat breakfast for fear the cereal had been there too long.

I wedge the stained chair under the door handle, lie down, and try not to think about bedbugs or intruders.

TRAFFIC ON THE interstate wakes me at seven fifteen in America's worst value inn. I have had just four hours' sleep, yet all seems somehow better; there is nothing to be afraid of.

And all really *is* well, except that the shower runs at one temperature only: too hot—but just bearable if you stick one limb in at a time and keep the curtain open to allow a cool breeze. And I test the cereal at breakfast; it's crisp enough.

43

COW TOWNS AND CATTLE TRAILS

In downtown Abilene I walked the streets that had been so dark and empty the night before. There still weren't many people, but in daylight the streets seemed wider and there was plenty of architecture to gaze at—and very little of it bland, postmodern, or even postwar. Much of the district seemed to have been built in the 1920s and '30s. Art deco apartment blocks and hotels scraped the sky, but weren't high enough to obscure it; and, in the beautiful tile and mahogany entrance to the Paramount Movie Theatre, a poster—with a black-and-white photo of a young, red-lipped, sour-faced Bette Davis—advertised *All About Eve*.

I hadn't known what to expect from Abilene, but I hadn't imagined tasteful architecture or a reputation for causing boredom. I knew the city's name from somewhere within the welter of Wild West entertainment I'd enjoyed as a child, and I associated it with cowboys and cattle trails. It had featured in the enactments of life as a cowboy that I played out with my school friend Quentin. I remembered standing in a corridor at school, squinting, puckering my lips, and rasping in my meanest cowpoke drawl, "Ah gotta ride out, pardner, gotta get t'Abilene,

gonna meet the purdiest girl yer ever seen." To which Quentin might reply, "Yep. Ah'm goin' t'Abilene mahself, as ut happens. Gotta stash some cash. Guess ah'll jest ride along with yer."
300 Then, cheeks sucked in and trying not to giggle, we would mime riding slowly—down the corridor, over the parquet, a hand on the reins, bodies rocking forward and back, feet lifting rhythmically—into a sunset, beyond which was Abilene.

We didn't know then that there are two Abilenes: Abilene, Kansas, and Abilene, Texas. At different times both were pivotal to the shipping of cattle from Texas to the rest of the U.S.—a business that began to take off in 1866, when herds of Texas longhorns were first driven north to a railhead at Baxter Spring in southeastern Kansas, whence they were conveyed to markets in the east. Very soon, though, farmers in eastern Kansas were objecting that Texas longhorns carried a tick that spread fever to other breeds, and persuaded the Kansas legislature to establish a quarantine line to protect the more settled eastern side of the state.

In the same year, a fur trader called Jesse Chisholm drove a wagonload of buffalo hides north from Texas to his trading post in Abilene, Kansas—and thereby blazed the Chisholm Trail (another name that arouses a frisson of nostalgia in us who grew up steeped in the myths of the Wild West). Abilene, Kansas, was on the railroad and was west of the quarantine line. The next year, 1867, a man from Chicago named McCoy, realizing that land around there had not been settled by homesteading farmers and would provide grazing for cattle, set up stockyards to attract the Texas cattlemen. Within months McCoy's stockyards were the biggest west of Kansas City, and Abilene had become the first "cow town," packed with saloons, gamblers, pimps, whores—and cowboys. And soon gunslingers and lawmen, including Wild Bill Hickok and John Wesley Hardin, arrived and added to the fun.

Some herds were driven a thousand miles and cowboys often spent months on the Chisholm Trail. They were forbidden to drink alcohol and were paid a dollar a day. An average herd, around three thousand head of cattle, was controlled by ten or twelve cowboys, each of whom needed three horses. The spare horses, known as the remuda, were looked after by a "wrangler," who was usually the youngest member of the team, a junior cowboy. Many cowboys were young—some as young as thirteen. The cook, who drove the chuck wagon, was likely to be an older, respected man who was also skilled at first aid; and the outfit was led by an experienced trail boss. Before hitting the trail, the crew spent days rounding up cattle from the open range and branding them. The herd then traveled about fifteen miles a day, with breaks for grazing to keep the cattle's weight up, and the cowboys worked shifts, day and night.

One-quarter of Texan cowboys, I'd learned in Dodge City, were African Americans—former slaves, freed during the civil war, who found less discrimination in Texas than farther east. And many Mexican vaqueros worked in Texas. Not only did they teach Texans how to ride horses and herd cattle, but their clothing—broad-brimmed hat, boots with pointed toes and heels, tight trousers with a smooth inside seam, bandannas, and shirts with padded shoulders—set the style that is still followed today.

Over five years, forty thousand freight cars left Abilene, Kansas, carrying 1.5 million animals to meat-processing plants in Chicago and Kansas City. However, by the end of 1871 the nearby prairie had been settled, and, under pressure from the new arrivals, the state legislature moved the quarantine line still farther west. And soon a new trail, the Great Western Cattle Trail, branched away from the Chisholm Trail to lead cattle and cowboys to Dodge City. As I walked about in the heat of Abilene, Texas, I didn't know that later that day I would find myself at a point where the Great Western Cattle Trail crosses 83.

Today Abilene, Kansas, is a small town with a population of sixty-eight hundred.

Abilene, Texas, on the other hand, has a population of 117,000. It was founded in 1881 by a group of canny ranchers and businessmen led by the appropriately named Claiborne W. Merchant. The group persuaded H.C. Whithers, who was "track and town site locator" for the Texas and Pacific Railway, to build the new railroad across their land instead of taking it to the county town of Buffalo Gap, twelve miles to the south. And Mr. Whithers was pushed into setting up a new town, from which cattle would be shipped. The railroad promoted the town as "the Future Great City of West Texas" and followed Claiborne Merchant's clever marketing idea of naming it after Abilene, Kansas—trading on the name of its celebrated forebear which was by then defunct as a cattle town.

The new Abilene grew rapidly and has been well managed ever since. It now brims, not just with churches, but with industries and military bases; it has the highest-ranked public educational system in Texas. Is it boring? Compared with Abilene, Kansas, between 1867 and 1871, yes. However, I suspect that the "Keep Abilene Boring" T-shirts, which are sold at Monk's Coffee House, are worn with a measure of irony. They come out of a line of Texas T-shirt slogans: "Keep Waco Wacko," "Keep Austin Weird."

WITH THE AIR conditioning turned to high, I try to drive south out of Abilene. I take a wrong turn and get lost in streets of smart modern homes with high garden walls draped with the puce and mauve of hibiscus and bougainvillea. For a little while, it is like driving in the hills above Nice in the south of France.

South from Abilene, 83 is a busy, four-lane dual carriageway. And roadside shields show 84 as well as 83! What! I stop to consult the road atlas. There they are: 83 and 84 together.

84 begins at the Atlantic coast and crosses four states before entering Texas; to the west it crosses New Mexico and travels northwest through Santa Fe into Colorado. 84, like 83, is a U.S. route and part of the highway program planned in 1926. It piggybacks on 83 for fourteen miles before forking off to the left.

And instantly 83 becomes the familiar well-worn, two-lane highway that I love. From then on, the day—though it is already past four—gets better and better. I come off a slow bend onto a long, straight, almost flat stretch of road—and it is as if I can see infinity. Rows of lamb's-tail clouds straddle the road and I am driving under them as if in a tunnel—but the sun still shines and the sky between the clouds is blue. Green grass and small trees fill the plain. An endless line of T-shaped telegraph poles roll steadily by, and there is almost no traffic. It is the kind of time, the kind of place, where, if someone else were driving, I'd stick my feet out of the window and waggle my toes.

As it is, I put on JJ Cale's album *Roll On* and, nodding in rhythm, drive slowly to a pretty town called Ballinger. There I sit on a bench and eat a late lunch in a small quadrangle shaded by tall trees—at one end, an unpretentious bandstand; in the middle, rocks piled haphazardly in a low, bubbling fountain. I walk around the corner to Main Street, where the buildings are old, brick, and cared for. It is twenty-past five. People are shopping in a baker, a deli, a butcher—while upstairs windows are shuttered against the sun. If there is a Walmart anywhere near, perhaps it is losing the battle. In the square around the courthouse the grass has been mown and rolled, and a life-size sculpture of a cowboy standing by his horse stands high against the sky. The parents of a young man who died when his horse fell as he rounded up cattle put up the monument in 1919 "as a tribute to their son and all Texas cowboys."

I drive out of Ballinger on the wrong road, realize my mistake after two or three miles, turn off, and make a three-point turn. A man comes by on a tractor, waves, and calls out, "Howdy! You ain't the first."

304 THE EARTH SEEMS to be drying in the heat: parched grass supports a few sparse bushes and small trees. Then 83 begins to mosey over creeks, whose names—Pecan Creek, Spring Creek, Fuzzy Creek—appear on signs beside the road, and the green returns. I pass a county marker and know now, without thinking, that it will mean a change of road surface: from rough to smooth, loud to quiet—or vice versa. This one tells me that I shall soon be able to hear JJ Cale more easily.

I come to a town called Paint Rock where, Jamie Jensen says, more than fifteen hundred colored images adorn limestone cliffs on the north bank of the Concho River; some are more than one thousand years old and were made by Kiowa and Apache Indians; others were drawn by Comanches in the nineteenth century. Jensen says the cliffs are on private land owned by a woman who offers guided tours at a price. I stop by the river and get a glimpse of cliffs a few hundred yards away, screened by trees. But I can see no paintings, and begin to feel a little resentful of the woman who charges people just to look at pictures that were painted outdoors for all to see; after all, *she* didn't paint them. A side road, blocked by a padlocked five-barred gate, leads in that direction. I think about climbing the gate and walking, and quickly reject the idea: I might have to walk miles and, though it's nearly seven o'clock, it's still hot—ninety-one degrees, according to Prius. Besides there might be trouble if someone sees me.

The day begins to cool. The road curves around and over hills. Again the land seems parched, and again I want to stick my feet out of the window but, instead, put on some music: this time, Jim Hall's *Concierto*. Soon that great guitarist is off into a thrilling, twenty-minute version of Rodrigo's *Concierto de Aranjuez*.

I pull in to read a notice at the side of the road. It stands near a thicket of prickly pear, and is printed on a sheet of metal fixed to a slab of concrete about the size of a tombstone.

GREAT WESTERN TRAIL

Some seven million head of cattle and horses went up the Great Western Trail from 1871 to 1890 from Mexico through nine U.S. states into Canada with the major years being 1874 to 1886. This trail lasted more years, carried more cattle, and was longer than any other cattle trail originating in Texas... Longhorns... were herded north to Oklahoma, Kansas, Nebraska, South Dakota, North Dakota, Colorado, Wyoming, Montana, and on into Canada...

At the major railheads in Dodge City, Kansas, and Ogallala, Nebraska, buyers bought cattle for reservations, for eastern markets, or to establish ranches in the northern U.S. states, Saskatchewan, and Alberta, Canada...

Herds had been forced west by homesteaders, tick fever, and Kansas laws closing the Chisholm Trail...

Although the Western Trail lasted a brief nineteen years, it lived on as the legend and lore of the cowboy grew as tales of cow towns and gunmen and drovers and stampedes filled books, movies, and the imagination of the national and international community fascinated by a time unique to history, the cattle trail days.

The dates fit with the decline of Abilene, Kansas, and the rise of Abilene, Texas. And there, on this dusty roadside, is mention of a community to which I have belonged since I was a child.

A mile or two on, a vast sweep of golden grass ripples in the breeze. Seed heads nod and twinkle in the late sunlight. Low trees throw long shadows, and the plain seems like something out of Africa.

FROM THE TOP of a steep hill, I look down and see 83 crossing a narrow river shaded by spreading trees, then passing through a small town and climbing the other side of the valley. The town is Menard and the river the San Saba (rhymes with Ban Abba). Beside me are some low buildings and a sign: Motel 83. It looks fine but nothing special. Then I read, "American Owned and Operated." I think about it: surely this is a sly dig at the many motels run by Asians.

I hope—indeed, it seems likely that—there will be another motel in town that is free of prejudice. I don't want to stay in what Bill Maher would call "Whiteyville."

Sure enough, at the bottom of the hill the Budget Motel is run by a young Asian Indian couple. For dinner they recommend a restaurant with the strange name of Side Oats. The man comes out of his office, leads me to the edge of 83, and points. Side Oats is about two hundred yards away, a single-story building on the other side of the road.

Square dark-wood tables are arranged at a forty-five-degree angle to the walls, making—to my way of seeing—rows of diamonds. There are perhaps thirty tables, about ten of them occupied by people of all ages—which, for half-past eight on a Tuesday in a small town in Texas (pop 1,653), seems pretty good. And it *is* good. The waitress, a blond woman in her thirties—a badge says her name is Donna—takes an interest in my being English and in why I am there, but is too busy and polite to be intrusive. The food—fried chicken with mashed potatoes, vegetables, coleslaw, and a scone and butter—is some of the best of the trip. Side Oats doesn't serve alcohol, but has no objection to it. You just have to bring it yourself; Donna points to a supermarket across the road—where the beer comes in four-packs.

I've finished eating and am sipping a second beer when another waitress, a tall black woman, comes over. She's picked up that I am English, and wants to know if I have a connection with two Englishmen who came through Menard in 1982. They took photographs of her granddaughter—for a book, they said—and promised to send her copies of the photos and the book. But they failed to do so.

The bastards! By now the child will be over thirty! I apologize for their behavior, for their—to adapt W.B. Yeats—treading on people's dreams, and tell the woman that not all English people break their promises. (If, by some chance, those men are reading this, will they please get in touch with me via this book's publisher, or with the child's grandmother who works at Side Oats?)

THE PLACE IS emptying. As I pay the bill, I ask Donna about the restaurant and how it comes to be there. She says it was founded by a woman called Carol Taylor about three years before. She takes me across the room to show me two framed newspaper cuttings, and turns on a light so that I can read them. They are from Texas papers and full of praise for Side Oats and its founder, who started it, they say, because she wanted somewhere to meet her friends.

Back at my table, I thank Donna.

"You're welcome. Carol's over there, if you'd like to meet her." She points to a round-faced woman who is sitting behind a counter with a teenage boy who looks as if he might be Mexican. "She'll be interested that you're writing a book."

I go over, feeling a little presumptuous: do I have the right to interrupt them just because I come from England and am writing a book? I introduce myself and compliment Carol Taylor on the restaurant and the food.

She smiles and thanks me; she is small with a high forehead and reddish-brown hair pushed behind her ears, and is perhaps in her late fifties. "But credit for the food goes to the chef," she says. "He's called Michael. And this"—she gestures to the boy—"is another Michael. I'm helping him with his math." Michael looks up, waggles a pencil, and looks back down at his exercise book.

Carol and I talk for a few minutes. She asks questions about England and Route 83.

"Every year at Side Oats," she says, "we have a library festival; writers come and launch their books. You should come next year, or whenever your book is ready."

"I'd love to do that," I say.

Then she says that she lives on a ranch—and would I be interested in seeing it the next morning?

"Wow! Yes. That sounds great. I've never been on a ranch."

"Come for coffee, say about nine. I got a Gator, a little tractor-type thing. We can drive around. It's a beautiful place—if I say so myself." She takes a ballpoint and draws a map.

OUTSIDE THE AIR is still warm. I walk back to the motel carrying two cans of beer in a brown paper bag. On the way I pass a rattlesnake, squashed flat, like cardboard in the road.

KIND RANCHER

EVERY DAY NOW THE sun shines and the sky is blue—and today there are white clouds that might have been painted by a child, or by René Magritte.

The SSRR, Carol's ranch, is just twelve miles west of Menard on the San Saba; yet I arrive late, having got lost, despite Carol's map. While I was unsure where I was, I came to the entrance to another ranch. The Stars and Stripes and the Lone Star flag of Texas drooped in the hot, still air from flagpoles at either side of a metal gate which was padlocked with a heavy chain. A notice, in red capitals on a white ground, read:

NO TRESPASSING
VIOLATORS
WILL BE SHOT
SURVIVORS
WILL BE SHOT
AGAIN

Adrenalin surged through me and I shivered despite the heat. I got back into Prius quickly and drove away. After half a mile or so, I began to wonder if those words might be a joke. I couldn't be sure; everyone knows that there are some crazy people in the U.S.—especially in the remoter parts.

Carol doesn't mind that I'm late. "What's twenty minutes on a morning like this?" She has an open face and smiley eyes.

The ranch house is beautiful: low, light, airy, with stone floors, mosaics, sculpture, paintings, candles—too much for me to take in. And there are photographs. In one of them a handsome man smiles into the camera. "That's Jamie, my husband," Carol says. "He died June 27 last year—in an accident. We just had the anniversary."

I say that I'm sorry. Carol murmurs something, but she's walking away into the kitchen. I think about it: this fit-looking man died just a year and ten days ago. I go into the cool, white kitchen where she is making coffee, and she asks about the motel I stayed at. "It's owned by Indians, right?"

"Yes. Indian Indian. How do you say that? Not Native Americans."

"India Indians," she says. "You know, the hotel up at the top advertises 'American run.' So a friend of mine: she thought they maybe didn't realize how offensive that could be. She went in there to tell them and they said, 'No. That's what we wanted to say!'"

"I saw that sign, and decided not to go there."

"Yes. Very prejudiced."

We sit with the coffee on a terrace high above the San Saba River, and I can see for miles: dense treetops and dry golden grass. The river is still, a murky, but very pleasing, green toward its farther bank—within it are bright reflections of shrubs and small trees; on this side the water is blue-gray, a washed-out copy of the sky.

"It's wonderful, isn't it?" I say.

"It's made a change in *my* life," Carol says. "I came from Minnesota where the woods are comfortable and cozy and you snuggle in during the winter. And then, when I got down here, it's all taking a deep breath and opening up."

She tells me about a book she loves and thinks I would like, *Comanche Dawn* by Mike Blakely. "It's about the Comanches' trip down from up north when they got the horse. They came all the way south and then they were the Apaches' main foe here. The land we look at when we're on the peak out there"—she turns and points west along the river—"is where they roamed around. It's a huge expanse, and I picture the Indians on their horses there." She drops her arm and looks back at me. "There's a place up there where I know they sat and made smoke signals."

"Really! I'd love to see... Is that far away?"

"No, no. We'll drive up there in the Gator. And I can just *feel* the Indians walking around there."

I'm sitting across a table from Carol and facing the way that she pointed. I lean back and look up at the sky. A hummingbird hovers by a honey-feeder hanging from the ceiling of Carol's veranda—and is joined by another. I'm amazed by what she said—and at my luck in being invited to this place.

Carol is telling me about historians and archeologists. There have been digs on her land and plenty of evidence of Indians. Then she says, "What I love about it is that it's *so* restful and undistracting. And yet the life here is intensely current and we're connected with all the greater issues of the world." She pauses, then goes on, "When we bought this place we knew it was kind of a gift to us that we were able to. And we decided it wasn't just for us. I'd sit out here on the porch and think, it can't be just for me; it's too beautiful. So we do what we can to share and—"

A black dog with a white nose and chest, a medium-sized mongrel, appears and puts his head on my knee.

"Hey, Fella! You are such a pest!"

"Oh, I don't mind." I pat his head. He sniffs around and trots back into the house.

She turns sideways in her chair, and looks out across the river. "They always say that Menard is a city that sits facing west, while Mason, which is thirty miles east of here, faces east. So Mason faces Austin and the more sophisticated life of east Texas, and Menard faces the oil wells and the big open country. Jamie went hunting for mule deer on a ranch that had thirty thousand acres. He gravitated toward that side."

I discover that Carol and Jamie moved here from Minnesota about fifteen years ago, and I ask if she now feels a loyalty to Texas.

"Oh, I'm *glad* to be a Texan. I have a bumper sticker that says, 'I wasn't born here, but I got here as soon as I could.'" And she tells me about her uncle and aunt who raised apples in Minnesota and oranges and grapefruit in McAllen, in the very south of Texas, and how she visited them as a child. And how she grew up in the early years of television and watched Tex Ritter and Roy Rogers.

I interrupt to call out, "Me too!"

"Did you? And I just loved them," she says. "So—when I met my husband—he had a southern accent and he was a cowboy. He was *really* a cowboy; he wasn't an *east* Texan. He was a lawyer, but he was a cowboy and I think that's one reason I fell in love with him."

"So you met him up north?"

"Uh-huh. He went to law school and then he thought he had a job down here, but it didn't happen. Never dreamed of going to Minnesota. Texans don't; they don't know where Minnesota is. They know it's above the Mason–Dixon line. And that's about it."

Jamie, I learn, worked for a publisher of law books in Minnesota. He and Carol lived in a suburb of St. Paul, Minneapolis (the twin cities whose baseball team, the Twins, Joe and Eli in Minot support). Jamie worked for the publisher for thirty-four years, and then the company was bought. Jamie and Carol had stock, sold their holding, and came down to Texas to buy a ranch—because Texas was Jamie's home and ranching was what he had always wanted to do.

"My folks were pioneers up there in St. Paul, Minneapolis, homesteaders," Carol says. "Great-grandfather settled there along the Mississippi. My dad cut ice from the river as part of his job in refrigeration, and then he had a truck farm and raised vegetables. And my uncle was governor of Minnesota for a little while." The dog that she called Fella came back. Carol reached a hand down to him, and went on. "We have strong ties to Minnesota. But it's funny, Minnesota doesn't elicit the same kind of loyalty that Texas does. I'm not a Southerner, and there is a core to Southerners that my husband had that I never could understand. When I watch *Gone with the Wind,* I see it in the Southerners. It's a *blind* loyalty that prevents them analyzing, or looking objectively at, other factors. It's the conservatism of the South too. I don't get that, but I sure do love Texas. I love the variety and the openness, and how the people are so hospitable."

I mutter my agreement—and Carol goes on, "I like the boundary they set. They're very helpful, but not invasive. Once you get to West Texas, they're very individualistic. They don't mess in anybody else's life. And, you know, there are people who have thought Menard and this part of Texas got too crowded and moved on to Iraan [she pronounces it Ira Ann] and some of those other West Texas towns."

"People could think this is crowded? I come from London... It's a funny idea that this is crowded!"

"Yeah, it is funny. But they go: 'Ooh, traffic! Too many people! Someone telling me what I should do! I'm not sticking around here—I'm moving on!'"

"I sympathize with that bit of it: people telling you what to do," I say. "But—I passed that sign on the road that says something like, 'If you come in here you will be shot.' Is that serious?"

Carol laughs—and I laugh. "No, that's a joke! But..." She thinks about it. "They could do that... They feel pretty much that way, and if they catch you on their property, they can shoot you—almost. That's *almost* OK around here." She turns away, hand to her mouth, thinking. "In Menard there have been stories of people who were shot because"—she drops her voice and then speaks quickly—"they deserved being shot."

I laugh at this, perhaps nervously, and say, "What? People didn't like them?"

"Interesting," Carol says, and I realize that this isn't funny. "A man who's killed a man who abused his sister in a marriage relationship, because he deserved being shot. And nothing done. Actually I know two cases like that—within the last ten years."

"What, and the police just don't do anything?"

"No. It just settles out. They believe things are simple and—if you need to talk too much about the differences in your opinions, then there's something wrong. Things should be easily settled. Kinda like with a gun—or not!"

"Really? Gosh!" I say, sounding more and more like an Englishman created by P.G. Wodehouse.

"That is part of the culture of West Texas. I always loved diversity—cultural differences—and Jamie was the most diverse person that my mother would let me date. The culture of Texas was *so different*. And it's just so clarifying to have huge differences that we need to talk about, so we need to address where we come from. It makes it a little harder on kids, but it does make a marriage awfully interesting."

Carol used "we" with both past and present tenses. This made sense to me. She and Jamie had had a long life together and for many years that life had been here, on this ranch which to me—and clearly to her—was a magical place. She was continuing with that life, in which he belonged absolutely.

She suggests we go for a ride in the Gator. We stand up, and she points to a circle of stones close to her veranda, above the slope down to the river. "You know that's my cathedral right there. This is the place we have Easter sunrise service, and this is the place where the historians said probably the Spanish and the Indians celebrated their first Easter—right along here someplace, very close. And I decided I didn't need to put a dome on my cathedral because, when you get out there it's—"

She paused, and I finished her sentence. "It's the sky."

"Yeah, the dome is already created."

We go through the house to the front and walk to a small stone building which Carol calls The Little House. I stare out at long contemplative vistas of cliff, river, and the plain that sweeps away into the west as well as to the north. I find myself saying, "I'm having difficulty not just going—'*Fantastic*.'" And then, "Have you ever been to Africa?"

"We went to Tanzania."

"This reminds me a bit of Kenya and Tanzania. I've only been there once," I add quickly—perhaps to let her know that I'm not some swanky person who spends his life traveling.

She smiles. "We sat in—I forget where we were: somewhere in Tanzania—but we sat there and it looked like Texas . . . until a giraffe walked by."

She points west along the ridge. "There's a scissor-tail that comes there, a little roadrunner that comes by, and good fishing." She turns and shades her eyes against the sun.

We walk back toward the ranch house, to the Gator. I ask about oil, whether there is drilling around Menard, and she says that they were approached by an oil company. "But Jamie never wanted to do that. There are oil people in town exploring and setting up new wells. If you go farther west, just here, along Route 190, you'll see that it changes the look of the things."

I tell her I've seen it farther north in Texas—and in North Dakota; I describe the nodding donkeys that I saw up there.

"Those are pumpjacks," she says with a smile. Then she begins to tell a story. "I like stories and I usually add a twist to them after I hear them." She's still smiling. "In Menard here, when we had oil a few years ago, two ranchers were exploring for oil and they went to their bankers: two different banks. One of the ranchers said, 'We just need a few more days. We're close.' The banker said, 'No.' He closed him out. Oil was found on that land. A week later the guy came back and shot the banker.

"The other one: the guy came in; the banker said, 'OK'; and a week later they discovered oil. Now, that rancher is always held to be Jimmy Powell, who is now one of the top ten landowners in the United States, owns all this land up near Fort McKavett and all over: huge, huge land holdings and he's huge in raising cattle. Hereford cattle are his. He raises the bulls and every year in October, he has a bull sale out there that is broadcast nationwide across the west and in Canada, where people buy his bulls."

"They buy them on television?"

"Yep. And on the internet. We cater that. That's just a *wonderful* event in October."

For a moment I'd forgotten that Carol owns and runs a restaurant as well as this ranch. "So he got going because the bank lent—"

"Yes. That's the connection I've made."

"And the other banker got shot?"

Carol nods—and we both have a good laugh at the fate of the mean, foolish banker.

She tells me that the ranch is eight hundred acres, and I ask whether there are cattle somewhere.

"We don't have cattle. We have goats. Since Jamie died—he had six hundred goats, six to eight hundred, and it wasn't too tough—we're going to sell off our goats, and we're going to lease our land that's good for cattle and goats to someone else.

And then they'll take care of that and I won't have to."

We get to the Gator, a little, open, green truck with yellow seats that, from the front, looks like a cartoon alligator. Another dog is there with Fella, and they are both coming with us.

As I get in, Carol calls from the driver's side. "Those tires look blown up over there, don't they?"

"Yes," I say. "I think so. They're not squishing out."

The sun beats down as we drive through scrubby grass and between trees. The Gator's engine chugs slowly like a Harley Davidson, while roaring like a lawn mower. We pass a grizzled-looking man sitting on a small tractor; he's wearing a checked shirt, jeans, and a straw cowboy hat. He waves.

"Eddie's our hand," Carol says. "And he walked all the way here from Mexico—two hundred miles—when he was twelve years old. He worked on ranches and then he walked back to Mexico, and then he walked back here again. Got his wife here. So he's been here a long time. Never worked for more than eight dollars an hour. His wife saved money to buy a house out of that and raise five kids."

"Wow!" I say. "So they live close by?"

"They live in town."

She tells me that the ranch is currently infested with grasshoppers, which reminds us both of the Oklahoma dust bowl, John Steinbeck, and *The Grapes of Wrath*.

"When we were looking for ranches," Carol says, "Jamie wanted a ranch that he could *work on*. That means removing cedars and prickly pear and pruning to increase the pasture. The ranch was overgrazed when we got it. Jamie had a five-year plan and he did that. He had a chance to play with all that equipment and he turned it to pasture that was good for grazing again." Three young deer leap across in front of us and skip away into the trees, hind legs kicking. "Aren't they gorgeous? When they run like that it makes your heart jump," Carol says.

We have been driving in a semicircle and now we come back to the cliff above the river, some way west of the ranch house. We begin to climb and the engine shrieks with the strain. And then we stop, and walk to the edge of the cliff. A little way below, a bench stands on a flat rock that juts out high above the river. And once again, there is nothing to see but sky, the winding river, and miles of plain covered with grass and trees.

"Gosh! This is like all the Westerns come true," I say. "All those movies I've watched!"

"Oh yes," Carol says, "that's what I remembered, all my old Western movies."

"Gosh!" I'm muttering to myself. "Happiness!" And maybe I'm a little crazy with the excitement of childhood imaginings suddenly made real.

For a few moments we sit in silence, just looking out. Then Carol points to a clearing beside the river. "Now that's where they did their archeological dig. There's a big midden—everything that was left when the Indians moved on. They used detectors, radio—all the latest archeological tools." She held her hands out, flat above the rock where we sat. "This is where you can picture the Indians really having their eyes open for people approaching."

"Right here, where we're sitting?"

"Yeah. And there's a place up there too." She pointed higher up the cliff and a little to the west. "I'm sure that was part of where they sat and watched all this."

"Would there have been buffalo here then?"

"Yes. There would."

"Buffalo came where there were trees as well as grass?"

"Yes. I think the buffalo were a little farther north, but they would trade their buffalo here. Buffalo is what they lived on."

A huge bird is soaring high above us. "Is that an eagle? Do you have eagles?"

“We do have eagles, though most of those probably aren’t eagles, but we have had golden eagles along the river. We have some large owls and some turkey vultures.”

“Can people cut trees down, as long as it’s their land?”

“Yes. Jamie did that. See—that’s the nice thing about it. It’s called the Free State of Menard which means you can do whatever you want. And it almost extends to killing someone if they need killing! There are no codes. That landowner”—she points across the river—“cleared a lot of that. And I had no say in it. He cleared a lot of mesquite.”

“Mesquite” was a word I’d picked up as a teenager reading J.T. Edson; his fictional cowboys were prone to sit beside campfires under the stars eating mesquite beans. “Which is the mesquite?” I ask.

She points across the river, northeast. “The lighter green, the small trees: that is all mesquite. They suck up huge amounts of water, and so do the cedars. The cedars take, like, thirty gallons a day. Here, on the cliff, we leave the cedar, but out in the field we take them all up. Jamie cleared the mesquite from our pasture.”

We walk back up to the Gator through dry grass, rocks, and cactus. She says, “Of course, we have to watch out for rattlesnakes here. Jamie said he lived for thirty-four years in Minnesota and, just about the time he quit looking for rattlesnakes, he moved back down. You always watch where you’re stepping.”

We drive down a gradual slope and the broad bank of the river, a small flood plain below the cliff, comes into view. Over the noise of the engine, Carol says, “Jamie was clearing the river with a shredder on the back of his tractor, and the grass was so tall—Eddie had had a sick spell and hadn’t been working, so Jamie was doing more of it himself—and the tractor wheel caught a hole and flipped the tractor, and it landed on him, and he died instantly under the tractor wheel." She speaks clearly, as she has about everything, from Indians, to mesquite, to how she fell in love with Jamie because he was a cowboy. "These tractors are like little death traps, I guess."

"Were you nearby?"

"Well, he did that in the afternoon. Our hunters were here—so when I came home from the restaurant, they came... Something was a little different, I could tell. Jamie is usually up—it was dark. The hunters came over and said, 'Why don't you and Jamie come over and have dinner with us?' And I said, 'He's not over there with you?' They came with me to look, because we knew he was... and they found him. I didn't. I guess I just didn't want to. And they found him and... thank heavens they were here. So..."

I say how sorry I am.

"Yeah," she says. "It was... He was doing exactly what he *loved* to do." Her voice seems to crack just a little. "We know he was planning on doing it for twenty more years."

"Yes... Yes," I say, with a sigh.

There is just the clatter and howl of the Gator, until Carol says, "There's deer tracks in this mud here. I want to go down to the far end and show you the bur oak. And then we'll go over to the island, and then we'll come on back. OK?"

We drive along the riverbank and reach a group of old trees. Carol points out a pecan, and then a giant tree with spreading, tangled branches: a bur oak. We stand in the shade of it. The river is still and the same murky, jade green that I saw from the house.

Carol tells me there are caves hidden in the undergrowth on the side of the cliff that were used by Indians. "There are twenty-five sites on the land where Indian activity has been found. One of them was a station where they made tools."

We drive back beside the river and on west. Carol steers

the Gator down a slope and into the river and through shallow water to an island. There's a pool, six to twelve feet deep and perfect for swimming, a place on the bank for diving, and another where Carol sets up chairs for picnics.

"Then we have baptisms up here—because our pastor says it looks like the Jordan." She chuckles. "Most Texans think they never have to travel outside of Texas, because they can find whatever they need right here. And I think they might be right!"

We drive up, away from the river toward the house, and meet Eddie again. He tells Carol where her goats are, and we go that way, jolting across rough grass. We stop beside a loose clump of ten or twelve tall trees. "Live oaks," Carol says. "They stay green all winter, and in the spring they turn yellow and the new leaf pushes the old leaf off." She spreads her arms as if to embrace them all. "They grow in motts like that, in stands. Without them, it'd be pretty depressing here in winter. I needed these, because I had all those pine trees up in Minnesota."

We talk about grass: the mesquite and prickly pear have been removed from this part of the ranch so that it will grow better. And I discover the origin of her restaurant's name. "Side oats is the state grass of Texas, and it's the most nutritious grain in the pasture." About twenty goats stand together and stare at us, then skitter away, tails up, and come to a halt a way off, their white backsides pointing our way.

We get back to the ranch, to the kitchen where Carol gives me a glass of water, and somehow we get to talking about politics. Carol is a progressive Republican, a new term to me; it sounds like a contradiction. She says she doesn't want America to go backward. "I grew up in the fifties and sixties—I'm sixty-five right now—and I don't want to go back there. It wasn't good for women, or for lots of other people. I think what we're seeing with our black president is that racism is still around and well. There's been an increase in hate groups since he was elected."

She chuckles. "Here in Texas, when Obama won, those of us who were for Obama, the five of us in town, we had our little celebration."

When I ask why, as a Republican, she voted Democrat, she says, "Can you *imagine* where we'd be if McCain was president? I think we would be..." She seems unable to express the horrors that would have ensued. "We needed the brain that Obama has, the ability to see the whole picture." She pauses again, and smiles. "I just really admire what he's trying to do, but it shows how hard it is to do it. I really like his attitude toward people. He knows a kind of life that's different. I think we are becoming an oligarchy here in the United States, government by the few who are rich, and I think that's a crime."

"He's broken that mold for sure," I say.

"They said he wouldn't have won if he wasn't black. I certainly think it helped him."

"Because a lot of blacks voted for him?"

"They voted, period. Saw him as an opportunity. But it's hard for him to make improvements. You see conservatives, like Jamie, southern conservatives, don't like it if you think we need to improve things. They think America is fantastic."

"Fine as it is?"

"Perfect. And if you say that things could be better, then you're being critical. To me, that's not addressing the problem—and there are people who have problems. It's like saying they don't exist. So it's a double slap in the face. 'I'm doing fine. Why don't you just get on with the program?'"

"I suppose that's why I'm Labour in England," I say. "Whatever else, they have always seemed to care more."

"Oh, no doubt! We should not go to war. I would have a more socialistic health-care system. But we prefer to spend our money on war." We are sitting on stools at a bar in her living area. "I think there are two sides always—not always called

Republican and Democrat. There's the side that thinks the answer to everything is power and might; and the side that thinks it's cooperation and collaboration." She picks up a glass and puts it down again. "Maybe that's what we call enlightenment a little bit. You go beyond the power and might... Sometimes I'm hopeful. Sometimes I'm not."

She tells me about a woman she knows whose mother died of cancer because she couldn't pay for treatment. "She's Mexican. She remembers going to the doctor's office with her mother, sitting in the waiting room and the doctor not seeing her, even though she was dying of cancer."

I express horror, and say that that wouldn't happen in England.

"Have you seen Michael Moore's film, *Sicko*? [I haven't.] After I saw that, I was ready to move to France or any place else—Canada. That's what we do: we say things like, 'Canada? Huh!' or 'Oh, socialized medicine?' But we don't know how good that is." Moore interviewed doctors in France, she says, and they told him that they had good lives, even though their incomes were limited. "What bothers me is that here in the United States, people say, 'It's not good if I can't make as much money as I want.' That seems to be what we have set up as the ultimate. 'If I want to make a whole bunch of money, hey, don't you stop me! And don't tax me! Because I'm motivated by making a lot of money.' Well"—Carol drops her voice—"you can't build a *society* on people who want to make a lot of money."

She pauses, and goes on. "I think we might even be doing this in school here now. I think we're starting younger and younger to have them make that decision: go for the money. And it's interesting what happens with Mexicans. They have a hard time going for the money; it doesn't make sense to them. They're just really family orientated and they don't mind living on a little bit of money. So they don't fit in very well. They don't do well at school because they don't care if they win. They don't care if they're number one."

Again, she stops talking and thinks. "Most of the kids who go through high school here have no concept of what they would like to do, or who they are or what their talents are. They have no sense of what life could be. They've lived in Menard all their life and that's as much as they see, even with television. So there's a lot of drug use, a tremendous amount of drug experimentation."

"Here in Menard?"

"Yes, because we're on the border. When we first got this place, I called home to Minnesota from a Pick 'n' Pack—a convenience store on 83—to tell them. Afterward someone told me, 'If you sat in that Pick 'n' Pack long enough, everyone on the Ten Most Wanted list in the United States would pass through—would stop at that Pick 'n' Pack.' That's because we're on the route to Mexico. 83 is. They go from here over to Iraan and head down about eighty miles. Or we're two hours from Del Rio, on the border. So they're running: lots of drug traffic."

"So the drugs go up 83?" I want to be sure.

"Yes. And then San Angelo—northeast of here on 277, the road that goes down to Del Rio—they just busted a big ring. In fact, one of Eddie's sons is in jail for fifteen years, in the federal prison for drug trafficking. His wife got them associated with some Mexican mafia—and they're not nice people. One of them has a dairy out there in a little town... There's nothing around there. You know, we're in perfect country for that kind of thing."

"The dairy is a front, you mean?"

"Yes. Everybody knows it. They can't—"

"Even the police?"

"Certainly the *local* police don't know much. They're pretty unsophisticated and they end up letting informers free, to use and deal in town if they turn in users. Users would be in trouble if they turned in dealers. To me a user is more of a victim." She shrugs. "But that's being out in the country like this."

I tell her about the university professor in Minot, North Dakota, who said that 83 had been a route for running alcohol into the U.S. from Canada during Prohibition. "So a lot happens on 83."

"Oh yes." She smiles—and then turns serious. "One of the reasons we opened the restaurant—" She breaks off—and continues. "First of all, I was sitting out there on the deck, saying, 'God! Man! Thank you, this is beautiful! I'm extremely happy. But surely this isn't what you're all about in the world: making *me* this happy? Surely there's more to it than that.'

"So, our bridge group would talk about what we needed in Menard: a restaurant. And we talked about what kind of restaurant for maybe two years. And then I noticed there was no place to go in town and meet someone.

"So, I prayed every morning as I was out there on the deck. And I definitely got the message: you know, *you* could open that restaurant. And I thought, I'm not in the restaurant business! It came every morning for months, and pieces started to fall into place. And eventually, with help, I got it started.

"We're still working to make it a healthy human organization that promotes our development and growth—and is more than just a place to work. The thing I'm most excited about is most everybody's off drugs; they're not off alcohol yet, but they're off drugs—they've been heavy drug users."

I'm startled at this. "The people who work there, you mean?"

"Yes," Carol says. "Restaurant people are always drinking. Several of them are in AA locally, so they're really getting straightened out. And two young women just went back to school. One of them wants to be a lawyer."

Carol says her financial advisers have told her she is going to run out of money and has to do something to generate some cash. "We're not making a lot of money yet," she says, "but we're paying all those salaries and we've probably put three million dollars into the economy over the last three years. Last year we only lost a thousand dollars, and I think that was really good. I thought this year we'd make some money, but now we've had new air conditioners that we needed, we might not."

Carol says she has done research on businesses, like Ben and Jerry's, that have what she calls a human model. "They help humans flourish. Organizations should help human beings flourish, just like a family should help a human being flourish. But it's not the way..."

I tell her about John Lewis, the chain of shops in England that is owned by the people who work for it.

That's what she wants for her restaurant, she says. "I think that's possible. And, of course, what they hit Obama with on that is, 'It's a share-the-wealth socialism.' I think, if we choose to be socialistic with our money—which is, I think, what we're supposed to do—we should go ahead. But it's an individual choice."

"It's unfortunate that word has so many connotations," I say. "The U.S.S.R., the Union of Soviet Socialist Republics: it conjures up all that."

"Yes. That is too bad," Carol says. "To me, when I look at all that—at people owning the businesses they work in—it supports my faith more than any other." She pauses and goes on. "To be a Christian and a capitalist is kind of a stretch, a little bit of a stretch."

"Yes, it is," I say.

"I just think it's a great thing to support and develop talent. You know my outlook has changed, especially since Jamie died, I guess." Her voice drops almost to a whisper. "I don't have any short-term goals any more. Just look at the long term. I'm not going to be here soon, some day, so what happens to me right now is not inconsequential. I think the longer-term goals make more sense now. So,"—she takes a breath—"*what* between now and the time I die? *What* can we do? Jamie was very generous. He was a good man. Let's be generous."

"Yes, yes," I say. And then, perhaps because we have reached a kind of accord, "Gosh! I should let you get on."

"I'm afraid I kept you too long," she says.

She hasn't, of course. I could talk to her for weeks. But a friend of hers is at the door, and I must drive on.

45

THE SMILING MAN FROM PHARR

I DRIVE SLOWLY THROUGH THE heat—windows down, elbow out—back past the humorous sign that threatens death to trespassers—and on along the dusty road to Menard. It's twelve thirty. I was with Carol for three hours.

I remember the carpet of plain beyond the San Saba River, and trying, prompted by Carol, to imagine the Comanches living there—and again I'm reminded of those two-inch-high plastic Indians, bought from a small-town toyshop in England and drawn up ready for battle on Richard's parents' sitting-room carpet. The Comanches, *my* tribe, were not a pleasant people, not at all noble, according to Ian Frazier. Great fighters, especially on horseback, they frequently captured their enemies and tortured them. And, if their captives made too much noise—enough, say, to keep the Comanches awake at night—they would cut out their tongues. They liked to steal women from other tribes and, Frazier says, those women rarely lived long. Not surprisingly, they hated all white Americans. But they saw Texans as different from the rest. Texans didn't give presents, or enter discussions, and were quick to pull out a gun; they hated them most of all.

Real Comanches were small and bandy-legged—Frazier calls them "the jockeys of the plains." They did, however, keep the southern United States supplied with horses by stealing them from the Spanish in Mexico. And two creatures mentioned by Carol were special to them: they wore the tail-feathers of the scissor-tail flycatcher on their shoulders like epaulettes; and they hanged the skins of roadrunners, athletic birds that prefer running to flying, in their tepees as good-luck charms.

I STOP CLOSE to the San Saba in Menard and walk across the low, concrete bridge that carries 83. It spans a grassy, wooded flood plain, through which the river winds. It's shallow here. I know that because four boys—two of them, pale, Nordic; two, dark-skinned, Hispanic—are standing in the middle, with the brown, fast-flowing water below their waists, splashing each other. I stroll back to Prius and drive around town, a place of wide streets, old brick buildings, and towering trees.

Leaving Menard, I put on the sound track of *Oh Brother, Where Art Thou?*, beat time on the warm paintwork of the car door, and mosey slowly through thirty miles of rocky grassland and low hills—the start of the rugged Texas Hill Country.

APPROACHING THE SMALL city of Junction, 83 meets Interstate 10 in a welter of concrete bypasses, dual carriageways, and viaducts. I keep to 83 and find myself in a town whose old center is in the shade of a vast mountain—and where the air is cooler. I park and stroll along a Main Street where, as so often, many essential goods are unavailable. But there is a furniture shop, a café, a realtor, antiques, and an odd dilapidated place with warping shingles on its roof and a plastic Christmas tree in its window. The Texan Cinema, a castellated, art deco building, appears to be shut. On its marquee, in three shades of washed-out red, are these letters:

UN T D

WE

STAN

I can't recall a film with that title, but I know that the song from the 1970s took off all over again after 9/11.

A little girl, pretty with dark hair, about ten years old, passes me on a skateboard. She laughs as the board runs away in front of her. "Hi. How you doin'?" she says.

"Fine. Thank you," I say, and keep walking.

She skates along behind me and the board runs away again, under a car this time. A boy, her size with blond hair, arrives from somewhere, also on a skateboard. She says, "Sorry," to him—and he helps her retrieve her board.

He smiles and says, "I'm the only one allowed to do that."

THE ROAD WINDS up and up out of Junction—and on up, around the mountain. Near the top, a steep and stony track, signed Viewpoint, leads to a small, empty car park. There the Stars and Stripes flutters over cactus and dry grass as if to claim ownership—not just of the drab mountaintop, but of the waves of tree-covered ridges that billow, green and gray and blue, in the infinite haze to the south, east, and west. Way below, but close by, the South Llano River curls between cliffs and dense green forest, like a tributary of the Amazon.

I wander about taking photographs that I know will be puny reminders of the immensity of the landscape.

A silver SUV draws up, and two men and two women get out. They wander with their cameras where I have wandered. One of the men smiles, and we all get chatting. They are on vacation from a town called Pharr which is on 83 not far from Brownsville. The man who smiled offers to take my photograph—with my camera, of course. Would I like to pose against the hills and sky?

I thank him, and ask if he'd mind photographing me by my car instead. He seems puzzled but is keen to please.

A black plastic ledge continues out from the racy downward slope of Prius's rear window. Tits who like to drive fast might call this ledge a spoiler and think that by some magic it makes Prius go faster. Perhaps it does, but for me it provides something more valuable which I have used more and more as I have moved south and the weather has grown warmer: a place to rest my notebook and write. I park in shade and write standing up in the open air; the ledge/spoiler is a perfect height and width for this.

I explain this to the smiling man from Pharr, who continues to smile as he takes a photograph—of *me* writing *his* name in *my* notebook. Thank you, Ricardo Longoria.

THE ROAD WINDS back down the mountain and, after a brush with the utilitarian Interstate 10, wanders on, following a procession of telegraph poles through wooded hills and rocky valleys—more of the vast Hill Country. I stop and stare through a gate at a curiously neat ranch. Discreet notices are positioned inside the fence. A clump of trees is labeled Live Oaks—a mott rather than a clump, then—and there are more motts in the distance. Another notice says that turkey vultures live around here. I look up into the blue and, sure enough, two huge birds with fringed wings are soaring way above. Perhaps, like stately homes in England, this place is opened to the public sometimes.

The road climbs to rocky moorland where the view is again immense and wild; rusty wire sagging from weathered posts is all that humanity has managed here. And then the road drops to a broad, flat valley where lush grass pasture is spattered with trees and walled in a mile to the east by white limestone cliffs—of the kind that Carol loves—and nothing much is growing on the bosomy hills above. The air is warm, almost hot.

I stop at another ranch gate. A rough sign gives the ranch's name; the Stars and Stripes dangles, and another looms in faded paint on a board fastened to the fence. Mature trees are planted in rows—a pecan orchard—and beehives sit in the long grass beneath. In the distance, a dense forest coats a ring of hills.

The town of Leakey straggles in the cleft of a long valley, a makeshift sort of place, where there is much that is Mexican—shop-front signs in Spanish, windows skirted with patterned tiles, the thick low walls and rounded arches of adobe architecture. I walk from one end of town to the other, and back more slowly, catching the scent of wood smoke and the soft slur of Spanish.

A tall, white American, in checked shirt and Stetson, skips down steps from a brick-built bank and climbs into a shiny black SUV. Outside the low, arched police station, a young blond policeman, blue shirt coated in badges, sits in a black-and-white car—STATE TROOPER, TEXAS HIGHWAY PATROL. Farther along, at the roadside, a woman is barbecuing fish. The mingling of cultures is plain. Mexico is just seventy miles to the southwest.

I drive on through fields where dry grass lies beneath trees that surely have deep roots. Then on, up into hills that are almost alpine and, after twenty miles, down again into fields that explode with glossy maize, where phalanxes of giant metallic spiders bestride the land spurting water—as they do in the wheat fields of Kansas.

On again, and the green mutates into an unwatered desert of drab bushes and brown grass that extends to the city of Uvalde, an oasis where spiky palms and spreading oaks line the road.

AT TRAFFIC LIGHTS in an old square shaded by oaks and palms, where buildings are faced with tiles, stucco, and curving Mexican-style parapets, I turn left onto U.S. 90 which is also Uvalde's East Main Street. U.S. 90 is a major route east to

San Antonio, site of the Alamo and Texas's second-largest city, and west to Del Rio on the Mexican border. It's 7 PM. East Main Street is full of slow-moving traffic. People drive rather than walk; there are no pavements, just grass verges. Motels and the usual fast-food restaurants stand isolated in their own car parks.

The Inn of Uvalde is large, fronted by palm trees, and has a bar with a separate entrance. I am given a cool, dark room at the back. Outside, crickets chirp loudly, and it is still warm.

The bar is called Lunkers and turns out to be as it sounds: a vile place where you pay three dollars to join a club, inside which is overloud fatuous music, a smell of vomit, and waitresses who bark at you while sending empty bottles crashing into a bin. I sit on a bar stool alongside three lone taciturn men, facing two barmaids: one blond, one brunette, both surly. The blond asks what I want, snaps the top off a bottle of Coors Light, plonks it down in front of me, and wanders away.

I finish the beer quickly and ask for the check. And, for the first time, the barmaid looks at me. And wrinkles her nose. Perhaps the smell is getting to her—because she can't be thinking: Why did this man who talks funny join this stylish and welcoming club and then leave so soon? Can she?

I FIND A restaurant called The Town House—no logo, no chain. Just a friendly waitress called Chrissy, Latin jazz at low volume, and a menu that lists Spanish food and reveals that The Town House has been here for twenty-five years.

"All home-cooked," Chrissy says.

I order *carne guisada,* meat in sauce, with a cheese enchilada.

The food arrives with flatbread tortillas—wrapped in paper, inside a red plastic container to keep them warm.

As I eat, I get to like the plain, functional look of the place: cool tiles, chrome, red plastic, neon beer signs. Before I leave, I ask Chrissy if I may take a photograph.

She crosses the room. The owner is at a table with a friend. Thickset, proprietorial, he turns and smiles. “Of course. Be my guest.” He lifts his hands with the largesse appropriate to a man who founded a successful restaurant twenty-five years ago. “I hope you had a good meal.”

“I did. Thank you.”

46

189 HEROES AND A MAN WHO LOVED HIS CHILDREN

I DROVE OUT OF UVALDE, thinking about the weather. Or was I, by then, talking to myself?—"And on it goes, Highway 83. The difference this morning, folks, is that the sky is cloud covered and gray to the south. It looks like rain ahead. Perhaps not a bad thing. And I think I can hear thunder far away."

And I was thinking about making a detour to the Alamo, an important part of Texan and U.S. history—and officially, by statute, "the Shrine of Texas Liberty." Davy Crockett and Jim Bowie, two heroes from my childhood, died there fighting for freedom from Mexico; and, when I was about eleven years old, I was moved and excited by the film directed by and starring John Wayne. However, it might turn out to be an overhyped tourist attraction—a pastel reconstruction of the real thing, like Dodge City.

I stopped to read a plaque at the side of the road commemorating a camp set up in 1862 to protect supply lines from Mexico to the Confederate Army in the civil war. The text went on to break down the names of the 254 counties of Texas into categories: "10 commemorate colonizers. 42 have Indian, French, or Spanish names. 12 honor Washington and other American patriots. 96 were named for 1836–46 heroes of the Republic of Texas (including 15 who died in the Alamo)."

The mention of deaths at the Alamo—I knew there were a lot more than fifteen—somehow pushed me toward it. A few miles on, at La Pryor, I could turn left and go east; the last half of the journey would be on an interstate, so the trip shouldn't take long.

But still I wasn't sure. I thought about it as I drove. The cloud thickened and the colors of the earth dimmed. When I got to La Pryor, a small town with a school by a road junction... I turned off.

The road was a U.S. Route, numbered 57, two lanes, and similar to 83. The sky grew darker and darker and then murderous, and it began to rain. For a few seconds the water came in big drops, and then it poured, strafing the roof and windshield. I set the wipers to fever pitch, switched on the rear superbright fog light, and followed the faint red lights of a car about fifty yards ahead. I was driving at 30 mph.

I stabbed at the radio, hoping to find a station with weather news. But everything was in Spanish. I found a Mexican music station broadcasting jolly dance rhythms and chirpy tunes, and turned it up loud; it cut out the roar of the rain and the manic swish of the wipers, and cheered me up.

After a while, I lost touch with the car in front and could see almost nothing. I had driven through storms and driving rain many times, but this was fiercer, wilder. I once lived through a violent squall on a small, bobbing boat in the Mediterranean—I went below deck to keep dry, and could see nothing through the cabin windows but swirling water. I didn't feel sick now, but otherwise I felt as I had then: disoriented. I pulled off the road as soon as I could, into the gateway of someone's home or ranch. I sat, hazard lights flashing—and wipers swiping, so that I wasn't encased in rushing water.

A line of cars—all I could see was their lights—straggled past, slowly, each following the one in front.

The rain eased a little. I was able to see a short distance. I set off again, with wipers on full and happy Mexican music. Headlights appeared in the mirror and stayed there. Again the storm worsened—until I could barely see ten yards. I stopped on the forecourt of a blur of a building and watched seven or eight cars crawl by; they had all been following me.

I got moving again, and this time reached the interstate—for once a refuge, with its width and lanes and the red and white lights of slow-moving trucks and cars piercing the gloom and the lash of the rain.

I SWOOPED DOWN from the interstate into downtown San Antonio, caught a glimpse of the Holiday Inn, and pulled into its car park. I ran in through the rain and helped myself to a leaflet advertising trolleybus tours; a map on the back showed the Alamo in bold type.

By the time I'd parked in an overpriced car park, the rain had almost stopped. Hopping over puddles, I passed souvenir shops and an ice-cream parlor, and saw that I was on Crockett Street. I hurried on, turned a corner—and it was there, fifty yards away: a small, gray-stone building that surprised me because it seemed familiar to the point of being welcoming, even enticing—a little like coming face-to-face with the *Mona Lisa* in the Louvre, but without the crowds. I have seen pictures of the facade of the Church of San Antonio de Valero—the smile, as it were, on the Alamo's Mona Lisa—many times: first, probably, when I saw the film in 1960; and most recently, a few minutes ago, when I came upon it, bathed in silvery sunlight, in the leaflet I picked up at the Holiday Inn.

It is small, a chapel more than a church. From outside it appears to have two floors, with windows on both levels and a front door in the middle—like a child's drawing of a house. But it is far more than that, because a wonky curving gable rises from the roof creating a soft and friendly silhouette, and a rounded arch over the door, set between four gracefully carved columns and a pair of scalloped niches, echoes the shape of the gable above. The place seems rough and refined at the same time, and has an inviting, battered look that comes with age and the marks of cannonballs and bullets—so, in truth, more a late Rembrandt self-portrait than the *Mona Lisa*.

The church was part of the Mission San Antonio, which was built in 1724 as a home for Spanish missionaries and their Indian converts. It ceased to be a mission in the 1790s, and became barracks for a Spanish cavalry troop in the 1800s. The cavalrymen named it the Alamo, which means cottonwood, after their hometown. Back then, and thirty years later when the siege and ensuing battle took place, the church stood at the southeast corner of a walled compound, roughly the size of a football field. It was the compound, including the church, that fewer than two hundred men defended against a Mexican army of about three thousand, commanded by General Santa Anna, for thirteen days from February 23, 1836.

The issue was the independence of Texas from Mexico and, in the end, the men inside the Alamo died for that cause. They were a mix of Texians (American Texans) and Tejanos (Mexican Texans), led by Colonel William B. Travis, who was supported by the coonskin-hatted frontiersman and former congressman Davy Crockett, and the almost as famous Jim Bowie, bravura knife-thrower and inventor of the Bowie knife. (To me, as a child, these three men were, respectively, Laurence Harvey, John Wayne, and Richard Widmark.)

Before dawn on March 6, columns of Mexican soldiers attacked and were twice beaten back by cannon and rifle fire. At the third attempt they scaled the walls and overwhelmed the Texans with their own cannons. The end came in a bloody hand-to-hand fight. One hundred and eighty-nine Texans died there that day; the last left standing, wielding his rifle by its barrel above his head and clubbing Mexicans on all sides, was Crockett—in the film, anyway.

Only the church and a narrow stone building, the Long Barrack, remain. The rest is under a couple of roads, a lush tropical garden, and the "sales museum," which was built in sympathetic style in 1936.

I went inside. The church was refreshingly cool, yet warmly lit. There was no upper floor; instead the walls rose to a vaulted ceiling, appropriate for a church and for the "sacred memorial" that, according to Texas law, the building now is. Flags hung from the east wall where the missionaries would have had their altar. People were queuing against the south wall to my right; I wasn't sure what for, but I took my place at the end and shuffled along among stern-faced tourists for a few minutes. Near silence seemed to be required. At the east wall, we turned left and walked slowly past inscriptions giving the names and places of origin of those who died. We met a few people coming the other way—as it were, from left to right. They were carefully avoiding us sheep, who had apparently lined up so as to read the names in reverse alphabetical order.

Many of the dead, some with Spanish names, came from Texas; others were from Tennessee and perhaps came with Crockett, who was from there; there were men from most of the states and from England, Scotland, Ireland, and Germany. The penultimate name is Zanco, Charles—he was from Denmark. And the final name is written as "_______, John a Black Freedman."

Reading the names of the men who died in the cause of freedom in this place 174 years ago, I felt sadness and sympathy, of course, but I found myself feeling angry as well—angry with the men who died, because, when their deaths seemed almost inevitable, their own leader offered them a way out.

In the early days of the siege, relief was expected from several sources, including the Texan army under Sam Houston. Colonel Travis wrote a letter addressed "To the People of Texas and All Americans in the World," asking for reinforcements; it ended: "If this call is neglected, I am determined to sustain myself as long as possible and die like a soldier who never forgets what is due to his own honor and that of his country. *Victory or death.*" Travis gave the letter to a messenger and it was widely circulated. Some reinforcements arrived—notably thirty-two men from Gonzales, a nearby town—but not enough.

By March 5, General Santa Anna's troops surrounded the Alamo, and he sent a messenger with a letter demanding surrender or else all inside would die. At this Colonel Travis—who was twenty-six years old, divorced but close to his young son, who was safe elsewhere—is said to have called the men together, read them Santa Anna's letter, and declared that he would not surrender, rather he would die fighting for Texas. Then—in one version of the story, and in the film—he drew a line in the sand with his sword, and asked any man willing to stay and fight with him to step over it. Many historians dispute the drama of the line in the sand, but most agree that Travis called a meeting and gave the men the choice of staying or leaving. All but one "walked across the line," following, I suspect, their leaders—and perhaps their mates—as soldiers often do. And the next day they died: either blown apart by cannon and rifle fire, or butchered with bayonets.

And what about the lone dissenter? Was he a coward, as he has been called, or a hero of another kind? His name was Louis Rose. At fifty-one, he was one of the oldest men there; years before he had fought, bravely some said, with Napoleon in

Russia and Spain. He climbed over the wall of the Alamo on the night of March 5 and smuggled himself through the Mexican lines. One account says that he gave as his reason for leaving that he loved his family and his children; and another that he went on to live a quiet life in Louisiana and, when asked why he had left the Alamo, said simply, as if it were obvious, "By God, I wasn't going to die."

Why did only one man out of 190 choose life over death?

We sheep moved from the names into a small space, the north transept of the church, where there was an exhibition. Paintings hung on the walls—among them Davy Crockett, young, bareheaded, fresh faced—above cases of memorabilia: Travis's ring, Crockett's buckskin shirt, a Bowie knife, a flint-lock rifle used in the battle, books, letters, weapons, and clothes belonging to those who died. I inched my way round, trying to take it all in.

Outside in the gardens it was warm, the rain had stopped, and the sky was gray but unthreatening. I looked at the high rear wall of the shrine, at the curving roof, and at a window where, in 1836, a cannon was mounted. From there I walked through a walled garden past a well that had served the Spanish mission, to the Long Barrack, a low, gray-stone structure with rounded arches, where infantry and artillerymen had lived. Early in the morning of March 6, 1836, it would have been at the heart of the Alamo compound, between Travis at the north wall; Bowie, sick, bedridden, and useless, but close to the south wall; and Crockett, outside the church at a low wall facing southeast.

The interior of the Long Barrack has been turned into a museum with glass walls—and a small theatre where I waited with others to watch a seventeen-minute film, produced by the History Channel. After that I headed for the shop, passing on the way "The Wall of History," where the story is told outdoors on weatherproof panels. There was nothing wrong with any of this informative stuff. But it didn't move me, didn't send my imagination back to those heroic and tragic events, as the shrine and the outer walls of the old barrack did.

Out there, in the gardens, people in shorts and T-shirts milled about pointing cameras. Two couples with small children came toward me, excited, chatting loudly; they seemed to have just arrived. A gardener was nearby, fitting a hose to a tap. "Gee!" one of the men called out. "They had running water at the Alamo!"

One of the women—perhaps his wife and the mother of his children—screeched with laughter. Eventually she calmed herself and saw that the other couple weren't laughing. Maybe they hadn't heard. She pointed at the tap and screamed, "Did you hear what Greg said? He said, 'Gee! They had running water at the Alamo!'"

And all of them, including the children, broke into thigh-smacking hysterics. And good old Greg smirked, triumphant.

In the shop I bought Alamo bottle openers for my daughters' boyfriends and—I don't know why, perhaps because she can play the piano—a harmonica for my wife.

Then I left the Alamo, bought an ice cream, and drove out of San Antonio as fast as I could.

I had been there for about an hour and a half. As I drove, I couldn't get those men out of my mind—the paintings of them, their books and swords and trinkets. Did they *really* volunteer for death in the cause of freedom? When they decided not to leave, did they *expect* to die? Were they heroes in that self-sacrificial sense?

Don't soldiers tend to think they will survive, even if others die? And don't they sometimes, in extreme circumstances—such as when they're threatened by a despised aggressor like Santa Anna—get embroiled in a kind of collective madness?

Surely those men, despite pledging to fight a more powerful enemy and accepting that they *might* die, thought—perhaps crazily—that they *might* win; or that significant reinforcements *would* arrive, after all; or that they *might* somehow escape; or that the Mexicans, for all their threats, *might* in the end spare them and take prisoners.

There is some evidence that they weren't resigned to dying for the cause. As late as March 3, when a messenger brought news of more than six hundred Texan troops on their way, Travis had hopes not just of surviving, but of winning. In a letter to a friend who was caring for his son, he wrote: "Take care of my little boy. If the country should be saved, I may make him a splendid fortune, but if the country should be lost, and I should perish, he will have nothing but the proud recollection that he is the son of a man who died for his country." And there are accounts that suggest that, close to the end, Crockett and a small group of survivors tried to surrender, and that a Mexican officer who might have allowed this was overruled by Santa Anna.

There is, perhaps, an irony about the deaths of the heroes of the Alamo. A few weeks later, on April 21, at the Battle of San Jacinto, Sam Houston's army defeated the Mexicans, captured Santa Anna, and forced him to grant Texas independence. But that may not be simply ironic. Perhaps there is causation. Houston had a puny, largely untrained force, but his men are said to have gone into battle bellowing the cry, "Remember the Alamo," while hearing those words resounding all around them. So maybe they wouldn't have won without the men at the Alamo and the vengeful fury that followed their deaths.

By going there and looking at the place, and feeling it a little, maybe, and thinking about those men, I found out what I should have known already: the story I'd accepted for fifty years, the one shown in the John Wayne film, was, like so much of Wild West history presented as entertainment, hugely inaccurate. The truth was less romantic, and the heroism more ambiguous. Later I read that the two historians who worked as historical advisers on Wayne's film both demanded that their names be removed from the credits; and that another Alamo historian, Timothy Todish, wrote, "There is not a single scene in *The Alamo* which corresponds to a historically verifiable incident."

47

A BIRTHDAY IN CARRIZO SPRINGS

ON THE ROAD BACK to La Pryor I drive in the middle much of the time to avoid pools of water collected at the side. There's a little blue in the sky and I can see the land around me, which again, and despite the deluge, is a desert of brown grass sprinkled with small green trees, shrubs, and the odd cactus. Some miles on, something low and green is growing in rows: spinach. Crystal City, a little south of La Pryor, claims to be "the Spinach Capital of the World."

The rain begins again and is almost back at storm strength as I reach La Pryor, where I turn on to 83 and head south. Again the wipers are on full and I can't see far. I put *Artie Shaw's Greatest Hits,* a surefire seat-bouncer, into the CD player. At Crystal City I stop under the porch of a motel, manage to go in without getting wet, and am told they have no rooms. There's another motel about a mile on, the receptionist says, at the other end of town.

It looks posh and new, mock something—perhaps ancient Greek—with columns, and there's a spacious porch for dry parking. The rain is heavy and it's about seven o'clock; I'm looking forward to staying here. But a charming young man says that they too are full.

"Oh!" I say. "Why? What's going on?"

"They found oil," he says.

"What? *Today?*"

At this he laughs and shakes his head and looks at me as if I'm some great wit—or perhaps a nutcase—who has suddenly arrived from somewhere strange. "No. Not today." He shakes his head again, while smiling. "A few months ago, but since then all the hotels have been full."

"Oh. Well—"

"Are you going south?" He's looking through the glass doors at Prius.

"Yes."

"We got a sister hotel in Carrizo Springs, about twelve miles on. I'll phone and see if they have a room. They're full of oil people too—but they might. It's possible."

The sister hotel, which is called the Texan Inn, has one room left. He asks my name and reserves it for me, and for some reason—I can only think he likes me—arranges a 10 percent discount.

LIKE ITS SISTER, the Texan Inn is swish and new, ideal for oil people: an immense bouncy bed, armchairs, coffee and coffee-making equipment with which I can make tea, television with a remote that works, *two* ballpoints, and a notepad. The receptionist suggests I eat at a restaurant across the road—the road being 83. She doesn't seem to be actually recommending it; it's more as if it's the only place. I can see it through the rain from the porch outside my room: an enormous sign, Lee's STEAK HOUSE, rising from the roof of a low square building built of red corrugated material that might be plastic. It's about thirty yards away, so I wonder whether to drive since it's raining and I'm in America.

But I don't. I run across with my jacket draped over my head, and am welcomed by a small, compact waitress dressed in black, who ushers me to a table and brings beer. The table is in a corner and, of course, I sit facing out. There are plenty of tables; seven or eight are occupied, most of them by groups of young men in checked shirts who might be oil workers. Fans, ten or twelve of them, hang from the ceiling, wobble, and whirr. The walls are enlivened with stuffed deer heads, most of which show no expression—but one, self-important with antlers, and fixed above a door in the far wall, has a supercilious sneer—as if he has decided that we happy humans eating meat are beneath him in more ways than one. Between two deer heads, a notice reads: "Gun control is being able to hit what you aim at." On another wall, a stuffed turkey stands on a small platform staring at the ceiling, wings behind its back as if on parade.

From time to time, as I chomp a tender steak, the door in the farther wall, below the sour-faced deer, opens and someone—usually one person, occasionally two—goes in or comes out—and, for a few moments, I hear loud music, voices, and laughter. Most, but not all, of the people who go in and out are fattish or fat young women.

What's happening in there, I wonder—and I ask the waitress.

"That's our bar. Lee's bar. There's a DJ tonight and dancing. It gets pretty lively."

I order an ice cream—and find that I'm remembering the Alamo, the coolness and the yellow light inside the church.

When I pay the bill, the waitress points to the door across the room. "Why don't you go in? Have a drink."

"No, no. I'm too old for that type of—"

"Go on! Mingle with somebody. It's fun. There's all ages in there."

It's true. I've seen one or two gray-hairs going in and coming out.

All right then—*mingle with somebody!* I stand up, heave on my jacket, button it, and stride across the floor.

IT'S A SMALL room, much smaller than the restaurant. The lighting is dim and the room is warm, almost too warm. A lot of people are standing up, crammed together, and there is fast, rhythmic music and raised voices. I move toward the bar in the corner, squeezing between men and women, stomach in, shoulder first, muttering, "Excuse me." People move to let me by and resume their conversations, oblivious.

The bar is long and narrow, built of rough, scarred pine, decades older than the building. A barmaid gives me a quick smile as she hoicks the lid off a Beck's and takes my dollars. I turn away, drink, and look around. Two men are playing pool, and two or three others watch. In a corner, behind a small, empty, highly polished dance floor, a man in headphones is sitting at a tiny table behind a microphone and a laptop. At the farther end of the room are tables and chairs—but no one is sitting down. People stand between the tables and in every sliver of space.

A lean man is here, beside me, half-turned away; he has a lined face and silvery hair beneath a clean white Stetson. He turns and looks at me. "Howdy," he says.

I am struck by the cool blue of his eyes. "Hi. Noisy in here," I say. What *else* can I say? I can't say, "Hi. I'm from England," in a place like this—certainly not to a man who looks like Henry Fonda.

"Sure," he says. "Lee likes it like this. Sells plenty of liquor." He grins and turns away and says something to a woman on his other side.

The crowd murmurs as a rotund man in a khaki baseball cap begins to dance with a girl who is taller than him. The rhythm is fast and funky, and they know the moves. People cheer and catcall, and some clap the time. More dancers arrive, filling the little floor, and soon they spill outward toward the bar and the pool table.

I edge away and somehow get talking to another man wearing a white cowboy hat. This one is big-bellied, friendly, prepared to shout into my ear and let me shout into his. He wants to know who I am and where I'm from. He puts out his hand and tells me his name. I have to ask him to repeat it, but he doesn't seem to mind and he spells it. His name is Ed Saig.

Ed leads me behind tables to a space by the wall and introduces me to his wife, his daughter, his stepdaughter Eva, his friends Robert and Mary-Lou.

They all nod and smile and mouth, "From England, huh!"

It's Ed's daughter's birthday, and there's a cake on the table. Ed buys a round of drinks. Eva cuts the cake, a kind of strawberry trifle, and hands out gooey, dripping triangles.

I talk to Eva. Her job is teaching migrants—kids from Mexico, El Salvador, and elsewhere—and she cares about it and them.

When Eva goes off to dance, I talk to Robert, a handsome man with a goatee beard and a black cowboy hat. I ask about his work.

"I'm a cowboy," he says.

"Wow!" I say.

He smiles. "By that, I mean I ride a horse at work. I'm involved with hunting."

A young woman with a tray delivers drinks to a group standing nearby. I get her attention and order a round for my new friends.

Everyone dances. Even big Ed and the pool players take their turns. Robert and I are the only wallflowers. "I have to feel it," he says. "And the floor is a little small."

I just feel I have to have a partner—and I don't.

Eva is popular, back and forth from the dance floor. She is a writer, and tells me about her short stories and poems and where her ideas come from—until yet another man arrives and drags her away.

I begin to think that this music and this place and these people are somehow exceptional. Everyone in the room seems happy—even me and Robert. I tell him this and suggest that there must be something special about Carrizo Springs—perhaps the climate.

"No," he laughs. "It's just a small town like the others."

"Anything to do with being close to Mexico? Maybe Mexican people are more relaxed, and that gets into the air."

Again he disagrees. "On the right night you'll find people dancing all the way up your Route 83."

I'm not so sure. I haven't seen them—and, anyway, today is Thursday.

I stay with Ed and his family till closing time. They are going on somewhere that is open till 3 AM, and invite me to go with them. I'm not sure. Despite the beer, I'm *still* English; I don't want to intrude.

As I leave I speak to Johnny, the DJ. "Three types of music I play," he says. "Colobiana, Colombian; reggae, you know reggae?"

I nod. "Of course."

"And Tejano, Texan—but *Spanish* Texan."

I wander out to the car park and look around. I can't see Ed or Eva or Robert or any of them. So I cross the road back to the Texas Inn. It's probably better that way.

48

THE STREETS OF LAREDO

THERE IS NO ONE else at breakfast, which is a find-it-yourself flotsam of plastic knives and forks, Styrofoam plates and cups, plastic containers of sweet substances, preheated coffee, and a waffle iron in the shape of Texas. Over toast and coffee, I search through Ian Frazier's *Great Plains* and find what I'm looking for:

> A person can be amazingly happy on the Great Plains... Joy seems to be a product of the geography, just as deserts can produce mystical ecstasy and English moors produce gloom. Once happiness gets rolling in this open place, not much stops it.

Perhaps Robert was right, and it was the Great Plains themselves that brought about all that bonhomie in Lee's Steak House.

Last night, Ed warned that 83 might be closed farther south; there are floods down there, particularly in Laredo, where the Rio Grande hasn't been so high since 1965. This morning, the receptionist tells me to avoid Laredo. She has seen people being evacuated from their flooded homes on television, and it's *still* raining there. For that matter, it's raining here too, quite hard. She suggests that halfway to Laredo, about forty miles south, I leave 83 and turn east on to Route 44.

I make no decision about this—I'll see what happens—and drive off into the deluge. Here 83 is two-lane and the land, what I can see of it, is flat and empty but for a few shrubs and some low trees that I manage to identify as mesquite; I learned on Carol's ranch that from a distance mesquite trees look a little like olive trees, but close up, their leaves are more like willow.

Excitement this morning comes from driving through the rain, somehow passing a couple of tractors, and being rocked and sprayed by fast-moving trucks and SUVs. Meanwhile I play Geraint Watkins's CD *In a Bad Mood*, which was given to me by my wife and is a lot more fun than it sounds.

I slow at the junction with Route 44, see no Diversion or Road Closed signs and keep going. Twenty miles on, 83 arrives at a multilane junction and I find that, while I'm still on my road, I'm also on Interstate 35, a dual carriageway with entry and exit lanes and nothing much to look at. My take on this, of course, is that I-35 has joined 83 for a short distance—fourteen miles—which will take me into central Laredo. In effect, though, I have to drive those miles on an interstate—which isn't so bad, given the weather and that I soon come to a parking place where I can take a break and eat some apricots.

As I get out of the car, a wave of spray hits me in the face and soaks the seat and the steering wheel. When I get back, I sit in the passenger seat, fiddle with the radio, and find an English-language station broadcasting flood warnings, but also reporting that the water level in the Rio Grande is now subsiding.

83 and I-35 are soon belting through low-rise suburbia, and exits to districts with Spanish names are signed every few hundred yards. I stay in the slow lane, hoping for a sign to

downtown while being aware that, if I go too far, I will reach a bridge and the border with Mexico.

This is the biggest city on 83; it has almost twice the population of the next biggest, Abilene, yet from this elevated road I can see no soaring skyscrapers. A church spire and a couple of small office blocks stick up above a sea of single- and two-story buildings. A brown sign appears: Historic District. I turn off and find myself in a grid of narrow streets packed with small shops. Signs are in Spanish, except for Duty Free, which is everywhere, and it seems you can buy almost anything—from watches to satsumas, socks to cigars. There aren't many people around, but I feel as if I have arrived in another country, which perhaps isn't surprising since 96 percent of the population is Hispanic.

The rain has stopped but the streets still shine with water. Is this the center of Laredo? I'm not sure and, what's more, I'm lost in one-way streets that are clogged with roadworks.

I pull into a filling station and buy a ham and cheese sandwich sealed in plastic. As I give my money to the young woman behind the till, I ask for directions to the town center. She calls an elderly bearded man and they have a long discussion in Spanish, during which they keep glancing at me. After a while a younger man turns up and asks me in English what I want.

"The town center?—The city center?"

He turns to the others, says something in Spanish and suddenly all three understand. They confer with much pointing and arm-waving, and then the younger man gives me an answer which, for simplicity and rigor, is worthy of Einstein: "Straight on to Lincoln. Turn left. Straight on to Flores. Turn right. Keep going. And you will be there, in a square with a church."

He says this twice with hand gestures. I thank all three profusely, and as I walk back to the car the old man walks with me, smiling, and speaking in Spanish.

"*Gracias. Adiós,*" I say, and climb into Prius.

He waves and gets into an ancient, beaten-up Cadillac—the kind of car that thirty years ago was commonplace and called a gas-guzzler—with a rear-end like the wings of a seagull and a two-tone paint job in colors that, if the car were new, would be called cappuccino. It's full of stuff, cushions and bedding in particular, and looks as if the old man lives in it. Perhaps he does.

For once I remember the directions, and in about five minutes arrive in an old square filled with trees and benches. There's a church in one corner, a smart colonial-style hotel, a small museum which is closed, and expensive-looking cars parked at the curb. I squeeze Prius between them and wander around the square. It's warm; the sun is out, throwing shadows under the trees; and the red-brick road is already dry.

Glancing between two buildings, I see a vast gray river. I am one steep block away from the Rio Grande, and there, not far off, is Mexico! The trees and buildings beyond the river are in Nuevo Laredo, a city with a population even larger than old, American, Laredo.

I can't get closer to the river. All but one of the streets that go that way are closed with tall steel fences. The one that's open slopes down to a fortified customs point. There, in front of yellow-painted barriers, a gang of policemen and soldiers loiters, hands resting on guns. A group of workmen digs up the road. A couple of cars cook in the dust by the curb. Small groups of onlookers stand a little way off—waiting, perhaps, for friends or relatives to arrive from Mexico. I walk downhill, stand close to them, and wait a while to see who or what might emerge...

And nothing does. Perhaps there's a traffic jam on the other side. Or a drug bust on this side.

Four road bridges link the two Laredos. This one, Gateway to the Americas International Bridge, joins their main streets. Eleven thousand pedestrians and numerous private cars cross it daily, while many of the five thousand trucks that come through every day from Nueva Laredo use it too.

Forty percent of the goods imported into the U.S. from Mexico and Central and South America go through Laredo—as does a large proportion of imports to the U.S. from China, after shipping to the Mexican port of Lazaro Cardenas. The U.S. depends on this trade, which seems to include almost everything—and certainly, for example, car parts, clothing, chili peppers, computers, and oil. Ninety-seven percent of these imports—including the produce of the maquiladoras, the sweatshops strung along the Mexican side of the border—are legal. The remaining 3 percent are drugs. In the other direction the same percentages apply: cash and guns are smuggled south in payment for cocaine, heroin, methamphetamine, and marijuana.

In his excellent and eye-opening book *Amexica: War along the Borderline,* the war correspondent Ed Vulliamy describes a visit on a Sunday afternoon to a gun show in Pharr, Texas, six miles from the Mexican border. There he watches one part of an insane trade that happens all along the border on a terrifying scale: "Americans selling guns that arm the cartels that kill each other so as to peddle the drugs that kill Americans."

I GO BACK to the square—it's called San Agustin—and go into the church, which has the same name. It turns out to be a cathedral, parts of which date from the founding of the city in 1755. Inside it's cool and Catholic with bright hyper-real paintings, sculptures, and stained glass. I sit down and enjoy the silence, alone and away from the world—and am startled when two women loom out of a side chapel. When they've gone, I stand and look into the chapel. A woman is sitting, gazing down at a painted plaster cast of a recumbent Christ, pale and naked but for a loincloth. She seems rapt, perhaps in tears.

Somehow it's already three o'clock. I fetch the ham and cheese sandwich from the car, take it to a bench under a tree, and realize that I bought this brand once before. The sandwich itself was just about all right, but the packaging—bendy but extremely thick plastic—impossible to open with mere human hands. On that occasion, much exasperated and not having a chainsaw or even a knife, I used the only sharp implement I do have, nail clippers. Now, carrying the sandwich and feeling a bit of an idiot and hoping no one is watching, I go back to the car, rummage through my luggage, find the clippers, and clip my way through to the clammy bread that surrounds the ham and cheese. By the time I've achieved this, rain is falling again. None the less, I return to the bench, determined to enjoy the darned sandwich.

I WANDER THE shiny, slippery streets looking into shop windows. This famous old city seems very quiet. There are very few people around now. Well, it's siesta time on the day after the Rio Grande rose to its highest level since 1965.

Out of curiosity, I go into a small snack bar. At the back of the shop there's a glass cabinet filled with cold drinks. I pull out a bottle of pineapple juice and take it to the counter. The proprietor asks me something, but I don't understand. There are four other people in there. I have almost no Spanish and none of them understands me. Why should they?

The proprietor goes into the street and returns a minute later with a young girl who speaks English.

Speaking slowly and enunciating thoroughly, she says, "Do you want to drink it in, or take it out?"

"Drink it in, please."

This is relayed in Spanish to everyone present. They all smile and nod. The proprietor leads me back to the drinks cabinet and points to a bottle opener screwed on the wall next to it.

She watches as I remove the lid, smiles, and returns to her station at the counter.

I sit on a high stool by a shelf against the wall. It's a small, knocked-together kind of place, paneled with white Formica. The menu is behind the counter written with plastic letters pressed into plastic boards. Most, but not all of it, is in Spanish. "*Pechuga Rellena de Jamon o Broccoli*—$5.75" is followed by "Buffalo Wings—$5.75," "*Flautas de Pollo o Carne*—$4.99," and "Club Sandwich—$4.50." A few people come and go, most of them women, smallish and olive skinned, wearing tight jeans.

These people, like more than four million other Texans, are Tejanos, Texans of Mexican descent, which means ultimately of Spanish or Native American descent, and probably both, because the two races began to get together when Spain, represented by Hernán Cortés, conquered the Aztec Empire in the 1520s. (Texas was essentially ungoverned land until Mexico formally claimed it in 1710. From then until the Battle of San Jacinto in 1836, Texas was part of Mexico. After that astonishing victory, it was independent until 1845 when it was admitted to the United States as the twenty-eighth state.) A few Mexicans settled in Texas soon after the Spanish conquest—so there have been Tejanos since then—and more and more arrived over the centuries; certainly some Tejanos died at the Alamo fighting for Texas against Mexico.

AS I DRIVE out of Laredo, I'm caught in a three-lane traffic jam. Inching forward, I see a flooded underpass and water deep enough for swimming.

A little way out of the city and 83 is on its own again, a four-lane highway with diagonal, don't-drive-here stripes in the middle. T-shaped telegraph poles stretch away on the left and, once more, shrubs and small trees fill a flat landscape that reaches a distant place where the earth seems to end. Yet I'm no longer on the plains, no longer—after all these miles—traveling south. 83 points southeast now, and will veer more and more to the east, following the Rio Grande. There is no rain, and the gray-white wash of the sky is streaked with blue.

The town of Zapata rambles along the highway and is duller than a town named after a Mexican revolutionary hero ought to be. I stop at a gas station and come away with coffee in a Styrofoam cup. Beyond the town, at a picnic place on a low pimple of a hill, I drink the coffee and gaze across the Rio Grande. I can see the river widening into Falcon Reservoir, a twenty-five-mile-long lake, created by a dam in the south.

The sky clears. The sun is hot on my back. I move to the shade of a canopy set above a concrete picnic table, and stay there for half an hour, sitting, staring.

"That road goes to Mexico." Not far now.

83 IS TWO-LANE again and straight. Twice it becomes a causeway, barely above the water, as it crosses spurs of the Falcon Reservoir. Otherwise the terrain is dull, level, low-growing green. After Roma, where there are old colonial buildings, trees, and shade, 83 widens to four lanes again and is filled with evening traffic.

Rio Grande City spreads along the highway for miles, spoiling the view of the sky. A clump of old, balconied buildings with the word "Hotel" hanging from one of them, makes me stop and turn back. I find a yellow-brick house with a paved courtyard and geraniums, like an old inn in Spain. But it has just three rooms and they are taken.

The rest of Rio Grande City seems to have been built recently out of concrete and red brick. With a silent sigh, I check into Best Western. And it's fine—mainly because of an unusual receptionist whose eyebrows are plucked, angled, and painted brown so perfectly and with such mesmeric symmetry that I have to look away for fear of being caught and suspected of ogling. I fill in a form, push it toward her, and manage to look into her eyes while ignoring what is above them.

She smiles and comments on my accent, and I tell her where I'm from.

"What in the world are you doing in Texas?"

I tell her that I have driven slowly down 83 from Canada.

"Cool!" she says. "Wow!" And gives me a suite with sofas, armchairs, a big television, and a functioning remote, at no extra cost. It even has a kitchen and a trouser press. And not far away is a machine that dispenses cold beer. And I've been avoiding Best Westerns all the way, just because there are some in England.

SLOUCHING TOWARDS BROWNSVILLE

THERE IS NO SIGN of eyebrows behind the reception desk in the morning—just a smiling woman in a white shirt. I smile back, collect toast and coffee, and look at the map: a mere hundred miles to go—but I fear it will be dull driving. For the rest of its journey 83 is, at the least, a four-lane dual carriageway; and, for the final seventy miles, a freeway—which seems to differ from an interstate only in that it doesn't cross a state line. After more than two thousand miles, my road's status as a U.S. Highway will change. No more country road—and probably no more slow road, no more dawdling or turning back to take in a view. The Rio Grande will be a few miles away and out of sight, and there don't seem to be any hills; on paper the Rio Grande Valley looks like a plain rather than a valley.

THERE ARE CLOUDS in the sky and the heat is oppressive. I will drive, at least for a while, with the windows up and the hiss of air conditioning. I swing into a line of traffic on 83 and slouch for a few miles in the slow lane past a soporific sprawl of cheap, functional buildings—shops, offices, homes, warehouses. Then, on a curve a couple of hundred yards ahead, I see a low, pleasingly proportioned structure with a dome and a long, openwork wall of the type that lets in light and air. It looks like—can it be?—a mosque. Here?

I drive on around the bend and slow down for a better look. It's a beautiful building. And there's a sign—First National Bank.

Farther on, and for many miles, palm trees grow on the strip of grass in the middle of the road. They appear regularly, planted perhaps one hundred yards apart, and are the smaller type whose shape, though pleasing, resembles an upended lavatory brush.

I see a sign to Los Ebanos ferry, the only surviving Rio Grande ferry that is hauled across by hand. I turn off and follow an uneven tarmac road past small, painted wooden houses. Children play outside, and look up as I glide slowly by. Two small boys, bare chested, brown skinned, Hispanic, shade their eyes and wave, and I wave back.

After three miles the road ends in a rough clearing where twenty or so cars and pickups are parked. I leave Prius and walk toward the Rio Grande, which looks like a lake surrounded by trees. To my left is a customs shed, apparently closed; and in front of me a shelter for travelers. A notice says that the ferry isn't running because the river is too high. The ferry itself, a gray-painted metal platform that can carry three cars and a few foot passengers, is tied up and too high in the water to load cars.

In the shade of the shelter and the trees a small crowd is gathered. Some people stand; others sit on benches, plastic chairs, and on the ground leaning against tree trunks. It seems that they have come just to look, chat quietly, and point.

A man wearing a mustache and a black porkpie hat smiles at me, and for some reason—he looks so Mexican—I say, "Do you speak English?" And instantly regret it; it was surely patronizing and rude.

But he smiles again and says, "No." And gestures to the woman sitting beside him, who might be his wife—there are two little girls with them.

"These people are here," she says, "because none of us have ever seen the river so high. It is amazing." She looks toward the water, raises her arms, and smiles. "It is easy to get across usually." Normally, she tells me, Mexico is just seventy yards away. "Today," she smiles and shrugs, "because of rain, it's three times that. Incredible!"

Crossing into the U.S. from Mexico *is* easy as long as you have the right papers: a visa or a border crossing card, which is issued only to those who live close to the frontier. In his book *Amexica,* Ed Vulliamy describes the border as "simultaneously porous and harsh... Families live astride the frontier, workers, shoppers, relatives, and schoolchildren commute across the line." On the other hand, Mexicans who have no papers take huge risks to get across, though many are unaware of the degree of danger until it is too late. Some trek across the Arizona desert, where it is estimated that, since 1994 when the U.S. strengthened its border defenses, ten thousand have died: lost, gasping for water, and robbed of their savings by "people smugglers."

The U.S. has been building a fence. I saw it at the ends of the streets in Laredo. In 2010 about one-third of the twenty-one-hundred-mile border had been fenced. The more, Vulliamy says, the U.S. builds its fence, and the more it erects a technological barrier of infrared cameras and sensors backed by soldiers and SWAT teams, the more people—about a million a day—cross legally.

Some who cross legally stay beyond the date set for their return and become illegal. Between ten and twenty-eight million Mexicans—estimates vary—live in the U.S. illegally, while twelve million Mexicans and twenty-eight million Mexican Americans live there legally.

From 1740, until the Los Ebanos ferry was set up in 1950, there was a ford at this place. A plaque, set into a concrete post under an old, spreading tree, says that at different times the ford was used by Mexican soldiers, "Texas Rangers chasing cattle rustlers," and "smugglers in many eras, especially during the American Prohibition years." The ferry, which is named after the Texas ebony trees that grow here, is "the only government-licensed hand-pulled ferry on any boundary of the United States."

IN THE SLOW lane of 83 again, I reflect that this is yet another part of the road that was used, it seems, for smuggling during Prohibition. A few miles on, I again turn right toward the river—on a whim, this time—following a sign to a wildlife center in a small town called Penitas. I am certainly slouching towards Brownsville, making the slow road slower than ever. I want to get there, yet I don't want the journey to end.

I get into a queue of cars on a narrow road. Maybe they are all going to the wildlife center. I put JJ Cale into the CD player—and come to a pair of rusty gates that are padlocked shut. The wildlife center is closed forever, defunct, kaput, gone. So, where are all these cars going? I move back into the traffic and drive on, looking for somewhere to turn. I'm behind a smart-looking SUV with its tailgate open and what looks like an old refrigerator poking out. It's Saturday morning. And soon I find myself at the entrance to the Penitas municipal dump.

BACK AT THE junction with 83, in the full heat of the sun, a lean old man, in jeans and cowboy hat, pushes a mower up and down the grass outside a gas station. A boy rides a bike, pedaling lazily, knees out, along the side of the road in the wrong direction. I sit alongside many others, cool, inert, air-conditioned, at the traffic lights, watching.

83 becomes a raised freeway and all I can see is concrete and sky and slender poles that stretch both arms to hold a light over each carriageway. Evenly spaced, they sashay toward me like models on a catwalk, and somehow keep in time with JJ Cale. Entrances and exits come and go; vehicles mingle and separate at narrow angles that make 83 seem like a circle with numerous tangents—a circle so large that its curve goes unnoticed. I pass an exit to Pharr, host to gun shows and home of the photographer Ricardo Longoria. I'm getting hungry. I'd like to buy some fruit. Near the exit to McAllen, the tops of a forest of notices wave above the parapet: Taco Bell, McDonald's, Dairy Queen, Exxon, HEB. I don't know what HEB means, but below the logo are the words "low prices every day." Perhaps it's a supermarket.

I drive down the ramp and manage to steer Prius into the right car park. HEB is a vast supermarket: not quite Walmart, but there's plenty of fruit. I choose a banana and an apple, and queue up to pay behind a waddling-fat young man, who, as we get closer to the cashier, sticks out a fleshy arm to grab an outsize bottle of spring water. I think about the water I have bought over the past weeks—two bottles from a gas station near Winnipeg, refilled from a motel tap every morning since—and I remember my childhood in postwar Britain, when the suggestion that drinking-water should be bought in bottles would have tickled the Queen and brought down the government. As I leave HEB, I see a notice: "Sandwiches and salads food stampable." Water can't be stampable. Can it?

The supermarket's car park contains no greenery save for some skinny palm trees that are supermodel tall, yet just one-third the height of the sign advertising HEB. It is no place for a picnic of fruit and almonds. I return to the road and half an hour later come off at Harlingen, where I find a small park with mown grass, trees, tables, and blue litter bins labeled Don't mess with Texas. The park fills a city block. One end faces a busy road where chain stores and fast-food franchises simmer behind their car parks. I drive to the other end and, opposite the park, find shops and old brick buildings boarded up with their windows smashed. A small sign high on a wall states that this is Main Street. The cheek-to-cheek proximity of shiny new and discarded old seems, at best, tactless. But perhaps it was calculated. Perhaps the birth of the new was precisely positioned to bring on the death of the old.

I park beside an old, dark green saloon whose windows are wound down, and notice two stickers: VIETNAM VETERAN in a side window, and MARINE VETERAN in the rear window. Then I see a row of bumper stickers, some of which are a little startling. I want to record them, but I don't want to stand in the road copying them into my notebook; there's a group of men at a table in the park, and one of them probably owns the car. Instead I walk toward the abandoned shops and take a couple of photographs while pretending to look in another direction. Then I fetch my laptop, and my apple and my almonds, and go to a table under a tree some distance away. I load the photos onto the laptop, blow them up, and read the messages.

Most of them, such as "The Most Dangerous Place is Between A MARINE and His COUNTRY!," are innocuous. There is one that bothers me, "WE PROMISE YOU SLEEP DEPRIVATION, MENTAL TORMENT, AND MUSCLES SO SORE YOU'LL PUKE, BUT WE DON'T WANT TO SUGARCOAT IT," until I decide that it's a mock recruiting slogan. I'm disturbed, though, by one in the middle of the car's bumper, just below the Texas license plate, "Some People Just Need KILLING. That's Why We Have MARINES." It seems like a warning, almost a threat: "I'm a killer and proud of it, and I might be provoked into killing again, so—you can mess with Texas, pal—but don't mess with me."

But perhaps it's a joke, like the notice on Carol's neighbor's ranch gate. Maybe messages like this are commonplace in the United States, and people just shrug. We English are supposed to be good at irony: some of our stand-up comedians say the most outrageous things and we—most of us, anyway—know they don't mean them, and we laugh. Somehow the solemn declarations of being a marine and Vietnam veteran make the joke more sinister.

From Harlingen the freeway turns southeast. There are only twenty-six miles to go.

THE BRIDGES TO MEXICO

A SIGN WELCOMES ME TO Brownsville, and the freeway sweeps down to ground level. Motels, shopping malls, office blocks appear to my left; to my right low-rise buildings are built on land that slopes a little toward the Rio Grande.

I follow signs to the Brownsville Visitor Information Center, and there meet an urbane, dark-haired man who tells me that the city's hotels are strung along a highway to the northeast—he means places like Holiday Inn and Days Inn—while the interesting part of Brownsville is the historic downtown to the southwest.

"Are there no hotels downtown?"

He consults his computer. "Well, there are two, but they're not exactly upscale." He marks them on a map and tells me how to get to the old downtown without going back to the freeway. I must take a road called Old Alice. He traces it with his finger on the map.

Downtown Brownsville is a grid of narrow streets. The buildings are old—some of them Spanish colonial—and few are more than two stories high. Streets with names—Madison, Jefferson, Washington, Elizabeth—run from northwest to southeast and are filled with small shops, many of which display signs in Spanish—hardly surprising in a city where 93 percent of the population are Hispanic. These streets are crossed by numbered streets where small houses open straight on to the pavement.

The first hotel looks a little flyblown and grungy, and turns out to be closed. The second, the University Inn, is painted pink with turquoise trimmings and looks like a giant dolls' house built in the shape of a Swiss chalet. It's on the edge of downtown by the Rio Grande. Palm trees of both kinds, loo-brush and supermodel, grow in the grounds along with bougainvillea, hibiscus, and well-mown grass. The receptionist is like the building: welcoming and colorfully painted. She gives me a key and I drive Prius twenty yards to my front door.

IT'S FOUR O'CLOCK and very warm as I walk back into downtown. The streets are crowded with cars. Shops are jammed together, each built onto its neighbor, many of them perhaps one hundred, others nearer fifty, years ago. The older buildings are graceful, with wrought-iron balconies and finely arched windows; the newer, squeezed between the older, are bland, postwar commercial. I come to a low building with a curved portico and miniature minarets. It might once have been a cinema. Now it's a clothes shop. A hundred shirts and T-shirts hang face-out on hangers, filling four plate-glass windows. Inside, jolly music plays as a crowd of women and children picks things up from tables—skirts, jeans, trousers, shirts, socks—shakes them and puts them down again. It's a little like Macy's or Harrods at sale time, but more friendly and without woolens—who needs a sweater here?

I want something to eat, but can see no bars or cafés. I'm about to try a small supermarket when I see Church's Chicken on a corner. It's a small, L-shaped space in which bright lights burn down on white plastic. I wait in a queue behind two dark-eyed, teenage girls who swivel and spin with boredom; eventually I receive two pieces of fried chicken on a cardboard plate, a paper bag filled with crinkly french fries, and a plastic beaker of ice flavored with Sprite. I take some paper napkins—there is no cutlery—and find a small table covered in the remains of someone's lunch. I remove it and eat with my fingers while vile music plays. And I watch a small girl, who seems to be about ten years old, try to sweep detritus from between the legs of chairs and tables and people who act as if she isn't there.

I leave as soon as I can, walk a few blocks, and gaze at the oldest building in Brownsville, which was built in 1848. It is plain and delicate: two stories and a wrought-iron balcony that runs the length of the upper floor. From up there, a local judge delivered a stirring speech during the civil war.

I walk a short block to the southeast and find the Gateway International Bridge. It stands, low and unspectacular, on circular concrete pillars. Beyond it, a hundred yards away, I can see Mexico: thick trees and a drooping, green, white, and red flag. I look down at the Rio Grande, broad, brown, and flowing fast. Branches of trees race by, their leaves trailing in the current.

I walk on and, as I reach the corner of Elizabeth Street, a couple with three children come toward me. The man has blond hair and is wearing shorts. He says, "Do you speak English?"

"I *am* English," I say.

He shows no surprise. "OK," he says. "Do you know where the bridge to Mexico is?"

I tell him it's round the corner and point the way. He thanks me and rushes off—in a hurry to leave the United States, it seems. And I spend another hour drifting about looking at old buildings.

Back near the University Inn, I walk through the long grass that grows between the road in front of the hotel and the river. On the riverbank, slender steel bars form a tall fence that runs both ways for as far as I can see. Between the bars I can see the Rio Grande—and, again, there is Mexico, just the width of a football field away. There are three bridges in Brownsville, one of which takes trains as well as cars and trucks; every day numerous people and huge quantities of freight cross between Brownsville and Matamoros, the city on the other side. Movement across the bridges is, of course, monitored by border guards and customs officials, and passports and border crossing cards are scrutinized by computers. The river in front of me is out of sight of bridges and customs posts, so this fence—twenty-five feet high and built, probably, since this is the USA, to resist nukes—must be here to deter people from swimming or crossing in small boats.

IT'S AFTER SEVEN and there is something I have to do. The trip isn't over yet: there are still five miles of 83 before it reaches its end at the Veterans International Bridge. I drive through the old downtown, back along Old Alice, and past the visitor center to the point where I left 83.

For three miles the road is raised and walled with concrete, over which only the tops of palm trees are visible against a hazy sky that is turning pink. Streetlights, lit, though it is by no means dark, stand on both sides, heads bowed as if to acknowledge my arrival.

83 drops to earth once more, and it's not far now. A silver SUV is in front, in my lane, waiting at red traffic lights. A shield signing 83—identical to the one 2,271 miles north of here in Swan River—is fixed to a post in front of a line of palms. I slow down, lift my camera with my right hand, and click. Then I drive through the traffic lights and on for a couple of hundred

yards. And find that I'm about to drive out of the United States and onto the bridge to Mexico.

I didn't mean to come this far! I haven't even got my passport. Cars behind me! Headlights in the mirror! I turn right at an unsigned turning a few yards before the customs kiosks, and stop on a small square of tarmac. There is nowhere to go from here: NO ENTRY to the right, NO ENTRY to the left, U.S. CUSTOMS OFFICIALS ONLY straight on. What can I do?

I see that, if I drive past a no-entry sign, I can cross the lanes that go to Mexico and turn left into one that leads back into the USA.

I get halfway across, and have to wait as a few cars come from my right—from Mexico. I turn left and follow them. No sirens scream. All is well. At this border crossing no one has noticed Prius or me—and no one, except me, knows that we've reached the end of the road.

51

TEJANO

NEXT MORNING, A TALL, good-looking young man is behind the reception desk at the University Inn. As I pay my bill, I ask if he knows of anywhere that might show the World Cup football final on television.

He suggests a place on North Expressway, a road that sits in the lee of a raised section of 83, where there are shopping malls, motels, and restaurants.

"Is there nowhere in downtown?"

"There isn't really anywhere." He pauses. "Well, there are places you can have a drink. They call them saloons. They're full of smoke and there wouldn't be a television anyway."

We talk about football and the final between Spain and Holland; he doesn't care who wins, and nor do I. I tell him that I'm at the end of a long trip, from Canada down through the Great Plains.

He seems rather amazed. He had no idea that 83 goes so far north. "There should be a photograph of you, at the end of your journey," he says. "Have you got a camera?"

I stand in the sun beside Prius—and try to look nonchalant in front of a bright blue sky, the border fence, and, a long way off, the Mexican flag flying above Mexico.

He clicks the shutter.

I thank him and ask his name.

"Manuel Casanova." He pauses, as if wondering whether to go on. "The third."

"Wow! What a great name!" I say.

"Well." He shrugs. "We are Mexican, but we have lived in San Antonio for generations." He speaks with a Texan, southern, accent. "I'm a student here. In fact, I'm here to learn Spanish."

We talk some more before I shake his hand and leave. As I drive, I reflect that Manuel, with his need to learn Spanish, is a Tejano in the old, and strict, sense: someone from a Mexican family who was born in Texas. And so are his mother and father and grandparents. Only recently has the word's meaning been loosened to include new arrivals, and there are comparatively few of them: more than 80 percent of Mexicans in Texas were born in the United States.

LATER I SIT in cool comfort at the bar in Vermilion, the place Manuel recommended. The room is dark and windowless, with six screens so that you can see the action wherever you are. I chat to a small Latino barman and drink nonalcoholic beer called O'Doull's. There are some posh-looking people here, thirty or forty of them, old and young, male and female—some of them waspish, preppy, in the American sense. All of them are supporting Spain. The referee, Howard Webb, is English and so are the linesmen and the fourth official. Webb's shaven head gleams. He looks fit and authoritative, and a little natty in a turquoise shirt and a white belt.

AS THE GAME wears on, I do a sum in my notebook using figures from Prius's odometer. I've driven 5,152 miles since leaving Swan River—more than twice as far as I would have if I'd driven straight here, 2,271 miles, with no detours or doubling back.

I remember that I tried to set out free of expectations, ready to look, see, listen, and hear—to enjoy a trip into the unknown, an adventure such, perhaps, as children enjoy, and fear, when they swim in a new sea, enter an unknown forest, meet someone new. I have learned a lot, much of it by chance—more perhaps than I might have, had I set out with an agenda.

I have learned, for example, that many of the Indian tribes lived collectively as farming communities; that relatively few tribes subsisted as hunter-gatherers. I have learned that there were no horses until Hernán Cortés brought a few from Spain. And that cowboys rarely fought against Indians. The U.S. military did that. Cowboys occasionally defended themselves.

I have learned that Kit Carson and Buffalo Bill were not heroes. Both attacked Indians as well as, at other times, defending them. Later Buffalo Bill exploited Indians and created the stereotype or myth. After the civil war one-quarter of cowboys in Texas were black. Hispanics taught Americans how to ride horses and herd cattle—which reminds me that Indians taught early American settlers how to farm. There are cowboys now—several men told me that they are cowboys: Robert at Carrizo Springs, Mick Barth at Oberlin, Phil Greeley at North Platte—and Carol Taylor told me that her husband, Jamie, was a cowboy and that was why she fell for him. Many cowboys have inherited a way of life; some work with cows.

Davy Crockett was a brave man and, as a senator, he took on Andrew Jackson over the Indian Removal Act. But at the Alamo he behaved like an idiot rather than a hero.

Indians were not all noble, peace-loving people provoked into belligerence by white men. Many tribes fought each other, often cruelly, for territory, women, buffalo, or horses. I remember particularly the Comanche, the Hidatsa who kidnapped Sacagawea, and the Sioux who attacked the Pawnee at Massacre Canyon.

Numerous people on the plains are the descendants of homesteaders, and many of them farm their ancestors' land. Some have added to it; some have sold much but not all of it; some, as the result of a marriage—I think of Fran Greenwood, who sat and spoke quietly with a baby on her lap—have two farms from two sets of grandparents.

People used to be embarrassed to have Indian ancestors. That has changed, perhaps thanks to Martin Luther King and the civil rights movement.

The myth of the American road follows on from the myth of the pioneer trail. Traveling in wagons became a thing of the past, but traveling in search of the new hasn't—look at me!

The plains are indeed flat, but there is respite in the form of occasional rivers, valleys, and hills.

Many parts of Texas are beautiful. Most Texans vote Republican (if you vote Democrat, you may have to keep it a secret), but not all Texan Republicans are conservative.

The people of Kansas, and by inference of the rest of the plains, are not all bigots bent on voting against their own interests.

Beef is crucial to the economy of the plains south of Pierre, South Dakota, but the way it is produced bothers me—though not enough to prevent me eating it.

The obesity phenomenon was triggered by the building of interstates and is perpetuated by the greed of a handful of fast-food and sweet-drink corporations. A tiny bit of socialism, in the form of taxes on sugary drinks and burgers, to temper those corporations' capitalism might help America and the world to lose weight.

Generalizing is difficult and, as I have said, I have tried as far as possible to explore as a child might, free of preconceptions. However, I've picked up a sense that in this region of Middle America, which has a reputation for conservatism and

Republicanism, there is—with notable exceptions—much liberal thinking and tolerance, more than I and many in Europe might have expected.

I remember Carol Taylor saying, "I don't believe in being cautious. Sensible but not cautious." America seems, and is, new rather than old; instead of established ways cautiously guarded, I have seen—again, with some exceptions—hope and potential.

EVENTUALLY, AFTER EXTRA time, Spain wins the World Cup by one goal to nil, and I walk outside into hot sun and a hair-dryer breeze.

Earlier I asked Manuel if he knew where I could buy a postcard.

"You will need to go to Port Isabel or, maybe, South Padre Island," he said.

"How far is Port Isabel?"

"Twenty miles. There is nothing like that here." He sighed, as if embarrassed by Brownsville's shortcomings. "Unless... possibly," he said, "Sunrise Mall. Up there past Vermilion."

I find Sunrise Mall, park in a giant car park, walk around indoors for fifteen minutes, look into shops, and ask people. There are no postcards in the biggest shopping mall in Brownsville.

So I drive to the post office on Old Alice, go in, and buy a stamp. Then I search among my notebooks, find a postcard that I bought three days ago, and write:

> Dear Stuart,
> Made it to Brownsville yesterday, and they have no cards. Here is a picture of the Alamo instead. Back to England tomorrow from Houston. Thanks and warmest wishes,
> David.

ACKNOWLEDGMENTS

I WANT TO GIVE A Toyota Prius's tank full of thanks to Nancy Flight, associate publisher at Greystone Books. Without her this book would be a limp replica of itself; she has boundless patience and a terrific editorial eye, both for the unnecessary and for the necessary that is somehow not-there-yet. Rob Sanders (rhymes with pandas), publisher of Greystone Books, also has terrific eyes—and quite a nose and a dazzling smile—and I have benefited from his excellent advice as this book was being planned and, as draft succeeded draft, from his ability to encourage while being critical. Editor Maureen Nicholson's advice and attention to detail have been invaluable. My agent, Tony Peake, has read and commented on the text more times than he should have had to; his opinions and enthusiasm have been invigorating. My wife, Penny Phillips, a professional editor, has read, commented, suggested, argued, corrected, and edited—in many places, including the car, at all times of day and night—and she showed up in Denver, Colorado; I am a lucky man.

My thanks also to Claire Davies, Toby King, Judy Hevrdejs, Colleen MacMillan, Roy Williams, David Downing, Ben Yarde-Buller, John Smallwood, Charlie Fairey, Martha Reynolds,

Grace Scott, Rose Reynolds, Andrew Jarman, and Freddie Broome. And to four Manitobans, Garry Harris, Wilbert Schoenrath, Douglas Gourlay, and Dale Wiebach, who took time to tell me all they could about the road.

Stuart Harris, who celebrated his one hundredth birthday in March this year, has been the source of many good things. In this instance, he showed me the road and sent me down it. I shall always be grateful.

Finally, my thanks to everyone I met on, or close to, Highway 83.

SELECT BIBLIOGRAPHY

THE DATE GIVEN IS THE DATE OF FIRST PUBLICATION.

Stephen E. Ambrose, *Undaunted Courage: Meriwether Lewis, Thomas Jefferson, and the Opening of the American West* (1996)

Paul Benson (Ed.), *Great Stories of the Wild West* (1957)

R.B. Bernstein, *Thomas Jefferson* (2003)

Mike Blakely, *Comanche Dawn* (1998)

Bobby Bridger, *Buffalo Bill and Sitting Bull: Inventing the Wild West* (2002)

Hugh Brogan, *The Penguin History of the USA* (second edition, 1999)

Dee Brown, *Bury My Heart at Wounded Knee: An Indian History of the American West* (1971)

Bill Bryson, *The Lost Continent: Travels in Small-Town America* (1989)

Bill Bryson, *Made in America* (1994)

Jenni Calder, *There Must Be a Lone Ranger: The Myth and Reality of the American Wild West* (1974)

Truman Capote, *In Cold Blood* (1966)

Willa Cather, *O Pioneers!* (1913)

Cowboy Picture Library, *Kit Carson and the Man Who Hated Redskins* (ca. 1957), collected in *High Noon, Wild West Picture Library Collection* (2008)

Gene Dattel, *Cotton and Race in the Making of America: The Human Costs of Economic Power* (2009)

Christopher Davis, *North American Indian* (1969)

Simone de Beauvoir, *L'Amérique au jour le jour* (1954), trans. Carol Cosman as *America Day by Day* (1998)

Molly des Baillets, *Cultural Pluralism and Social Capital in Garden City, Kansas* (2008)

Barbara Ehrenreich, *Nickel and Dimed: On (Not) Getting By in America* (2001)

Emily Ferguson, *Janey Canuck in the West* (1910)

Thomas Frank, *What's the Matter with Kansas?* (2004)

Ian Frazier, *Great Plains* (1989)

Stuart Harris, *Autobiography* (unpublished)

Stuart Harris, *Durban* (1986)

William Least Heat-Moon, *Blue Highways* (1983)

Ted Hustead, "Wall and Water," in *Guideposts* (1982)

Clay S. Jenkinson, *A Lewis and Clark Chapbook: Lewis and Clark in North Dakota* (2002)

Jamie Jensen, *Road Trip USA: Cross-Country Adventures on America's Two-Lane Highways* (fifth edition, 2009)

Jack Kerouac, *On the Road* (1957)

David Lavender, *The Penguin Book of the American West* (1969)

Claude Lévi-Strauss, *Le cru et le cuit* (1964), trans. John and Doreen Weightman as *The Raw and the Cooked* (1969)

Tom Lewis, *Divided Highways: Building the Interstate Highways, Transforming American Life* (1997)

Barry Lopez, "The American Geographies," *Orion* (1989), collected in *About This Life: Journeys on the Threshold of Memory* (1998)

Elgin Ostrum, *Memories of the Good Old Days* (unpublished)

George Packer, *The Unwinding: An Inner History of the New America* (2013)

Michael Pollan, "Power Steer," *The New York Times Magazine* (2002)

Annie Proulx, *That Old Ace in the Hole* (2002)

Jonathan Raban, *Bad Land: An American Romance* (1996)

Mari Sandoz, *Cheyenne Autumn* (1953)

Simon Schama, *The American Future: A History from the Founding Fathers to Barack Obama* (2008)

Eric Schlosser, *Fast Food Nation* (2001)

Brock V. Silversides, *Prairie Sentinel: The Story of the Canadian Grain Elevator* (1997)

John Steinbeck, *The Grapes of Wrath* (1939)

John Steinbeck, *Travels with Charley: In Search of America* (1962)

Mark Timbrook, *The Last Hurrah: An Account of Life in the Mouse River Valley, Bone Town, Little Chicago, and the Magic City* (2008)

Ed Vulliamy, *Amexica: War along the Borderline* (2010)

Carl Waldman, *Atlas of the North American Indian* (third edition, 2009)

David Foster Wallace, "The View from Mrs. Thompson's," *Rolling Stone* (2001), collected in *Consider the Lobster and Other Essays* (2005)

Clark Wissler, *Indians of the United States* (revised edition, 1966)

DISCOGRAPHY

Jimmy Buffett, *Songs You Know by Heart*

JJ Cale, *Roll On*

Bill Evans, *Waltz for Debby*

Charlie Haden and Pat Metheny, *Beyond the Missouri Sky*

Jim Hall, *Concierto*

Hot Club of Cowtown, *Continental Stomp*

Van Morrison, *Keep It Simple*

Mozart, *Piano Concertos Nos. 9, 25, 22* (First movement—CD 1 of 2-CD set), Alfred Brendel, Academy of St. Martin in the Fields/Sir Neville Marriner

Several artists, *O Brother, Where Art Thou?* [sound track]

Artie Shaw, *22 Classic Hits*

Bruce Springsteen, *Born to Run*

Marcin Wasilewski Trio, *January*

Geraint Watkins, *In a Bad Mood*